With The Gurkhas

With The Gurkhas

India, Burma, Singapore, Malaya, Indonesia, 1940–1959

Scott Leathart

The Pentland Press Limited
Edinburgh • Cambridge • Durham • USA

© Scott Leathart 1996

First published in 1996 by
The Pentland Press Ltd.
1 Hutton Close
South Church
Bishop Auckland
Durham

British Library Cataloguing in Publication Data.
A catalogue record for this book is available
from the British Library.

ISBN 1 85821 420 3

EAST GRID STAMP

BB		SS		MM	
BA		SB		MW	
BT		SC		MC	
BR		SD		MD	
BY		SE	7/92	MO	
BC		SW		MY	
BG		SL			
BH		SV			
BS					
BN					

To the Gurkhas and
their Families who shared
it all.

ACKNOWLEDGEMENTS

I wish gratefully to acknowledge the help given to me, in their several ways, by Sir John Chapple, Chris Matthews, John Mole, Evan Powell-Jones, Bill Towill, William Shepherd and Denis Wood; and to record my gratitude for the friendship and support of the many colleagues who took part in this story.

Particularly do I recognise both the encouragement given to me, in a very special way, by Dr May Reed, and the loving support which I have enjoyed from my wife, Betty, these last 40 years.

CONTENTS

FOREWORD

by

Field Marshal Sir John Chapple, G.C.B., C.B.E., formerly Colonel 2nd. K.E.O. Goorkhas (The Sirmoor Rifles), Chief of the General Staff and Governor of Gibraltar.

Scott Leathart served during a particularly interesting period in the history of the Indian and British Armies. Although his total military and police service covered less than two decades, he managed to pack in a great deal in a wide variety of places. The 1940's and 1950's were challenging and fast-moving times. Great changes were taking place, not always apparent to the participants. This memoir has a special value by recording events in a number of different theatres and campaigns at this time of great change.

It is essentially a record of regimental soldiering, full of small observations of daily life. These are things which major military histories omit, but they bring the memoir vividly to life and give a sharp feel to the routine of soldiering in a Gurkha Battalion and serving with the Gurkha Police. For me the interest is enhanced by extracts from letters to home and by details of the flora and fauna, of which Scott is such an acute observer.

His service in the 9th. Gurkha Rifles, the 2nd. Goorkhas and the Singapore Police gave him experience of all the tribes and clans who traditionally serve in Gurkha units. He recounts with clarity and modesty soldiering on the North West Frontier; fighting in the Arakan; campaigning with the 2nd. Chindit Expedition; post-war service in Java, Malaya and Sumatra; the run-up to Independence and Partition; the transfer to British service (and a new regiment); the beginnings of the Malayan Emergency; and the early years of the Gurkha Contingent of the Singapore Police which Scott Leathart raised and commanded for nearly ten years. There are particularly vivid accounts of the actions in Burma, and a very succinct description of the events leading to the Maria Hertogh riots in Singapore.

Above all this book is a record of service with Gurkhas. It adds to the many other accounts which pay tribute to the qualities, courage and loyalty of the Gurkhas. It also recalls the close bonds between British Officers and the Gurkhas which all who have been privileged to serve with Gurkhas will readily recognise.

Although my own service only overlapped with Scott's for about four years, I can remember some of the events he describes, and relive some of the experiences. More than this, I can respond directly to the rapport he established with his soldiers and policemen.

I commend this valuable and important memoir.

John Chapple

6th January, 1996

PREFACE

These pages are not just fond recollections dragged from the failing memory of an old man years after the events; they come from letters written home at the time and from a daily diary kept without a break since January, 1948. There is nothing spectacular about them, nothing to 'rubbish' leaders or contest military decisions. They merely chronicle the actions and thoughts of a junior officer, proud and privileged to serve with Gurkhas in days long past; fortified in boring and hazardous times by an interest in wildlife, and particularly in birds. A pointless day in the clammy heat of Bengal made memorable by the first siting of a Jerdon's Chloropsis; the menacing hum of a Japanese plane searching for us in the Burmese jungle matched and muted by the distant call of a gibbon or the whine of a Great Hornbill's pinions as it skimmed the tree canopy.

Lord Louis Mountbatten, Supreme Commander of South East Asia Command, when asked by a British soldier about the 'Forgotten (14th) Army', is reputed to have said 'Forgotten – You've never been heard of!'. I do not think that we in Gurkha regiments ever worried much about whether our folk at home were interested in our doings. We lived in a world of our own, with a job to do, never doubting that, with the men we led, it would be done to the full.

The decade 1949/1959 saw the Gurkha Contingent of the Singapore Police formed and expanding *pari passu* with the political progress of the colony to an independent republic, a significant role being played by the Contingent, as part of the Police Force, in the maintenance of internal security.

The raising of this new unit, its integration into a somewhat sceptical Force and the special conditions of service needed for its expatriate members,

1

often resisted by the Secretariat, are described in some detail, as are the exciting as well as the more humdrum yet important duties. The loyal steadfastness and cheerful impartiality with which the Gurkhas performed their tasks were soon appreciated by the public, whose admiration and affection for them steadily increased as the years went by; so did mine.

It is now some 55 years since I first started to share a life with these wonderful hillmen of Nepal, but my gratitude and admiration remains undimmed, and I find myself as deeply moved as ever by Professor Turner's tribute, written after he had served with Gurkhas in the Great War:-

'As I write these last words, my thoughts return to you, my comrades, the stubborn and indomitable peasants of Nepal. Once more I see you in your bivouacs or about your fires, on forced march or in trenches, now shivering with wet and cold, now scorched by a pitiless and burning sun. Uncomplaining you endure hunger and thirst and wounds; and at the last, your unwavering lines disappear into the smoke and wrath of battle. Bravest of the brave, most generous of the generous, never had a country more faithful friends than you'

Scott Leathart

CHAPTER 1

PASSAGE TO INDIA ROUND THE CAPE

As the troop-train made its uncertain, darkened journey north, the blind-covered windows streaming with condensation, I sat huddled in my ill-fitting greatcoat with seven other cadets, each alone with his thoughts, at the start of a journey which was to end physically some eight weeks later on the other side of the world, where another journey, much longer and even more uncertain, that of a new life in itself, was to start.

To the incessant drumming of the carriage wheels, the rhythm changing as we crossed over points, and the swish and roar as we entered tunnels, I reflected on my sheltered past and wondered what my future in a war-torn world might be.

I was born in Birkenhead just a year after the Great War ended, the second son of an ENT surgeon who had his consulting rooms in Rodney Street, Liverpool. My mother came from a well-known Liverpool shipping family – the Beazleys. I have two brothers, one who became an Air Commodore and the other a chest physician, and two sisters, one married to an air traffic control officer and the other to a rubber planter in Malaya. We lived in a residential part of Birkenhead.

Like all moderately well-off middle class families in the 1920s, we had adequate domestic help: a cook, a house/parlour maid, as well as a Shetlander nannie whose strict discipline and rigid nursery timetable seemed irksome at first. But the ordered way of life thus instituted soon became the expected routine and the basis of the security for which children unwittingly crave.

Too soon, though, this safe, well-ordered life came to an end when my younger brother and I went to our prep-school, The Leas, Hoylake. Here we were, with shattering suddenness, introduced to life with some 90 other small boys after the misery of apparently being abandoned by our parents at the school gates. Slowly, we became inured to the stress of communal life but for my part, I was never really happy there and it was a relief to go on to my public school, St. Edward's School, Oxford, in May, 1933. Here, for an annual fee of £120, one received as good an education as anywhere in the world. True, life was rather spartan; cold showers every morning throughout the year, indifferent food, the cane if you put a foot wrong, chapel twice a day, compulsory games and, perhaps the worst hardship, the lack of privacy, at least until one became a prefect. But we were very well taught by dedicated masters both in the classroom, and in my case, on the river. Most of us emerged well-prepared for whatever the world was to throw at us; for me two years at St. Edmund Hall, Oxford reading forestry, followed by war.

Although forestry was a reserved occupation, and I could have applied for a post in the Colonial Forest Service or the Forestry Commission, such was the parlous state of our country in the summer of 1940, when I took my finals, that I felt compelled to join up; and being in the Oxford University Officers' Training Corps, it would only have been a matter of time before I was called up anyhow. So in July I left Oxford and returned home to await events and, in the meantime, joined the Local Defence Volunteers (later to be called the Home Guard). As possible invasion became more and more imminent, we used to do duty guarding road-blocks and essential buildings, mostly at night. Oddly enough, our platoon commander was a bank manager with the name of Wilson; but the similarity with 'Dad's Army' ended there. We were equally dedicated and certain that we were helping the war effort but we saw none of the farce which daily accompanied Capt. Mainwaring's activities. The important thing was that we were convinced that we were helping, and the public in general thought so too. In such a situation morale remained high, and that was everything.

In September I received a letter from the India Office asking if I would like to go to India as a cadet and attend the Cadet College at Bangalore and, if subsequently commissioned, join the Indian Army. I accepted at once: two of my uncles had served in India; one in the 54th. Sikhs (later to become the 4/12th. Frontier Force Regiment) and the other in the Indian Civil Service. Furthermore, my elder brother had three brothers-in-law serving in the 9th. Gurkha Rifles at that time. It subsequently transpired that 500 members of university and public school O.T.C.s had been similarly approached, and a further 500 men already serving, most of them with similar backgrounds, were also given this opportunity to volunteer for service in India.

We all gathered in Willems Barracks, Aldershot a few days before Christmas, 1940 and those of us with no parent regiment were enlisted into the First of Foot, the Royal Scots. The days at Aldershot are somewhat blurred in my memory. We endured medical inspections, inoculations and their consequent fevers; we were issued with kit, including ill-fitting balmorals, the official headgear of the Royal Scots, and with solar topis. We stencilled code letters onto our tin trunks (a special concession to cadets) – these were RCHDM J11; it did not dawn on me, as it might well on an enemy agent, that J11 meant 11th. January, our subsequent sailing date. We were not much harassed by the regular N.C.O.s despite our unofficial but envied status as cadets. But a fellow cadet, writing 50 years later, had more vivid memories:-

'Looking back, I think the time spent in the old Victorian Willems Barracks was probably one of the worst periods of my life. The living conditions were appalling with 24 soldiers in one barrack room. There were no indoor recreational facilities and the only heating was a small coal fire in our barrack room. I seem to have spent the whole time on cooking fatigues, cleaning vegetables, washing up in tepid, greasy water and helping in the preparation of uneatable food. To add to the misery, the N.C.O.s appeared to be morons. The difficulties were compounded by the fact that being a polyglot lot and not belonging to a proper unit, we had not the time to establish that corporate comradeship and sense of humour which is so essential when things are bad. The one consolation was that I was proud of my Royal Scots badge and liked wearing my glengarry (sic) Highland headdress.'

After what seemed like many days and almost hourly rumours, we marched out of the barracks, with our solar topis strapped on to our packs, to the station and our train journey north. In the cold, grey dawn of 9th January, 1941 the train drew into Gouroch station. We marched down to the jetty and embarked on a lighter. Out on the waters of the Clyde was an assembly of great grey-painted ships and beyond them the snow-sprinkled mountains of Argyll. We had been given tickets marked with cabin numbers and the fact that so many numbers were the same had seemed very odd; perhaps, we surmised, the cabins were very large. With a clanging of telegraphs our lighter left the jetty and headed out into the Firth of Clyde, as we sat on our kitbags with our balmorals distorted by the stiff, icy breeze. Beneath the towering *Empress of Britain* and the *Windsor Castle* we sailed, heading for a much less inviting vessel, the *Highland Chieftain*, of but 14,000 tons, against which we moored. In single file we climbed the steeply sloping gangway and went on board, snaking along the labyrinth of passages into our 'cabin' – a converted refrigeration hold previously used to ship beef carcases from the Argentine.

That several hundred of us could live and eat in such a small space seemed impossible. We were dismayed at the conditions, which were foully cramped beyond our worst expectations; to make matters worse, we had not eaten since 2200 hrs. the previous day, nor did we get any food for several hours more, so great was the confusion. Protests were futile, brushed aside by the regular N.C.O.s; 'we were in the army now and just had to lump it'. This 'Black Hole', as it was quickly named, had no port holes and was reached by steeply-angled metal ladders. A central aisle ran between narrow rows of mess tables and benches and there was nowhere to stow any kit; nothing but bare steel bulkheads and steel decks above and below. Hammocks and blankets were issued and handed round with difficulty in the tightly packed assembly, but even the large number of hooks intended for meat carcases were insufficient for more than a third of our number to hang these devilish contraptions. For the rest of us, after protests, mattresses were issued to be placed on and under the tables. Thus we were to sleep in three tiers, the condensed breath of the many dripping from the ceiling on to those suspended in their hammocks. Luckily this appalling state of affairs lasted only while we were in the North Atlantic; as we approached the tropics, sleeping on deck was allowed and the nights became more bearable.

The galley was an open-sided shelter up on deck, manned by two African 'cooks' who prepared food in huge vats. The fuel was super-heated steam applied to whatever was to be cooked by thrusting the pipe into it. Chunks of meat, fat and onions, with added water, soon became a bubbling mass heaving about like some noisome volcanic mud. Potatoes and other vegetables would suffer the same fate in other vats; the twain met one another in a stew of monumental unpalatability! Bread came from the first class galley, tinned fruit and other imperishable items from the main store. Some measure of the hunger we felt from poor food in short supply (and the purchasing power of the cadets) can be gauged from the fact that a stock of confectionary in the Barber's Shop, estimated to last for eight weeks on a normal trooper, was completely exhausted in a fortnight. Two-pound boxes of chocolates were bought almost daily to share with friends and keep hunger at bay.

On the morning of 11th. January, 1941 the ships weighed anchor, heralded by the 'whooping' of the Royal Navy escort vessels, and slowly proceeded down the Firth in line ahead, past the snow-sprinkled Isles of Bute and Arran, round the Mull of Kintyre and out into the Atlantic, where we were joined by ships from Liverpool and the vast extent of the convoy became apparent. There were 40 merchantmen, many of them famous liners, and a large number of escorts, including two cruisers.

Before we sailed, boat drill had been vigorously practised, but it was abundantly clear that a torpedo strike and a quick sinking would find most of us going down with the ship, so crowded were we and so difficult was it to get up on deck. Most of the old soldiers amongst us were detailed to man anti-aircraft weapons – light machine guns of various types – and thus were excused the irksome fatigues which the less fortunate performed, such as swabbing decks, peeling potatoes and so on, as well as cleaning the latrines; these consisted of sloping troughs with batteries of rough wooden seats above them. Perhaps the most fortunate were those who acted as officers' batmen; not only were they excused many duties, but they also managed to cadge meals from the first class galley. I never discovered how they were chosen.

The weather soon deteriorated and the sea became very rough, with all the normal activities becoming that much more difficult as the ship pitched and rolled. I recollect overbalancing on the iron staircase whilst carrying my table's porridge ration. The large, steaming bucket went flying, spraying hot porridge all over the place. As this daily morning dish was one which was generally liked and which greatly helped to assuage our chronic hunger, there was general dismay, for there were never any second helpings. In the ablutions a pitching and rolling ship made life particularly hazardous. Trying to manipulate the taps so as not to be scalded or frozen, whilst bracing oneself against the bulkhead as the ship lurched this way and that, was a real struggle. Attempting to dry oneself afterwards, with nowhere to sit down, often ended in a collapse on to the duckboards, bringing down, in a struggling naked heap, one's companions similarly engaged.

This rough weather was not all grief; periods of sentry-go on deck at night were a real relief. Out from the fuggy, vomit-smelling wretchedness of the 'Black Hole' one emerged into the wind-swept freshness of the night. The starry heavens and the waxing moon gradually relieved the initial pitch darkness to reveal huge waves bearing down upon the stern, to lift it, with shudders from the partially exposed propeller, and plunge it once again into the trough with a juddering roar. As one stood on guard, bracing oneself against each mountainous wave, it was difficult to imagine that 50 and more other ships were ploughing through the same seas on parallel courses. As soon as the moon sank lower, fleeting glimpses of silhouettes appeared, accompanied by flashings of white from the plunging bows of the great ships as they zig-zagged in unison on the Commodore's orders. Standing there on deck, guarding hatch or vital door, one was quite alone; mercifully so after so much hugger-mugger down below. The wind whipped round the deck-housings and the spray, pouring from the rails, ran in rivulets along the scuppers this way and that as the ship wallowed in the waves. It was hard work just standing upright and harder still to sip the mug of cocoa brought round in a bucket halfway through the two-hour stint. If the watch happened to include the hour of dawn, one was witness to the most dangerous period of the day. U-boats, tracking the convoy with their sonars during the dark hours, might be poised to attack with the rising sun behind them; or a raider, homed in by a high-flying 'Condor', could well be hull-down on the S.E. horizon. So as the pink flush of dawn developed, all eyes scanned the sea and air. When the stern rose to the swell, the panorama of ships amidst the grey, white-capped waves seemed to be limitless, yet a few seconds later, as our ship sank into a trough, we seemed to be alone amongst the mountains of the sea and the sole likely prey. Only once in the North Atlantic did the alarm sound, when a 'Condor' was seen shadowing the convoy. An attack by U-boats, thus guided to us, was for some days expected but it never came, which, considering that more than 2½ million tons of shipping were sunk in the early months of 1941, was as remarkable as it was fortunate.

One circumstance which made our lives more civilised than they might otherwise have been was that our platoon commanders were all Indian Army Lt. Colonels called back from recent retirement. Their main task was to teach us Urdu. Every morning we assembled on the covered decks in the first class area to be taught the basic grammar of the tongue which was the *lingua franca* of the Indian Army. They also told us much of what we were to expect when we joined our regiments and, indeed, how to conduct ourselves as officers in this rapidly expanding volunteer army. Somehow this daily break from the tedious struggle to maintain standards in the crowded mêlée below decks, presided over by these kindly old gentlemen, who clearly realised how much this traumatic change in our life-styles had affected us, helped us keep up our spirits. These morning sessions were the high mark of the day and, as we sailed south, they began to be held on open decks beneath blue, cloudless skies, such as we imagined we would find in India.

In those early days of 1941 wearing a solar topi was still considered to be essential to avert sunstroke; so much so that when we reached the tropics it was forbidden for any cadet to go out on deck, even moving from one hatch to another, without wearing a topi. So fanatical were the 'medics' about this, that one of our number whose topi blew overboard was put on a charge and confined to the cells whilst we sailed in the tropics. To those of us who, in later years, played golf in the Far East hatless and shadowless with the sun directly overhead, and suffered no ill-effects whatsoever, this long disregarded notion now seems absurd. But it was a serious medical theory in earlier times.

After a wide sweep westwards into the North Atlantic, the convoy swung south and later east until, one morning, with 'whoops' from the escorting destroyers, about half the merchantmen, with a large proportion of the escorts, broke away towards Gibraltar. Meanwhile we veered south into increasingly blue and less troubled seas. Then I began to see new and exciting things: shoals of flying fish planing away from the ship over the waves in 50 yards or more of sustained flight, flashing silver against the blue sea; patches of red seaweed suggesting warmer water, and some African Grey-headed Gulls indicating that land was not far off. Then, one morning in late January, the convoy formed up in line ahead with the purple hues of West Africa's coast on the horizon. Slowly we steamed through the anti-submarine boom into Freetown's harbour. A fellow cadet, who later became Director of the Ashmolean Museum, Oxford and Fellow of Worcester College, wrote at the time:-

'Freetown: a sultry dawn, red and vicious, all done by Goldwyn Meyer in glorious technicolor, "thus we greet the great continent of Africa, the Dark Continent of Romance, while in the east emerges her shape, full of what horror, what mystery?". Indeed, shapes are emerging from the east, but it is probably imagination. The general effect is like arriving at St. Malo, but lacking the prospect of café-cognac and croissants to restore the sea-weary body. Later St. Malo turned into Africa with a golden strand and aloof tufted trees, with swaying trunks. Freetown the real thing, missing technicolor by a miracle; strange abrupt hills form undisciplined horizons. But their lower slopes and the brief coast are cluttered with grey and white roofs and occasional white facades of formal buildings, all set in an incomparable heavy green. A vague mist foaming from the highest hills gives the desired atmosphere of the steamy jungle. Sierra Leone, almost the white man's grave: fever port. But the most vivid impression was the first and sudden view of the hills, strange and fantastic against the sky: then the lovely approach with its white lighthouse and teeming foliage. And the delight of seeing land.'

Although it was disappointing that we were not allowed ashore at Freetown, it was understandable; in the convoy there must have been many thousands of troops, and it was only a small and potentially unhealthy place. But I was fascinated by what I saw during our few days at anchor in the harbour. I recognised four species of birds: Grey-headed Gulls, Gull-billed Terns, African Kites and an eagle. The kites were great scavengers, patrolling the waters in search of morsels flung from the ships, but the terns fished away from the ships and paid them no heed. The antics of the penny divers were astonishing. They leapt from their dugouts and remained submerged for half a minute or more to surface with as many as 5 pennies in one hand from half a dozen thrown in together. We all spent as much time as possible on deck where there was at least a cool breeze to make the humid heat bearable; below decks it was stifling.

As soon as the ships had taken on water, fuel and fresh supplies, our convoy sailed out through the boom and set a southerly course. We crossed the line without ceremony and our shadows on deck became progressively shorter until, at midday, they ceased to exist as we crossed the solar equator. Occasionally sharks appeared, their dorsal fins and tails cutting through the surface of the sea. Sooty Shearwaters, in small parties, flew beside the ship skimming the waves in swift and easy flight. The daily routine – P.T. on deck after breakfast, cleaning the mess decks for the Captain's inspection, Urdu lessons, the midday meal, lectures and tea followed by gatherings of new-found friends on deck in warm sea breezes beneath the great dome of stars – became less and less tedious as each worked out his own *modus vivendi*. And with so much more time spent outside the 'Black Hole' and with so much that was new to be seen, the voyage began to be bearable.

The sun would sink vertically into the sea at eventide, taking some three minutes from the moment its base touched the horizon, and a green flash accompanied its disappearance. As the darkness quickly enveloped us, the stars started to twinkle in their countless millions; the 'Plough' fell out of sight and the Southern Cross lay above the horizon. Southern hemisphere birds began to appear. Shearwaters skimmed the waves, appearing so suddenly that I sometimes mistook them for the dorsal fins of sharks, and one morning those most magnificent of pelagic birds, the Great Wandering Albatrosses, started to accompany the ship, gliding with consummate ease on their 12 ft. spread of narrow wings, or sitting, floating high on the sea, in small parties. Cape Hens too became very numerous and a second species of albatross, the Yellow-nosed, as well as Cape Gannets, joined the increasing throng of seabirds accompanying the convoy as we approached the Cape. Here the convoy split in two, one half putting into Cape Town and the other, including ourselves, steaming on to Durban. The weather at the Cape, albeit mid-summer, was cold, wet and windy; indeed, we saw little of Table Mountain as the ship wallowed in the waters where the Atlantic and Indian Oceans meet.

The morning of our arrival in Durban was memorable both because of the welcome we received from hundreds of citizens crowding the jetty singing patriotic songs (we might have been veterans of a victorious campaign rather than young cadets who had done nothing), and because of the news that we were to change ships from the *Highland Chieftain* to the *Windsor Castle*, a larger ship with ample deck space for us all. That evening we were given short leave and we stepped on dry land for the first time for several weeks, making a bee-line for a hotel, a bath and a decent meal. I recollect having an excellent 7-course dinner at the Beach Hotel for 2/6d. (12½p). Maybe our tattered, un-ironed uniforms and our generally wan appearance evinced compassion on the part of the manager, but even at £1.00, the meal would have been a bargain. Returning to the ship in a Zulu rickshaw along streets lined with pink oleanders and yellow allamandas, the warm air filled with exotic scents and ringing with the incessant singing of crickets, was an experience I shall always remember.

On the following morning the scents which assailed the nostrils of those detailed to unload and transfer our baggage to the *Windsor Castle* were very different from those enjoyed the previous evening. Each cadet had been allowed to bring a tin trunk, so one hold was stacked with a thousand of them. We, the fatigue party, did not do much physical work but we were obliged to be in the hold to supervise the Zulu dockers who were piling the trunks into nets for extraction by cranes. The heat was immensely oppressive, exacerbated by the arc lamps illuminating the nether regions of the hold, and the sweating dockers, clad in very little more than Gunga Din, gave off a pungent odour far removed from that of the roadside shrubs. They worked with a savage zeal which even the iron-bound trunks were scarce able to resist; the once pristine, shiny-black boxes, with names neatly stencilled in white on their lids, became chipped and battered travesties of their former selves as they were hurled higgledy-piggledy onto the spread-out nets, to be lifted aloft in groaning, creaking jumbles, out through the hatch and dumped with a crash on the dockside. The morning was far spent before we could come out into the cool sunshine.

Next morning we forsook the *Highland Chieftain* without regret and boarded the *Windsor Castle*: four of us to a former two-berth cabin with the luxury of a working hand basin, a locker each for our kit, proper baths, albeit only filled with salt water, and loos where privacy was again possible. Thus we set out on the final leg of our journey, drawing away from Durban north-east into the Indian Ocean, the sea-front hotels with the surf breaking only street-width from their doors and the green hills of Natal gradually sinking below the horizon. Through the Mozambique Channel we steamed at a steady 13½ knots, the sea a deep blue and oily smooth; so smooth that it was possible to see the vast numbers of minute organisms floating on the surface, in some parts so thick as to form a veritable paste.

We imagined that we would, after passing the tip of Madagascar, set a more easterly course for Bombay, but we suddenly found ourselves sailing slightly west of north, and rumour had it that a German raider was on the prowl in the north Indian Ocean, forcing the convoy to make for an East African port and temporary safety. Sure enough, one morning we steamed into Mombasa Harbour, and a memorable scene it was for anyone fresh out from England. At the time I wrote:-

'White houses lined the shore and minarets reached above the coconut palms. The tide was rising over rocky flats near the mouth of the harbour and on it turbaned Africans were carrying huge lobster-pot-like baskets on their heads. Behind, in the distance, was the Kenya Plateau. The shore of the harbour was lined with palms and large-trunked, branchy, bright-green trees. Here and there a native hut, white-washed and with grass roof, would peep through the foliage. In little gardens grew crimson-flowered shrubs. African Kites quartered the harbour in search of offal and Aden Gulls flew lazily about or sat inert on the water. We anchored and the day moved on hot and sultry, the ship swinging with the tide. Evening came and the sun sank behind the tall palms, silhouetting their feathery fronds against a sky of pink and blue. Overhead passed flocks of weavers and from the dense jungle came the cries of strange birds. Redder became the sky and amongst the palms parties of Wire-tailed Swallows hawked the myriad of insects which dusk had brought out. Still the strange birds called and the palms bent in the cool evening breeze.'

We stayed two or three days in Mombasa, but we were not allowed ashore. I remember watching a pair of African Sea Eagles perched on an old dead tree on the water's edge and only 100 yards from the ship, uttering strange cries; and on the morning we sailed it was exciting to see a flock of pelicans flying in V formation over the harbour. A few days later we crossed the Line and King Neptune came aboard to hold court. The ridiculous contrived ceremony, unusual in this instance, being performed as the ship sailed from south to north, was amusing to watch and made a change from the daily routine. We were all given certificates which were to give us immunity from the indignities which might be inflicted upon us in similar ceremonies should we change hemispheres in the future.

A week or so later we began to see Arab dhows plying between the Red Sea and India, suggesting that we were nearing our journey's end. Just before midday on 3rd. March, 1941 the port of Bombay hove in sight, the Gateway of India and the Taj Mahal Hotel being prominent objects in an otherwise rather dull scene. In the bay were hundreds of dhows – beautiful but rough boats – and overhead scores of Black Kites circled in the thermal currents, uttering their mewing cries soon to become so familiar. By early afternoon we were safely docked and our 12,000 mile journey had come to a mercifully uneventful end.

On the following morning we entrained for Bangalore with special apologies from the Cadet College officers who had met us for the conditions of travel we were to endure on an Indian troop train. The third class carriages had hard wooden bench seats, with a hinged shelf of similar shape and size above which provided a place to spread a blanket and lie flat. The windows, which let down, were slatted and without glass, and there was a native-style loo at each end of the carriage. There was no pretence at comfort, but as the journey was to take little more than 48 hours, and everything was new and exciting, we all accepted the gross over-crowding and made the best of it. The old soldiers amongst us were to be in No.1 Wing at the College and do four months training; while the rest of us were to do six months in No.2 Wing. At the time I wrote:

'This evening we entrained for Bangalore. As we drew away from the city, the Indian countryside began to spread itself before us. Paddy fields of brilliant green, dotted here and there with white egrets stalking frogs in the sodden soil; King Crows sitting on the telephone wires, humped-backed cattle heaving heavy carts and countless drab women kneading cow-dung cakes to dry in the morrow's sun for use as fuel. All these things appeared in a great and wonderful panorama, now so thrilling but later, no doubt, to become familiar scenes scarcely to be noticed. The engine panted frantically as we climbed the Western Ghats, but night had fallen and the famous scenery of these hills was denied us . . . This morning we woke to find ourselves on the Deccan Plateau several hundred feet above sea level. The country was intensely flat, supporting many villages whose inhabitants cultivated the stony ground with wooden ploughs drawn by skinny bullocks. The telegraph wires were still supporting many Drongos and, at stations, crows and ground squirrels came down near the train . . . Indian railway stations are weird and wonderful. A long dusty platform has, perhaps, one small building in the middle where works the Station Master – an exalted individual who wears a European topi as a mark of importance. His dignity is great and his stomach ample as he strides along the platform, monarch of all he surveys! Dotted about on the platform are groups of coolies, their authorised hireage written plainly on their maroon shirts. Some are smoking "bidis", some are chewing "pan", all are spitting and all are talking incessantly, none is listening. A traveller with his veiled wife leans heavily on a stick, waiting with eastern patience for a train which he has heard may arrive during the week. Naked children play in the dust or tease a lame pie-dog, laughing merrily and without pity at its limp-hanging foreleg, which has been crushed by a train. A wretched semi-naked beggar with sunken sightless eyes wanders up the platform waving a handless stump, beseeching money from apathetic passengers. A sacred Brahminy bull wanders up the platform. The heat is intense, the dust in swirling eddies engulfs a "bhisti" as he runs up the train pouring cooling water into many cupped palms outstretched from the carriage windows . . . This morning found us in slightly greener country. Bee-eaters replaced the Drongos and Paddy-birds strolled the fields. Towards evening we started to climb again and at 11.00 p.m. we drew into Bangalore station.'

CHAPTER 2

GENTLEMEN CADETS AT BANGALORE

As the train came to a halt the warm air, smelling of dust and cow-dung smoke, enveloped the carriage and the darkness beyond the platform lights was silky and intense. We could hardly believe our ears when a Sgt. Major came aboard and addressed us as 'Gentlemen', requesting us to pick up our kitbags and follow him in single file. Out through the station gates we went to the forecourt, where an assemblage of Indian buses stood in serried ranks. The order to move was given and the ancient vehicles came to life, each belching forth blue smoke and following one another in clouds of dust as we drove through the city to the cantonments, the smell of the hot Indian night wafting through the open windows. We were taken straight to our company messes, which were converted barrack rooms, one end for dining and the other an ante-room where white-clad, turbaned bearers, ignoring our unkempt appearance, served us with an excellent meal as though we were already officers and gentlemen. Then, by platoons, we marched to our quarters, where our personal bearers (one between four) were waiting to start their 6-month stint of attending to our every want. We were accommodated two to a room, each cadet having a charpoy, complete with a mosquito net, a chair, desk and almirah as well as a bedside table. The loos and baths, ample in numbers, were situated at the end of each block of ten rooms. To wash off the dust and dirt of days and to sink into bed between sheets, after being asked by the bearer what time he should bring 'chhota hazri', seemed heaven itself and sleep came quickly for what was left of the night.

Waking on that first Indian morning was an experience which I shall never forget. Once the feeling had passed of wondering where I was as I opened my eyes to find a little world enclosed in a mosquito net, the unaccustomed sounds crowded in upon me. The harsh cries of the House

Crows, the cackles of the Common Mynahs, the long quivering mews of the Black Kites all mingled with the man-made noises of the bearers ordering the bhistis to bring water, and the clatter of cups as the chhota hazris were prepared. The bugle call sounding 'Parade' for the resident Duty Company reminded me that I was in the army, although the bearer, padding softly into the room with tea and biscuits, was proof enough that this army had a very human face.

Our Company Commander was Capt. Stone, 7th. Gurkha Rifles, and our Platoon Commander was P.S.M. Davies (a rank invented by Hore-Belisha in the mid-thirties and soon to be abandoned) who said, on the first morning, 'I call you "Sir", you call me "Staff".' He was clearly at a disadvantage vis-a-vis the other platoon commanders, who were lieutenants and senior to him. Furthermore, the Company Sergeant Major, whose name was Workman, was also senior to him but held a post which was junior. Nevertheless, he quickly gained our respect, even our affection, and he was in fact much more professional and competent than the officer platoon commanders.

First parade each morning was at 0700 hrs.; in the early days drill followed and later field exercises. Bicycling to the parade ground under command of the cadet N.C.O. (we took this in turn) in the cool morning air was delightfully invigorating. The sun, which had barely started to show above the trees and buildings, gave little hint of the strength it was to muster in the next hour or two. Long shadows stretched across the shiny tarmac road as each platoon of cyclists, in files, sped past trundling bullock carts and heavy-laden tongas pulled by skinny ponies; India wakes early to beat the scorching heat. Drill parade over, we returned as we had come to our quarters at about 0800 hrs. and then walked over to the mess for a truly English breakfast of cereals, bacon and eggs and local fruit in season such as papayas or mangoes. The cantonment had its own dairy farm, so fresh milk and butter were always available, even if the butter did taste rancid at times. The messing in general was excellent although, as the weeks wore on, menus became predictable. But changes of scene were possible because we were all made members of the Bangalore United Services Club (B.U.S.), where sports facilities were available as well as meals. As far as sports at the college were concerned, there was none of the glorification which public schools lavish upon rugger and cricket. If you did not wish to play either, and I did not, nobody minded and there was no stigma attached. I found my recreation in occasional tennis, frequent golf, and shooting whenever possible, as well as bird-watching.

I find it hard to recall very much of our military training, but a colleague, writing 50 years later, had this to say:-

'Our training lacked any sort of realism and, although at the time I thought we worked hard, I can now see with hindsight that there was no real feeling of urgency. There was an acute shortage of transport and we went everywhere on bicycles. I never saw a military radio set at Bangalore and all our signal training was done using Morse code, either with an Aldis signalling lamp or semaphore flags which, after leaving the college, I never used again. Much of our tactical training was to do with the drills of piqueting on the North West Frontier. Modern mechanised warfare was only briefly mentioned and jungle warfare was not taught at all. The one subject that was taught most thoroughly was "Duties in aid of the Civil Power", i.e. riot drills. There was an acute shortage of modern weapons and training ammunition, so on exercises we represented firing by whirling rattles or waving flags.'

That may have been so, but we were mainly being trained to be junior officers with a very special status in an entirely professional volunteer army, and moreover one in which there was a unique and extra stratum of authority – the Viceroy's Commissioned Officer (V.C.O.). Whereas a British infantry battalion had an establishment of some 35 to 40 King's Commissioned Officers, an Indian infantry battalion had only 15, the rest being V.C.O.'s. In the early days of the war, these King's Commissioned Officers were nearly all British and, in the case of Gurkha regiments, invariably so throughout the war. But the V.C.O.'s were vastly more experienced than all but the most senior of the British officers because they were, without exception, promoted from the ranks and rarely had less than 15 years service before being promoted to the junior rank of Jemadar. The senior V.C.O. was the Subadar Major, who was the C.O.'s confidant in all matters concerned with the Indian ranks. Each of the four rifle companies and H.Q.Coy. had a British officer in command, with a Subadar as his 2 i/c. All platoon commanders were Jemadars, the Adjutant was assisted by a Jemadar Adjutant, and the Quartermaster, who was not an old soldier as in the British Army, but a fairly junior officer, was similarly assisted by a Jemadar Quartermaster. So every British officer had immediate and intimate advice at his disposal from V.C.O.'s of great experience and proven loyalty. Thus, what was of paramount importance in our training was learning the language which these V.C.O.'s spoke so as to take advantage of their expertise and gain their confidence. What our training lacked was any contact with these officers and other Indians. True, the Education Officer was an Indian, but his sole job seemed to be controlling the munshis who taught us individually the rudiments of Urdu. Our bearers, our only real Indian contacts, knew only Tamil and spoke to us in broken English. But for those of us who had been to English public schools, understanding our future relationship as British officers with V.C.O.'s was made easier, for the hierarchical set-up of an Indian or Gurkha battalion was very much like that of a public school: the C.O., the headmaster; the British officers, the masters; and the V.C.O.'s the prefects.

If the military training we received was to prove outdated and inappropriate, the middle East being the only likely theatre and the Japanese not being taken seriously at that time, the generally relaxed and calm atmosphere prevailing at the college was both correct and pertinent, calculated as it was to enable cadets to develop and show their qualities of leadership. We probably did not need the full six months at the college, but they were not wasted times and, for the most part, they were very enjoyable.

Much of our field training took place on Agram Plain – a hot, dusty almost treeless stretch of parched land near the college which became synonymous with sweltering, dirty discomfort. We would spend hours out there on section and platoon exercises, occasionally breaking off to sit under a scrawny tree and slake our thirst with warm, chlorinated water. Around us would be all the sounds of rural India; the monotonous 'tonking' of a distant Coppersmith, the mewing of kites, the singing of cicadas and the strident cries of bullock-cart drivers urging their beasts into momentary trots. Above, vultures circled in towering columns, keen-eyed for carrion, and pie-dogs, evicted from the shade by our presence, lurked nearby in cringing expectation of our early departure. Sometimes we did night exercises, when the eerie howling of one pack of jackals would sound across the plain to be taken up by another more distant pack; to and fro would they call like demented souls in torment until one was too distant to hear the other. Sometimes we saw them, red-eyed in our torch beams, loping along tail down and back arched. Between the jackal howls, which blocked out all other cries, the rattling call of the Indian Nightjar, resembling the sound of a stone skidding across rough ice on a pond, would mingle with the rasping of cicadas; and the chattering of a Spotted Owlet often joined the chorus. Those night exercises, beneath the velvety star-lit dome, with a half moon lying on its back above the horizon, although often tedious in themselves and robbing us of sleep, introduced me to the Indian night in a very intimate way and gave identity to erstwhile anonymous sounds.

Halfway through the course we were given a week's leave and I decided to go to Ceylon (now Sri Lanka) with a fellow cadet, Geoffrey Feiling, who also felt that the opportunity of seeing the island should not be missed. My notes, written at the time – June, 1941, recall my main impressions:-

'Arrived in Madras this morning to find it very hot and stuffy. We are staying at the Connemara Hotel, which is the acme of comfort. We drove round the city and saw various buildings of interest. It was refreshing to walk on the seashore in a cool breeze and interesting to see the fishermen, who live right down by the high-tide mark in little palm-leaf huts. It was very hot this evening and the "refrigerated" dining room was a cool sanctuary . . . Today we flew from Madras to Colombo, stopping en route at Trichinopoly. The plane was a 3-seater machine of American make with a top speed of 150 m.p.h. We flew at a steady 120 m.p.h. at an average altitude of 5,000 ft.. As it was my first flight, it was somewhat of an adventure and I greatly enjoyed it. From the air India resembled a parched, shimmering desiccated map. As we dived down onto Trichinopoly's grass-strip airfield, my ears popped and I became quite deaf. We devoured some sandwiches and tea, sitting uncomfortably in a little hut with a 60 m.p.h. gale blowing right through it. Taking off once more, we headed for the Gulf of Manar, which was shining blue and white in the distance. Over it the flight became very rough and Geoffrey's sandwiches, of which I thought I had seen the last, came on view again and were carefully placed under the seat in a greaseproof bag. Ceylon, green and steamy, loomed ahead and very soon was beneath us. Puttalam came and went amidst a mass of coconut palms as the shadow of our plane leapt across the landscape like a hunted stag. We circled round Colombo, dropping down to the green airfield – a reclaimed "maidan" in a jungle of palms. It was raining heavily and spray flew all round us as we touched down on the soggy ground. We drove through a greenhouse atmosphere to the Galle Face Hotel. . . . In a rather trippery fashion (our time is very limited) we "saw round" Colombo this morning. In a delightful park opposite the Town Hall was a banyan tree with 500 separate trunks. We watched lace being made and, shoeless, visited a Buddhist temple. Lamas with shaven heads and clad in saffron robes stalked stealthily about and eyed us with suspicious glances. Breadfruit and jackfruit trees grew in profusion round the temple and pretty little red hibiscus flowers peeped out from the green foliage. I ended the morning in the best bookshop, where I spent more than I could afford on a bird book. In the afternoon we motored up to Kandy in a hired car – an enthralling journey amidst palms, jungles, tea gardens and rubber plantations. Elephants were working in the jungle, lifting massive logs with their trunks. Flying foxes were suspended in swarms from trees lining the banks of the river at Mawanella. Our letter to the manager of the Queen's Hotel had not arrived, but Geoffrey argued with the rather pompous proprietor and eventually an indifferent room was wrested from him. The window overlooked the lake and I noticed a Common Kingfisher watching the water intently . . . Today we spent in motoring around the environs of Kandy. At Matale we again crept into a Buddhist temple, which had been hollowed out of a solid rock. These places rather bore me but they are the be all and end all of Geoffrey's existence and I have to follow meekly. Part of our route lay parallel with the Mahaweli Gunga, Ceylon's largest river, which was very muddy due to recent heavy rains; it averages 100 yards in width. We passed cocoa plantations, tea estates and rubber plantations and visited a tea factory. Rubber trees interested me; all were tall and clean-trunked, bearing a crown of glabrous, green entire leaves. Tapping is effected in a spiral fashion, the main channel having several tributaries of lesser size. The raw rubber oozes out as a white sticky liquid and is caught in small earthenware pots. The fruit is three-celled, containing three round black seeds slightly larger than a cherry stone. The size of the cocoa fruit surprised me; pinky green in colour, it averages about 8 in. in length and inside there are several 'beans'. I saw many Grey-vented Drongos (a species peculiar to the island), as well as Magpie Robins, Koels and Common Mynahs. We passed an elephant lying on its side in a river, being scrubbed by its mahout with a piece of coconut fibre. A visit to the beautiful botanic gardens at Peridynia ended the day (Earl Mountbatten set up his South East Asia Command H.Q. in these gardens in 1944) . . . This morning I went for a delightful walk on one of the hills above Kandy Lake. The start of the walk took me along a path overlooking a private garden where several birds were feeding. A Coucal walked clumsily about, White-vented Drongos, Red-vented Bulbuls and Magpie Robins consorted together in the shrubs. A female Purple Sunbird hovered over a hibiscus calling "phit-phit-phit", and a party of Jungle Babblers were having a squeaky conversation. The banks on the side of the road were covered with a curious plant which collapsed when I touched it (*impatiens*) and the hedgerow was ablaze with hibiscus flowers. Coconut palms and giant bamboos shrouded the paths and crows cried hoarsely. A Ceylon Loriquet flew screaming from a breadfruit tree, green and scarlet flashing in the sun. After lunch we motored up to Nuwara Eliya (6,200 ft.) through the most delightful scenery, which gradually changed from palms to tea gardens and finally to open country dotted with wild rhododendrons – all in the space of 65 miles. Although only six degrees north of the equator, we require a fire in our room at the Grand Hotel . . . This morning I wandered in the thick pine woods on the hill above the hotel. Ceylon White-eyes were feeding stealthily in the bushes, a dusky-blue Flycatcher sat disconsolate on a pine bough, feathers puffed up, Indian Grey Tits "sawed" loudly in the distance and Yellow-eared Bulbuls, in little parties, called "wheet-wheet-wheet" incessantly. Coucals uttered their uncanny calls which echoed up the valley. In the afternoon we visited a nearby botanic garden where I saw a Red-backed Woodpecker – a large handsome species (12 in.) with a brilliant red crest and back, closely related to the Indian Golden-backed . . . Today we returned to Colombo via Banderawella, Ratnapura and Avisawella through lovely mountain scenery. Two punctures on the way caused five hours delay, during which we were befriended by a planter near whose bungalow the incidents took place. By co-incidence he was a Northumbrian. As we sat on his verandah, hundreds of fireflies lit up the inky blackness in the most enchanting manner . . . We returned to Madras by air in very bumpy weather, starting at 0830 hrs. and arriving at 1315 hrs. We motored to Bangalore in 6½ hours.'

Golf at Bangalore on parched, stony ground with 'browns' instead of 'greens', was, to use a present-day cliché and give it a real meaning, a different ball-game. A topped drive would often go further than a well-hit shot, the ball scudding along the baked fairway, raising little puffs of dust to mark its progress; and a putt on the brown – smooth, compacted sand mixed with old engine oil and as level as a billiard table – went exactly where it was hit, unlike on a green, where undulations and different grasses cause deflections. A considerable hazard was the House Crow's liking for white golf balls, which they would swoop down upon, and carry off. To beat them, each golfer employed an 'agewalla', as well as a caddie, who went ahead, as his name implies, to where he hoped the driven ball would come. Here he would stand guard over it and, if nobody was looking, grip it in his toes and place it in a suitable lie so as to facilitate his sahib's next shot; for should he win, the chances of a more handsome tip would be enhanced.

Shooting round the jheels, paddies and sugar cane fields was fun. An extract from my diary tells briefly of a typical day:-

'John, Bill and I went out snipe shooting today. We shot over paddy and in sugar cane some six miles S.W. of Bangalore. The bag consisted of 41 snipe, 2 quails and a hare. The quails were very pretty little birds and, for a gallinaceous species, they are truly dwarf. A bevy 10 to 12 in number will rise up from the cane and fly absolutely straight with a whirring of tiny wings, to alight again quite soon and repeat the process until, if the guns are shooting well, there is none left. The hare was very small, no bigger than a rabbit.'

On another occasion my bearer brought to my room a man whom he called 'a very good shikari', who gave news of a panther near his village and said that he would make all the 'bandobust' for us to shoot it. John and I hired a taxi and drove 35 miles from Bangalore in search of evidence of this claim. The road was absolutely dreadful and the drive took much longer than we expected. But we did find what seemed to be pad marks of a panther and we asked the shikari to arrange for a bait to be put out. On the following Saturday we heard that the donkey had been killed by the panther and I rushed out here on the Sunday morning to sit over the kill. My vigil lasted two hours but nothing came, largely because vultures had played havoc with the corpse, and in any case my time was limited. In retrospect we felt that the whole thing was a put-up job. It would have been easy to fake the panther spore and any dead donkey would have been partially eaten by vultures and could easily have been placed, apparently tethered, to represent a kill. We payed the shikari Rs.20 for his services and Rs.30 for the donkey. No doubt both the shikari and the bearer received commission from the taxi driver who had driven us 140 miles at a price which I forget but which was certainly exorbitant. We were 'had for suckers', but at the time it seemed worth it for the excitement.

As Bangalore was 3,000 ft. above sea level, we tended to have reasonably cool nights even during the hottest weather, which occurred just before the monsoon broke in May. On one day when I recorded a maximum day temperature of 97°F, the minimum that night was more than 20 degrees cooler at 74°F. As May gave way to June, thunderstorms with gusty winds became quite frequent. Brilliant flashes of lightning followed by distant rumblings would herald an imminent deluge. A sudden strong wind would send up columns of dust between the buildings, and, far off but fast approaching, would come the swishing sound of rain, the noise eventually becoming deafening as huge drops splashed down, ripping leaves and flowers off the trees and shrubs. Thunder would crash and lightning hiss through the damp air. Suddenly all noise would cease, all would be still except for the squeaky calls of the mynahs and the harsh cries of crows as

1. *'Shikari Party', Author on right, Bangalore, 1941*

2. *Donkey killed and eaten by panther.*

they emerged from the trees to pick up grasshoppers drowned by the rain. The damp earth would give off a very special smell and the air would be delightfully cool. Yet on the morrow the earth would be as parched and dusty as ever and the heat would have a clinging, enervating stickiness hard to bear.

I suppose that I gained as much pleasure and relaxation at Bangalore from bird-watching as from anything else. I had bought Hugh Whistler's *Popular Handbook of Indian Birds* before I left home and thus had a good idea of the commoner birds I was likely to see. So my evening walks with my binoculars were full of discovery; rarely did I fail to see something new.

House Crows and Black Kites were the most omnipresent birds, with Common Mynahs running them a close second. These cheeky birds, a little bigger than a starling, were mostly very tame, striding with waddling gate amongst the buildings. Their scientific name means 'sad grasshopper eaters'; sad they never are, although some of their squeaky cries are less than cheerful, but hunt grasshoppers they certainly do, swallowing these leggy, uncomfortable-looking insects in just two or three gulps. Vultures too were always to be seen circling in the heavens. I remember on one occasion, when a dead horse had been dumped on Agram Plain, hundreds of vultures swarmed round the carcase in a vast, black mass fighting and bickering over the entrails. Most of them were the White-backed species, both young and old, but a few Neophrons, or Egyptian Vultures, sat on the edge of the proceedings waiting for their larger brethren to sate themselves. Many of the White-backs were so gorged that they could barely rise as I approached, and departed running with clumsy, flapping wings, their bare, gory necks outstretched, until they eventually became airborne in clouds of red dust.

The jheels (lakes) were some of my favourite places, the water attracting many different species. Always there would be one or two Brahminy Kites, much more handsome than their black cousins, with chestnut bodies and wings and white heads and necks, sitting watchfully on the tops of bankside trees. On the water would be Cotton Teal and Garganey swimming in little parties; and with them on one occasion was a Nutka with its strange fleshy beak knob. Sometimes Little Cormorants would be resting on nearby trees, their wings outstretched to dry after a fishing session, and Paddy Birds would stalk the banks in search of frogs, brown and drab but flashing white when they took wing. On the floating weeds Pheasant-tailed Jacanas, or Lily Trotters, walked as if on dry land, their absurdly long toes distributing their weight. A hovering Pied Kingfisher would plop into the water to emerge black and white and dripping with a small fish in its beak; and sometimes, to remind me of home, I would see the jewel-like flash of colour as a Common Kingfisher, disturbed at its preening, flew off with whirring wings, dropping a little speck of white into the brown water.

Round the barrack buildings and in the mess garden there would be the inevitable Mynahs, but high up in the trees were the birds whose calls are, to me, India – the Coppersmith or Crimson Barbet. Rarely seen, for it remained hidden amongst the leaves in the upper branches, its mellow call, 'tonk tonk', in which there was an unmistakeable metallic ring, would be repeated indefinitely (I once counted 115 tonks in 50 seconds), becoming a constant background noise on hot days. As the temperature rose so did the persistence of the birds increase. Indeed, the monotony of the call became exasperating in the hot weather.

While the Coppersmith remained hidden, the little Purple Sunbirds were highly conspicuous, their metallic plumage flashing in the sunlight as they flitted amongst the hibiscus flowers, sucking up nectar and picking off tiny insects with their long, curved beaks. Much less conspicuous, but betraying its presence by its strident, discordant calls, was the Tailorbird – an endearing little creature both because of its confiding habits and its practice of making its nest in a cup of growing leaves stitched together with cobwebs. In the garden too, where the lawns between the canna beds were kept mown and tidy by the industrious malees, the Magpie Robin would hop about on the grass, flashing black and white in and out of the shade as it picked up insects; and in the early mornings and again at eventide it would perch on a tree or roof-top to pour forth its delicious song, made the more so by the scarcity of songbirds in India.

Out in the country, beyond the college bounds, many loud and raucous bird sounds seemed to typify the hot dry vastness of the land. One in particular, known to everyone in India, was the call of the Koel, which, as the name implies, is an oft-repeated 'ko-el', increasing in intensity and ascending in scale to reach a frenzy of excitement before suddenly ceasing. Despite this persistence, which really can get on one's nerves, the Koel deserves respect as the only bird which regularly gets the better of the House Crow, for it is a member of the cuckoo family and lays its eggs in crows' nests, where the young are brought up by the tricked foster parents. Not so enduringly noisy, but only protesting when disturbed, were the Red-wattled Lapwings, long-legged and constantly bobbing when on the ground. They would fly up, always in pairs, uttering a penetrating 'Did-he-do-it, Pity-to-do-it' time and time again, to settle, bob and run before flying off once more, shrieking in protest. Where telegraph wires ran across country or along roads, Blue Jays or Rollers, would sit on the wires at regular intervals, dumpy and dull-coloured when at rest, but showing Oxford-blue wings and Cambridge-blue tails when in flight. On the wires too would be the King Crows or Drongos, black with gracefully forked tails, every now and then darting into the air to snap up passing insects with loudly clicking beaks, before returning to base on the wires.

All these birds and many more did I see and hear on my evening walks; those peaceful hours when the pressure of training was forgotten and when, for a short while, it was a pleasure to be alone. Sometimes I found myself oblivious of India's sights and sounds as my thoughts turned to home. Well did I share the feeling which prompted Robert Browning to write those famous words, 'Oh to be in England now that April's there'. How I yearned then to hear the Chaffinches singing in the plane trees lining Parks Road, Oxford, or the Blackbirds in the wych elms at home, the sawing of the Great Tits and the sad melody of the Willow Warblers! But these nostalgic musings did not last long; screeches from the Ringnecked Parakeets flying swiftly to their roosts, Red-rumped Swallows hawking round the rain trees, a sudden flash of colour or an unaccustomed sound, would soon bring back my thoughts to India. Long would be the shadows, cooler the breezes and stronger the scent of cow-dung fires as I returned to my quarters where Moonaswamy would be squatting by the door, polishing my boots and standing briefly to greet me before ordering the bhisti to bring my bath water.

This old man found pleasure in service; not for him the siren calls of Indian politicians promising Utopia when the sahibs had gone; he knew his place and had no illusions about promised betterment in this event. He had worked for sahibs all his life and knew them to be honest, just and caring. There were rogues, of course, amongst them, but how could they have ruled India for 200 years without the respect and affection of the great mass of people? Moonaswamy was one of that mass who found employment and satisfaction in the loyal service which he gave.

Towards the end of the course we spent several days under canvas out in the jungle some distance from Bangalore, carrying out company and platoon exercises, each of us in turn acting as company commander. The whole paraphernalia of college messing came with us, including mess tents and bearers, so there was no question of roughing it. We slept on palliasses on the ground, eight to a large tent, but the only congestion which occurred came at reveille, when eight bearers came in carrying trays of chhota hazri and found little space to put them down. Again, being out in the wild sleeping in a tent, the night sounds came close, many of them eerie and unexplained, to accompany the snoring of companions and the howls of jackals, quick to sense rich pickings round the camp.

On the final weekend before we left, my cousin John Beazley and I spent two nights in Mysore. Shortly after we arrived in Bangalore, John had bought a horse at the concessionary price for cadets of Rs. 50. He hunted it with the local jackal pack and helped the kennel-huntsman to look after the large pack of hounds. On this occasion he had entered his horse, Lottery, for one of the amateur races in Mysore. He was in illustrious company, for his co-competitors included the Maharajah of Cooch Behar and the Governor of Madras, Sir John Hope. John was not placed but we enjoyed the rest of the weekend at the new hotel near the recently constructed hydro-electric dam at Seringapatam. We visited the premises of the world-famous taxidermists, Van Ingen, where there were many trophies beautifully set up: sambhur heads, Himalayan bears, tiger and panther skins with superbly mounted heads and much else besides, including the skeleton of an Indian girl removed from a crocodile's stomach, with teeth marks on her bangles plainly visible.

So busy were we with so much of interest to see and do beyond our military training that the six months passed very quickly and the time came when our passing-out grades and regimental postings would be published. The threat of 'Return to Unit' (R.T.U.) had always been there, although, in fact, we had no units in India to which we could be returned. Indeed, relegation to the next course seemed to be the worst that could befall those who failed to make the grade, with a posting to the 'Rice Corps' (R.I.A.S.C.) being the actual fate of the marginally incompetent. On the great day I found that I had passed out fairly well and was posted to the 3rd/9th. Gurkha Rifles, the regiment of my choice, and my destination was to be the North-west Frontier. John Beazley too got his choice – the 4th/12th. Frontier Regiment, our Uncle Walter's old battalion.

CHAPTER 3

NORTH-WEST FRONTIER

It was a proud moment when we put up our 'pips'; anyone who affects to find no elation from the occasion is scarcely credible. Likewise, who could pretend that his heart was not stirred by the first salute to the commission which he has just received, or fail to be humble enough to realise that this act of recognition is to the commission and not to him?

Our first day as officers ended with a farewell dinner, and on the morrow, with our bedding rolls and trunks labelled to our several destinations throughout the sub-continent, we went to the station by the same route and the same transport as we had come by six months before. Hugh Power, who had also been posted to 3rd/9th (G.R.), and I headed for Bombay and ten days joining leave.

In September, 1941, the India which we were about to serve was on the point of radical change, but we were just in time to see the last of the old Raj. One of my fellow cadets, when asked to provide something to include in a commemorative booklet which I edited for the 50th Anniversary Reunion of the *Highland Chieftain* draft, sent me this:

'It is important to remember the India of 1941. First and foremost India was the "Jewel in the Crown" of the British Empire. It was a vast country of some 500 million people. Generations of soldiers, adventurers, businessmen and administrators had served and worked there to keep the "Pax Britannica" in the Empire's proudest possession. India was then composed of British India and 565 Indian states, large and small, ruled by maharajahs, rajahs and nawabs who each had an average of 11 titles, 5.8 wives, 12.6 children, 9.2 elephants, 2.8 railway cars, 3.4 Rolls-Royces, and had bagged 22.9 tigers. In 1941 India was not at war in the real meaning of the word. Pearl Harbour and the consequent advance of the Japanese armies to the very borders of India were yet to come. Life continued in the time-honoured way, servants were plentiful and one could live like a king on a pittance. For those in the Army it was a sportsman's paradise.'

Our journey to Bombay, especially that part of it which took us across the Deccan, was hot and uncomfortable; to make matters worse, we missed two connections, making us 12 hours late. But as we neared our destination and started to descend the Western Ghats, the country became most attractive. The train twisted here and there along the precipitous track amidst fresh green hills, lately bathed by the monsoon rains. All the dust and dirt, so much part of the earlier stages of the journey, seemed to have been washed away. The country of the Mahrattas was certainly beautiful at that time of year.

We booked into the Taj Mahal Hotel, where officers of H.M. Forces enjoyed a 50% discount, and were given a room overlooking the harbour, which was dotted with tramp steamers, liners and naval vessels. In the background, shimmering in the heat (it was 88°F and very humid when we arrived) was Elephant Island and its satellites; in the sky, wheeling in the thermals, were countless kites and a few vultures keeping an expectant eye on the Parsee Towers of Silence. Darting amongst the roofs of the hotel and other buildings was a myriad of Indian Swifts, their effortless twisting and turning punctuated by short dipping glides.

After our fairly strenuous six months at Bangalore, we were content to do very little in Bombay. I spent one morning at the Bombay Natural History Society's museum, mostly in the Bird Section, which I was surprised to find so limited in extent considering India's wealth of birdlife. On one afternoon we hired a sailing boat and went out in the bay, where it was refreshingly cool. Kites were quartering the dirty sea, picking up offal as it appeared and filling the air with their loud, wailing cries. I saw no gulls, although the Aden species was common enough out to sea, as I remember from our voyage; but for some reason, perhaps because of the kites, they did not frequent the bay.

On the evening of the 17th September 1941, we boarded the Frontier Mail – the most famous and longest distance through-train in India – which in those days left Bombay at 2000 hrs. and was due in Peshawar 46 hours later. It was dark, of course, when the train drew out of the station and made its way through the city's shanty town suburbs to the accompaniment of constant blasts on the steam-engine's moaning whistle, which served to clear the unfenced line of all who used it as a convenient highway. Dimly-lit dusty streets thronged with people, goats, cattle and bullock carts, gradually gave way to isolated shacks and shops, their pressure lamps stabbing the darkness to pick out a tonga or a wandering bull, until all was black beyond the light thrown by the carriages and we were in open country.

Although the dining car was air-conditioned in a somewhat primitive fashion – ice being stored beneath the floor with air blown over it into the carriage – there was no such comfort elsewhere on the train. Gyrating fans buzzed overhead, circulating the hot air round the bunks, but it was not possible to open the windows fully because of the dust, as well as the scope it would give to the light-fingered at stations. A fine gauze screen covered the windows, excluding the larger particles of dirt and the slightly cooler night air. So we sweated in our bunks and composed ourselves to sleep accompanied by rhythmic wheel noises and considerable lurching from the none-too-perfect track. I woke in the early hours, when the train stopped at a station, with a raging thirst. In what I thought was faultless Hindustani, I ordered two bottles of soda water; what I got was two buns and a glass of milk, all of dubious cleanliness, and I remained thirsty. But I did manage to get to sleep again, even through the stop at Baroda, and woke at 0600 hours as the steward brought in some very welcome tea. Hugh, meanwhile, had slept throughout the night.

As Indian trains had no corridors, we had to wait for a stop before being able to walk to the dining car; likewise, having finished a meal, we had to sit there until another stop before returning to our compartment. In those days the Frontier Mail was one of the few trains which had a restaurant car. The normal practice was that the train stopped at a station which had a restaurant, when passengers would alight and have a meal, the train waiting until they had finished with consequent disruption of the published timetable.

After breakfast on the first morning I watched Rajputana pass by the windows. The country ranged from flat to gently undulating and, so shortly after the monsoon, looked green and park-like. Peafowl abounded and even above the clatter of the carriage wheels their strident cries of 'mee-ow, mee-ow' could plainly be heard. Once some blackbuck scampered away, heads up and horns flat along their backs. Bee-eaters sat on the telegraph wires, swooping away to snap up passing insects and returning to their perches. Sarus Cranes stalked the maize fields like tall scraggy women, whilst those nearer the passing train ran bouncing and bumping like 1901 aeroplanes before hauling their loosely-made frames into the air. As the country became drier, the green crops growing in isolated patches between large expanses of brown parched earth, lines of camels became a feature, each beast roped to the one in front, marching along the dusty roads with their loads swinging and swaying to the rhythm of their long strides as they passed groups of women with pots of water or bundles of firewood on their heads. Indeed, the ceaseless toil of the peasants was everywhere apparent. Out in the fields some were cultivating the hard, stony ground with wooden ploughs pulled by skinny oxen; others were lifting water from wells in leather buckets hauled up by ropes or by compensating see-saws with a weight on one end and the bucket on the other. At bigger wells water-buffaloes yoked to booms described endless circles so as to turn water wheels raising the precious liquid in scoops to flow down sloping channels to the fields. Yet other workers were reaping crops, winnowing wheat or stacking maize in bullock carts – all in the shimmering heat and vastness of the Indian plains. Except when we moved to and fro from the dining car, I scarcely took my eyes off this fascinating panorama.

We reached Delhi after nightfall and saw very little of it; nothing more than the dimly lit outskirts and the railway station which, from the train, looked like any other, crowded with traders, coolies and beggars as well as travellers. Some of these were rich and prosperous and were followed by coolies carrying 'saman' on their heads; others poor and wretched clasped pathetic little bundles wrapped in dirty cloth. Not even the hissing of steam from the engines could drown the hubbub of strident voices as the whole platform seethed with jostling humanity.

Another night, less hot and stuffy as we moved north, passed off uneventfully and tea was brought as the train stood in Amritsar station – that town of legendary infamy – and we had breakfast in Lahore. Again miles and miles of flat cultivated fields, interspersed with expanses of sunbaked barren plains, composed the scenery as we crossed the River Jhelum and started to climb the rugged hills south of Rawalpindi, where we arrived at 1500 hrs., with a five-hour wait for our next connection.

The atmosphere in 'Pindi' was quite different from that in a town in southern India. I think it was the people who made it so. Tall, bearded and pale brown in colour – these seemed to be the chief characteristics of the men. The women were mostly veiled, the lines of their bodies hidden in shapeless, ample-length attire; although some were less shy, their faces visible, and dressed in shirts and jodhpur-like trousers. Beggars were few and the people prouder and less servile. Indeed, as we realised later, this was typical of a Muslim city with a very special frontier atmosphere.

At 2130 hours that evening, after a much-needed bath and an excellent dinner at Flashman's Hotel, we again entrained, this time on the overnight narrow gauge express to Mari Indus, one of the few places in the North West Frontier Province where there was a bridge across the Indus. We arrived there at 0700 hrs. on the following morning and, after a good breakfast at the station, we boarded the train affectionately known as the 'Heatstroke Express'. Well named, this comical little train followed the Indus south for some miles before branching off west along a tributary valley and then north to Bannu – a total distance of some 60 miles. On either side were barren hills which seemed to reflect the heat on to the train as the little engine, panting furiously all the way, hauled its line of toy, lurching carriages up towards the Afghan mountains. For some six hours we endured this ordeal beneath a whirring fan as we crept through this arid, scorching land, the windows wide open to catch the slight breeze which a speed of 10 m.p.h provides. With red dust still swirling round us, the shadows already lengthening and the fierce heat somewhat abating, we drew into Bannu station. The tonga ride to the Officers' Rest Camp through tree-lined streets and past identical, flat-roofed bungalows was cool and pleasant; the bells on the harness jingled merrily as the driver urged his skinny pony to greater efforts with shouts and cracks of the whip.

In those days a sizeable military force of several brigades was kept employed 'pacifying' the Pathans of the N.W. Frontier. These were a law unto themselves, living in permanent hostility to the British and in constant feuds with one another. The Indian Government's writ scarcely ran in Waziristan, yet it was vital to keep watch on the Afghan border. So hostile were the tribes, especially the Mahsuds, that only large military posts could safely exist in that wild mountainous country. Brigade garrisons were stationed permanently in such places as Wana, Razmuk and Kohat, with roads connecting them to more peaceful places such as Bannu. Not only had the garrisons themselves to be defended, but the roads leading to them were under constant threat and could only be used by lorry convoys protected both by armoured car escorts and by smaller garrisons and piquets at vital points along the roads.

It was in one of those convoys that we set out from Bannu. Once beyond the cantonment, we were soon in a country of barren hills sparsely covered with evergreen oak scrub, criss-crossed by deep nullahs, their beds etched by occasional flash floods. As the lorries laboured up the steep inclines, we passed groups of Pathans, rifles slung on their shoulders, daggers in their belts and bandoliers of cartridges slung across their chests. They eyed us with hawk-like curiosity, glancing over their shoulders to try and see what the lorries were carrying, which might have been anything from ammunition

Gardai Camp, Waziristan, taken from I.Y. Picket in 1941.

Gardai Camp, Waziristan, 1941.

to rations, or tents to personal effects.

Gradually the mountains grew taller and the nullahs deeper. We passed an old camp called Razani, recently abandoned because of a plague of rats, cockroaches and other unpleasant creatures which had defied extermination. It was replaced some miles further on by Gardai, our destination, which soon hove in sight. On a broad expanse of flat land surrounded by low hills was this 400 yards square camp, contained within an eight-foot tall dry-stone wall; the tops of hundreds of tents were shining white in the strong sunshine. Here and there wisps of blue smoke drifted up in the still air, giving the only sign of human occupation; it seemed as though we were approaching a dead city. But suddenly the broad-brimmed felt hats of the Gurkhas appeared above the roadside 'sangars' as they kept a sharp look-out for snipers in the scrub-covered hillsides. And then, in a small tent half buried in a deep wide trench, we saw some British officers, the black buttons of a rifle regiment on their blue mazri shirts. Some of them came out to watch us pass and gave us a friendly wave as we completed the last few hundred yards of our journey and turned into the camp gate, where the sentry shouldered arms to give us our first regimental salute.

We had often been told that on first joining a regiment, a subaltern's life was far from congenial: that he was at everyone's beck and call; he was to be seen and not heard and do more than his fair share of irksome duties; and to be looked upon as a general dog's body by the more senior officers. It was totally different in the 3/9th Gurkha Rifles, where we were made genuinely welcome from the start. Our C.O., Robbie Fawcett, greeted us in a firm yet fatherly fashion, making it quite plain that whereas he would brook no familiarity, he would do everything in his power to make us feel at home – part of a family of which he was head. He was quick to appreciate the fortes and foibles of his officers, encouraging the former and laughing at the latter. Once he had given you a job to do, you had his complete confidence and support; he gave credit when it was due and constructive criticism when it was necessary. We all loved him and, in consequence, we belonged to a happy battalion. Thus the other officers were pleased and proud to welcome us to its ranks and within a week we were completely accepted both by the British officers and by the Gurkhas who, being quick to appreciate our acceptance by those officers whom they knew, readily accepted our *bona fide* authority over them.

I was posted to D Company under Dudley Spain, who from that day to this, some 55 years later, has remained a close friend. The Company 2nd-in-command was Subadar Gumansing Mall, of the Thakur caste, with 25 years' service, and a man of commanding appearance complete with a curly, waxed moustache. He was extraordinarily kind and helpful to me and I owe him a great debt of gratitude, for within a few days of my arrival Dudley became acting Adjutant and I acting Company Commander with less than a month's service. Without Gumansing's unswerving loyalty and unstinting support I could not have coped.

To start with Gumansing and I conversed in Urdu, but I quickly picked up Gurkhali, and very necessary it was that I did, for the riflemen understood little Urdu and it was vital to be able to speak to them as soon as possible. In the early mornings Gumansing and I, both dressed in P.T. kit, would go out on to the football ground beyond the boundary wall and watch the platoons at their morning exercises. He would tell me about the other two Gurkha Officers in the Company – Jemadars Indrabahadur Khattri and Tekbahadur Khattri – about the N.C.O.'s and about himself and his long service with 1/9th G. R. Now and again he would admonish a rifleman for slack work or praise another for keenness, his sharp eyes glancing with pride at the men whom he had watched over and trained since the Battalion was raised and they came as recruits less than a twelvemonth before. After breakfast he would come to the office tent to report to me on the state of the Company: the number of men on leave, the numbers of those who had reported sick (usually bumps and bruises sustained during games on the hard, stony football pitch) and on letters received from Nepal by the men, reporting deaths or disasters requiring the early presence of the recipients. Many of these were bogus and I had to rely entirely on the Gurkha Officers to assess their worth. Hardly ever did he report a misdemeanour, for not only did they rarely occur but when they did they were usually dealt with by the Gurkha Officers in their own way. I was an acting figurehead, entranced by what I saw and heard; such enthusiasm, such faith in the C.O. and his officers, such pride in the regiment. As I walked round the weapon-training parades with Gumansing (we had just started to replace the old Lewis Gun with the new V.B.), I was amazed at the competence of the N.C.O.'s and at the keenness of the riflemen to learn and excel. What a privilege it was to serve with these men!

Twice a week the lorry convoy supplying Razmak was in need of our protection along the road through our area. As dawn was breaking, we would march out of the camp by companies to install platoon pickets on the hills overlooking the road. Never could a unit move, be it a platoon or a section, without another taking up a position to give it covering fire as it went forward. So, we would proceed by bounds until we were all in positions which commanded our surroundings and gave the road maximum protection. I, with Company H.Q., would move with a platoon, set up my headquarters in some central spot and await events. It was then, as the sun came up to take the chill from the autumn air, and as ravens wheeled and croaked high in the clear blue sky and a Lammergeier flapped slowly past, that Gumansing and I would talk of his home in far-off Nepal and I of mine in even more far-off and much less dramatic Birkenhead; of his shooting expeditions after chukor in the selfsame barren hills which surrounded us and after Kalij Pheasants in his mountain homeland; of fierce exchanges of fire with the tribesmen when he was a rifleman in 1/9th G. R. operating out of Razmak, and of distasteful duties performed during the Bengal rebellion in 1933.

Sometimes an orderly would come running up, stones clattering down the slope in his wake, bearing a message from a platoon; a suspicious movement had been seen, a rifleman had been smitten with a sudden fever or, more simply, could they boil water for tea? Bleeps from the radio would announce the imminent arrival of the convoy and the need for maximum vigilance. Far above us bright flashes betrayed a heliograph at Alexandra Picket (at that time the highest military garrison in the Empire at some 8,000 feet) making contact with a far-off outlier. A Hawker Hart of the R.A.F. would come droning up the valley ready to spot for the Mountain Artillery should a major incident occur. Gumansing would add a little rum to our hot, sweet tea to warm ourselves as the convoy snaked up the road and out of sight. Then we would return to the camp as we had come, each unit covered by another as it leap-frogged back to comparative safety. The spice of possible danger, the invigorating climate and the healthy, strenuous exercise all combined to give a real sense of achievement. A late lunch in the Mess was more than welcome.

The Mess was in two large overlapping tents, surrounded, as all tents in the camp were, by mud and stone walls. Coconut matting covered the floor and Military Engineering Service (M.E.S.) furniture gave the dining room a somewhat spartan look, but the anteroom, where there was a fireplace built into the wall, bore a more homely appearance with comfortable chairs hired from Bannu. A small tent on one side housed the Gurkha mess orderlies and all the paraphernalia required for serving drinks; while on the other side was the kitchen tent with a charcoal range and the mess butler's pantry. He was called Yussef Khan and, being only moderately effective, was generally known as Useless Khan, which was very unfair because he was a great deal of use and very clever at remembering the many different kinds of egg dishes which were ordered severally at breakfast; neither did he, despite his generally unprepossessing appearance, deserve the ironic nickname given him by Robbie – Angelface.

Our living accommodation was also in two-pole tents (known as EPIP), again with mud and stone walls and fireplaces, two subalterns to a tent and one each for the other officers. Indian charpoys were the beds, together with essential furniture. We each had personal bearers whom we payed Rs.30 per month, as well as Gurkha orderlies whose job it was to keep our personal arms (Smith & Wesson revolvers) in order as well as to clean certain items of our equipment, such as Sam Browne belts. They also came out with us on operations and remained close at hand ready for any emergency.

Messing was remarkably good, considering how far away we were from civilisation. This was due partly to Robbie's love of good food and to Dudley who, as Mess Secretary, was not prepared to let our isolation cause a slipping of standards. He ordered luxuries from Bannu to diversify the menus, supervised the cook and generally kept the Mess staff up to scratch. I cannot remember what our monthly mess bills totalled, but I know that out of my pay of Rs.400 per month (about £400 a year) I had a great deal left over after paying my bill and my bearer; and the bill included drink, of which there was no shortage, the most popular kinds being gin and bitters or gin piaz (little onions on sticks).

In the camp with us was Brigade H.Q., commanded by Brigadier Hungerford, formerly of the Mahratta Regiment and a very delightful man, and a British Battalion, the Royal Warwickshire Regiment. We had little contact with this regiment and I do not recollect any inter-mess visits. Once a month their band played in our lines, but what the Gurkhas made of this western music it was difficult to say. On one occasion there was much blowing of whistles in the Warwicks' lines and smoke rose in a black plume from a tent. It transpired that it was the Sergeants' Mess that had gone up in flames together with the mess accounts, which were reputed to be in disarray. That, I think, as well as a great deal of unnecessary night firing, was about the only excitement which the Warwicks provided.

To protect the camp from sniping and worse, there were permanent pickets of a platoon strength stationed on the hills surrounding the camp, each battalion being responsible for two or three. The personnel were changed once a week and the spell away from the rigid routine of camp life was generally enjoyed by the Gurkhas, although the conditions on the hill-tops were very cramped and there was always some danger of being overwhelmed by tribesmen at night, particularly when the moon was in its quarters. Alarms would occasionally occur when Verey lights would be fired to illuminate the scene. On one occasion, a reported attack during which shots were fired by the Gurkhas, left only a dead porcupine lying near the perimeter fence in the morning. I sometimes went up to a picket when one of my platoons was due for duty. They had to take all their rations, fuel, ammunition and water with them, carried by mules from the Brigade R.I.A.S.C. Transport Company. As always, we climbed up with one section covering another in leap-frog progression. At the picket the scene was superb. Below, on one side, was the camp looking compact and geometrical, to the north the tall snow-covered mountains of Afghanistan, with Alexandra Picket in the foreground overlooking the furthermost garrison, Razmak. Southwards the road snaked away between arid foothills, a tenuous link with civilisation far beyond the purple haze.

It was refreshing to be up at this lonely spot, well beyond the range of camp noises. Only the faintest snatches of bugle calls could be heard above the swish of wind in the sangar walls and the croaks of ravens wheeling in the sky. As I sat there while the change-over took place, my respect and admiration for the Gurkhas was further fortified by seeing how cheerfully they accepted the dangers and discomfort involved in spending a week hemmed in by stone walls, with only a single tent roof to keep out the rain and snow. In all weathers, day and night, constant vigilance was vital, lest the tribesmen should creep up and overwhelm the post, as indeed had happened, especially to British regiments. The tribesmen's object in attacking a post was to obtain weapons, both to shoot at the British as a kind of sport and to enable them to carry on their family feuds.

As the time came to return to the camp, the mules, much less burdened and carrying only empty water 'pakals' and the men's bedding, would make for home, dragging their straining muleteers as they slithered down the rocky path, sending streams of stones rattling down the steep slopes. The Gurkhas, sure-footed as ever and carrying heavy packs and pouches, would come down in measured bounds, instinctively choosing firm ground for their feet, their burdens a mere nothing to their short, stubby legs.

October and November came and went as I gradually gained confidence and became increasingly aware of my good fortune in my posting to a Gurkha regiment. The weather became colder, with frequent frosts and occasional snow which, in Gardai, never lay for long, though higher up it put a winter-long blanket on the gaunt mountains. Fur-lined boots and leather jackets were issued, and very welcome they were when the wind, sweeping down from Afghanistan, popularly known as the 'Breath of Death', blew for days on end, its chill factor accentuated by a relative humidity of some 3 per cent, as it cut through even the thickest clothes. For three days in October a dust storm raged; everywhere and everything became coated with a grey powder and it was hardly possible to see further than 100 yards. On the third evening the wind dropped, leaving the still air full of dust and the moon surrounded by a succession of haloes.

We did road protection about twice a week, and on other days weapon training and field firing on the range in a deep nullah near the camp. The tallest mountain which we had to climb was 'Camel's Hump'; its summit was 7,000 feet above sea level and 2,000 feet above the camp. Up there, again beyond the sounds of human activity, it was so peaceful and the scenery so dramatic. As we sat down and caught our breath after the climb, we could see the Safed Koh range, at first tinted pink as the sun rose up from the plains, and later shimmering white against the bright blue sky. Soon the sun became quite warm and little mid-blue gentians started to peep through the thyme mats which covered the stony ground, together with a tiny purple creeping daisy. I believe that the gentians became a favourite with Queen Mary, who had received some from General Wigram, a brother of Lord Wigram, King George V's private secretary and at one time commanding at Razmak. They were planted at Balmoral. I never saw them lower down than Camel's Hump. Lammergeiers would fly past, turning their heads to look at us without any sign of fear. These birds, sometimes known as Bearded Vultures, are mainly scavengers with a particular liking for bones, swallowing the small ones whole, but taking the larger up into the air, dropping them from a great height on to rocks and swooping down to eat the fragments.

Occasionally incidents occurred at night in the camp, mostly when snipers fired into the tents or at one of the pickets. This happened once when I was inspecting the perimeter posts at 0200 hours. The sound of the shots echoed round the hills in the still, crisp night air, causing numbers of kites and crows to fly up from the scrub oaks where they were roosting and flap about in bewildered flocks silhouetted black against the moon, calling loudly for many minutes. If one of the pickets was fired on, there was rarely any reply from the Gurkhas; but if the Warwicks were on the receiving end, all hell was let loose, with tracer bullets streaking across the sky and Verey lights giving a fireworks display. The whole camp would stir and wonder if it was about to be overwhelmed. Sometimes, even during the day, the mule lines, where 100 or more animals were tethered outside the perimeter, would be a target. Bullets would arrive with the familiar 'tuck-toom', spurting stones and dust in the air. Surprisingly, no mules were ever hit, but they would strain at their tethers and sidle here and there, sometimes braying loudly in protest; as well they might, for they had no protection either from bullets or from the weather, standing uncomplaining in hot sun and cold winds alike.

In late November, when the Japanese's aggressive intentions were becoming obvious, we were ordered to supply a draft of one British officer, two G.O.'s and 100 men to reinforce the 2/9th G. R. in Malaya. Volunteers readily came forward, some 20 from each company, together with Willie Taylor, then commanding B Company. Greatly were the chosen volunteers envied and much were they fêted before they left for what seemed to be a 'real war'. I bought a billygoat, costing Rs.30, for a special khana in honour of the D Company men who were going, and we had a memorable evening, the rum flowing freely and the men wildly enthusiastic about joining the 2nd Battalion. Within a few days of the order being received, they all departed in lorries to the cheers of those of left behind. Little did we dream that within a few weeks many of them would be dead, including Willie Taylor, and the rest prisoners of war in horrendous conditions for four long years.

Before I arrived in the battalion, Robbie Fawcett's second in command was Ian Roche. He had left on promotion to command 1/9th G.R. Somewhat to everyone's surprise, he was to be replaced by Major G.B. Matthewman, a Canadian who had retired shortly before the war started. Surprise there may have been, but there was no disappointment, at least amongst the junior officers, for when he arrived, just before Christmas, he proved to be wonderfully friendly and easy to work with. Although he was very sad at leaving his family in Canada so soon after retirement, he never complained. Robbie went off on leave as soon as Matt arrived. The happy atmosphere continued and our affection for Matt was scarcely less than what we had felt for Robbie.

CHAPTER 4

PUNJAB AND TOWARDS THE WAR

Just before Christmas, when many officers were on leave, including Robbie, we received orders to move to Jhelum in early January, 1942. It fell to us, a much depleted band of B.O.'s (Matthewman, Spain, Stott, Power and Leathart), to plan and execute the order; but before the work started in earnest, we were able to enjoy Christmas Day. Dudley had managed to procure a live turkey and two live Chinese geese, as well as other seasonable luxuries sent up from Dehra Dun, so we were not short of traditional fare. The weather was frosty but dry and we spent a very happy day, marred only by the increasingly grim news from the Far East where the battleships *Repulse* and the *Prince of Wales* had been sunk off the Malayan coast and our forces (including 2/9th G. R.) were in retreat.

Moving a battalion, especially one still on peacetime establishment, was no small matter. It was made more complicated because we were at the end of a very long line of communication and two modes of transport were involved – road and rail. Matt, left with but four emergency commissioned officers, seemed concerned at first, but he soon realised that both Dudley and Bertie, having worked with civilian firms in India before the war, were well experienced in administration; and that Hugh and I were perfectly capable of acting on our own initiative. The result was, as Matt said later, the smoothest and best organised move he had ever made.

Over a period of three or four days, all the stores and personnel were moved in lorries to the Rest Camp in Bannu. It was there, in the evening when I had arrived with the rear party, that I had an encounter with a retired Colonel Blimp. I was in a hurry to get from the station, where I had been checking on the morrow's troop train, to the Rest Camp and I urged the tongawallah to make haste. Sensing a larger tip and more time to engage other fares, he whipped the pony into a gallop up the tarmac road, sparks flying from its shoes and harness bells jangling furiously. Suddenly, about 50 yards ahead, an elderly man darted into the road holding up his arms. The driver reined up the pony which came skidding to a halt and the enraged sahib berated him for driving so fast. The tongawallah blamed me and the colonel came round and peered into the tonga. 'I never expected to see an Englishman galloping a tonga,' he said. 'You never see tongas being galloped in London. You ought to be ashamed of yourself.' I could but agree, although, as I told him, tongas are scarce in Piccadilly. We trotted on leaving him fuming in the middle of the road.

We left Bannu on the following morning in the military version of the Heatstroke Express, transferring to two other trains of different gauges before reaching Jhelum, where, for a few weeks, we enjoyed life in an Indian station on a peacetime basis, albeit with some feelings of guilt as the Japanese swarmed almost unchecked over South-east Asia. Clearly we would soon be mobilised.

The Mess and our bungalows were the traditional type of massively-built edifices with flat roofs. The men's barracks were large, cool and airy. Four of us B.O.'s shared a bungalow, each with his own room, leading on to a wide cool verandah, and a bathroom. Parts of a letter written home at the time seem relevant:

'My bungalow is in a pleasant situation, about 200 yards from the River Jhelum, which promises to be a good bird-watching area . . . Of the river birds, many of which are new to me, the first I saw was a Greenshank, pale coloured and bobbing like a Redshank. It was very tame and I had to clap my hands to make it fly. European Swallows were hawking up and down the river, waiting for more favourable weather in their breeding areas of Kashmir and further north. Rather to my surprise, some terns flew past diving for small fish. They were Indian River Terns, pure white with black patches on the abdomen, together with Black-bellied Terns. Two species of kingfishers were numerous, showing off both colour and fishing prowess – the brilliantly plumaged White-breasted Kingfisher and that black and white hovering expert, the Pied Kingfisher. Two wagtails, the White and the Large Pied, were ever-present, running along the river bank or 'chizziking' in dipping flight from one side to the other. Jackals are very common here. Last night at about midnight I was walking round the lines checking sentries. I had a torch with me and whenever I turned it on, the staring, yellow, menacing eyes of jackals glared at me from the darkness and the hideous cries of their kin out on the plain added to the eerie scene.'

The garden around the bungalow was spacious and bordered by trees, the lawns being of that slightly blue-tinged grass which requires so much watering for most of the year. There were a few flower-beds sporting cannas and zinnias and anything else which the malee had managed to persuade his friends, in the employ of higher ranking officers, to steal and sell to him for a pittance. The malee is a very Indian institution who ensures a colourful garden provided he suffers no interference. Much of the day he spends cutting the grass with a small knife, tying up the clippings into small bundles which he sells for cattle fodder. Flowers, grass and soil are his breath of life. Humble in the social scale he may be, and prepared to work for little more than £1 a month. Yet he is remarkably independent when it comes to the choice of flowers to grow. He may agree, with a salaam, that cannas should grace the front bed, but if he has already made a deal with a friend for some gladioli corms, the cannas which he would plant and for which he would charge an exorbitant price would somehow fail to prosper. A squirrel might be blamed for eating them or a sahib's dog for digging them up. The gladioli, however, would prosper exceedingly and no squirrel or sahib's dog, or anything else, would get near them.

I used to derive much pleasure from watching our utterly dedicated malee at work in the garden. He loved his plants and they seemed to respond to his ministrations; his careful cultivation round their roots, his regular watering at eventide, his gentle pricking out of tender seedlings and his pleasure and pride in their blooms. To be greeted, every time I returned to the bungalow, by this humble, industrious man was to share in the pleasure he obtained from the beautiful garden which was his life's work; for he went with the bungalow, as it were, and when we left he was employed by our successors and theirs to tend his beloved plants to the end of his days.

One duty which fell to my lot while we were in Jhelum was to command a two-company detachment at a place called Tarki, some 50 miles north of Jhelum on the railway line to Rawalpindi. Here there was a huge underground petrol store, making it an important vulnerable point. It was here too that the railway line swept round in a tight curve to cross itself as it climbed the Salt Range Hills. Although we were once again in tents, with a welter of tedious sentry duties to perform, the freedom from routine and the wild country were ample compensation for the discomfort and isolation. Part of a letter sent home from Tarki illustrates one reason why we enjoyed ourselves:

'I am out by myself on a special job with 200 Gurkhas. Being completely on my own is a pleasant experience, and as no one else speaks English, it is a great help in improving my Gurkhali (I spoke no English for three weeks). Today, being Sunday, Subadar Gumansing and I arranged a shooting party, our quarry being the Punjab mountain sheep or oorial. We set out before dawn, two G.O.'s, 15 men and I, carrying rifles and my Holland and Holland shotgun. It was extremely chilly and I was muffled up to the eyes in a greatcoat and khaki scarf, as well as my rabbitskin gloves, in which the Gurkhas took a great interest as the skin had been dyed to resemble some sort of spotted cat; they were incredulous. We eventually reached the reputed oorial area and started to climb the rocky hill. Almost at once one of the men shouted and pointed to a small flat grassy area on the hillside about 100 yards away. Standing there, watching us suspiciously, were nine female oorials. Immediately they began to bound up the craggy slope. I seized a rifle as one of the animals stood poised momentarily on a rock and I took a snap shot. To my surprise, the beast turned a back somersault and came rolling down the hill. The Gurkhas, shouting 'Shabash', rushed up to the animal and despatched it with a kukhri. We continued to climb the hill and, on reaching the top, almost stumbled upon another flock which contained two rams with superb curved horns. They made off at great speed along the ridge and we followed, eventually catching another glimpse of them as they rushed down the hill. Thinking it possible that they might circle round and climb up again behind us, we retraced our steps along the ridge. Then the rain started and wisps of mist hung about, reducing visibility to a few yards. So we sat down and lit a fire, heating up some chappatties and washing them down with some ration rum. Considerably warmed, both outside and in, we continued our somewhat hopeless quest. However, after much weary walking, the mist lifted slightly and old Gumansing, who has eyes like a hawk, dropped another female at a range of about 200 yards. Thus we returned to the camp in triumph bearing two corpses. An immense haunch was hacked off and presented to me, and my cook gave me roast oorial, cold oorial, oorial croquettes, oorial curry etc, for days on end. The meat was extremely good, far surpassing the best Indian mutton both in taste and tenderness.'

I enjoyed this spell of duty enormously. In the evenings I would go out with my shotgun and one or two Gurkhas in search of Grey Partridge. I shot a brace or two most evenings and sometimes bagged a hare as well. So my larder was always well stocked and the men had a change from ration goat. In the late evenings the G.O.'s would come to my tent to talk about their homes and their varied experiences during many years of service. These were memorable hours which added much to my respect and affection for these warm-hearted and courageous men.

The Battalion was not left in peace in Jhelum for long, nor did we expect it to be. Singapore had fallen, the Dutch East Indies had been overrun and the British Army had been driven out of Burma, across the Chinwin to the Assam border. Britain's standing in Asia had received devastating blows; the threat to India was acute.

The 3/9th, until March, 1942 still on peacetime establishment and scarcely 18 months old, in that month suddenly received a flurry of signals ordering mobilisation. The men's families, but recently arrived from Dehra Dun, were sent home. All leave was stopped, new weapons were drawn from Ordnance Depots, jungle green uniforms replaced the khaki and all was as much bustle and urgency as the increasingly hot weather allowed. Perhaps it was the arrival of the medical officer which made us realise that we were destined for active service; yet the man himself, an elderly Indian muslim, did not inspire much confidence. Poor fellow, he was to lead a lonely life, for there were no Indians in the Mess and he never came there. He had nothing in common with the Gurkhas either, and they found him as comical as we did as he stumped round the lines inspecting kitchens and latrines with his topi on the back of his head and his ill-fitting uniform creased and unlaundered. He remained with us for a year or more fulfilling the role of a dresser, which is what he really was, able only to give first aid and pass on more serious cases to the Field Ambulance.

Mobilisation complete, we said farewell to Jhelum and set out for an unknown destination in one of those long, uncomfortable troop-trains which, being obliged to give way to all scheduled services, took days to crawl across the vast and dusty land which is India. Not that time mattered much, for we were completely self-contained. At the rear of the train were all-metal wagons with sliding doors in which cookhouses were installed, powered by huge oil-fired blowlamps which added their own B.T.U.'s to the already stifling heat engendered by the sun beating down on the metal roofs. How the cooks coped heaven knows, but twice a day, when the train was shunted into a convenient siding, cauldrons of rice, dhal and vegetable curry, and piles of chappatties emerged from these infernos to be consumed by the Gurkhas squatting beside the railway line.

For officers' meals, our leisurely progress often allowed us to stop at major stations where we ate lunch or dinner in the restaurant. The menus varied little; brown Windsor soup, stringy roast chicken and, almost invariably, caramel custard. More enjoyable were the occasions when no stop at a station was possible and we were given curries from the men's cookhouse. For liquid refreshment, we enjoyed Solan beer (brewed in the hills near Simla) and put up with Nasik whisky and Haywards gin. These were poor substitutes for the real things, but were taken to conserve our diminishing stocks of English liquor, only occasionally served by the Mess Orderlies in the evening from a compartment set aside for them. Here they also made up iced 'nimbo pani', much in demand during the hot dusty days. Breakfast was usually taken while the men were eating their morning meal, our cook somehow contriving to fry, poach or scramble eggs on a charcoal stove in one of the wagons. It was all a strange experience. Here we were, a complete battalion on wheels, creeping across India, cocooned in our carriages yet functioning as though we were still in barracks. All the usual reports were made: the platoon commanders to the company commanders, the Jemadar Adjutant to the Adjutant and the Subadar Major to the C.O., showing that all was well with our tiny world, apart from a few men sick with fever, a Gurkha hat borne away in the slipstream, or a man caught buying forbidden fruit from a platform vendor.

Thus three or four days passed as we followed the Ganges valley eastwards. None of us junior officers knew where we were going until we received a clue on what turned out to be the last evening. This, unlike the previous ones, had become humid and oppressive as well as exceedingly hot. Coconut palms made their appearance around the mud-hutted villages which, to those who knew, meant Bengal. By our reckoning (oddly enough none of us had a map) we could not be far from Calcutta. Indeed we were not and our sleep that night was more than usually interrupted by stops, starts and shuntings as we skirted the great city. When the orderlies came to the carriage at dawn, with mugs of sweet condensed-milk tea, we were standing in a neat station with the sign JESSORE set against a background of white metal railings. This small town, some 70 miles N.E. of Calcutta, was far from any military cantonment and had no European residents.

A fleet of lorries and commandeered local buses was lined up beyond the white railings and these elderly, rattling vehicles took us a few miles out of town to a large Bengali village called Jhikagacha, from which all the inhabitants had been ejected. Here we were joined by the other two battalions of our brigade, the 6/11th Sikhs and the 8/8th Punjabs, to form the 4th Indian Infantry Brigade, commanded, we were glad to find, by Brigadier Hungerford. (An Indian Infantry Brigade usually consisted of two Indian Battalions and one British or Gurkha Battalion). With these two regiments and Brigade H.Q. we were to share the few brick buildings and the many mud huts recently vacated by their owners.

It was a dispiriting scene which confronted us, despite the efforts of the Advance Party to create order out of chaos. There was mud everywhere, such houses as had been allotted to us were mainly in disrepair and invariably filthy, and there was no order about the place; no building lines, just a jumble of dwellings facing in all directions, cheek by jowl, in which any semblance of barrack orderliness was almost impossible to create. Later 'bashas' (huts with coconut palm leaf roofs and interwoven bamboo walls) were erected for messes, clubs and canteens, but the initial shock of arriving in this steaming, smelly and disorganised outpost was considerable. To this was added a perplexed uncertainty as to why we were there. However, it was not for us to reason why and, with their usual cheerfulness, the Gurkhas soon made the best of a bad situation, which was just as well because almost a year was to elapse before we moved on to, as it happened, much more uncomfortable surroundings.

At the time of our mobilisation it had been assumed that our Thakur and Chettri Gurkhas would not take kindly to being British officers' batmen. So the Regimental Centre recruited some Limbus and Rais for us in Darjeeling. They presented a comic sight when they arrived just before we left Jhelum. They had had little or no military training or submission to discipline, their uniforms were ill-fitting, their Gurkha hats were too large and floppy, and their boots were only partially filled with feet unaccustomed to such incarceration. But they were all smiles and well able to see the joke. Most of them took to army life with a will and in a very short time became indispensable to those officers lucky enough to enjoy their services. Some were quite unsuitable and were discharged. They were not replaced because the reported reluctance of our Gurkhas to carry out batman duties proved unfounded and our erstwhile orderlies took on the dual duties.

The Darjeeling batman allotted to me was one Karandhan Rai, a man of strictly limited intelligence and of decidedly simian appearance, but with an unquenchable determination to do something, anything, to help and prove his worth. I was accustomed to keeping my shaving brush in an old pewter mug in which my shaving water was brought. On his first morning of duty, Karandhan, seeing other batmen taking their officers' tea to them in mugs, decided to do likewise, but he saw no reason to remove the shaving brush before doing so and it arrived half submerged in the tea. Perhaps he thought that one of the strange habits of the Sahibs was to suck tea from the bristles of a badger. But his attention to me was almost canine in its devotion. With his anxious looks to see if I was pleased with his efforts, it was difficult to criticise or correct his efforts and omissions; a tea mug considered well cleaned by a quick wipe with his dirty handkerchief, a bed deemed correctly made with the sheets on top and the blankets beneath them, a grey sock darned with red wool (who would see the repair anyhow, except him and his Sahib?) or a pair of boots, best placed for putting on, with the right on the left and the left on the right. Had he had a tail to wag when praised and to put between his legs when admonished, this appendage would have been in constant motion. He eventually became quite efficient, serving John Thorpe faithfully throughout our time in Burma.

Our stationing in this outlandish place north east of Calcutta was to enable us to act as a mobile reserve to counter any Japanese landings in the Sunderbands (the Ganges Delta) and elsewhere in South Bengal. But only once during the whole year during which we were in Jhikagacha was there any real alarm. That was when a Jap plane was shot down in the Khulna area after an air-raid on Calcutta. D Company with Dudley Spain went out in force to search for it, eventually finding the wreckage, after a long and difficult search, with very dead bodies inside it and no evidence that anyone had survived.

For the most part life was exceedingly boring, the boredom being compounded by the appalling climate. Everyone had prickly heat, especially the Gurkhas who were no more accustomed to the hot humidity than were the British officers, but lived in much more crowded conditions. We at least had a little hut each, albeit dark and stuffy and often shared with rats living in the loose thatch, but the men lived in tents which usually leaked and which, because it so often rained, had to have their sides let down at night, making them insufferably hot and airless. Water too was, paradoxically, a problem. A sluggish river seeped along one side of the camp but it was unfit for washing or bathing, let alone drinking. One thing which a Gurkha enjoys perennially in his homeland is a constant supply of cool, fresh water; without it he is greatly deprived. Bore-holes were put down and hand pumps installed which called for very considerable physical effort. It often happened that when these pumps were used with the sort of vigour which only a Gurkha can muster, the vital parts shattered. In any case they only produced a modicum of tepid water made the more unpalatable by the necessary heavy chlorination. So this vital commodity was never in sufficient supply and its uncertain provision was a constant worry.

Our humdrum training for war was overseen by the Divisional Staff, who had no personal experience of the defeat in Malaya or the retreat from

Burma and thus no conception of the problems of jungle warfare. Nor was there any jungle nearby in which to train, the countryside being mostly paddy fields and swamps. In the occasional exercise conducted by Divisional H.Q. we merely went up and down the roads, which the directing Staff designated as passing through deep jungle. We were not encouraged to avoid ambushes by leaving the road because the jungle was thought to be impenetrable. It is easy to criticise in hindsight, but though our senior officers (Division, Brigade and Battalion Commanders) were all men of great humanity and proven courage as junior officers in the 1914/18 war or on the North West Frontier, they had not, nor could they have, any conception of the problems which were to face us in the Burma jungles. Neither had we, the junior officers. All we could do, in the absence of any real guidance from our seniors, was to ensure that our soldiers could use the weapons issued to us. This we did by much range practice, both small arms and mortars (2 in. and 3 in.) as well as field firing. Thus, by the time that the Japs arrived on the Assam border and in the Arakan, we at least felt that we could give a good account of ourselves whilst learning the hard way on the battlefield.

My personal contribution was initially as the Carrier Platoon Commander and later as M.T.O. Shortly after we arrived in Jhikagacha I went on a three-week carrier course at the Small Arms Training School at Saugor in the United Provinces. The carriers were open armoured track vehicles powered by Ford V8 engines and steered by braking the track on one side or the other as required. Everything about them was difficult of access; many were the knuckles skinned and tempers frayed whilst attempting to do the simplest maintenance. They were called carriers because they were intended to carry a light machine gun and crew, in comparative immunity from small arms fire, to a tactical position from which they could give covering fire either from the vehicle or from a better hidden position on the ground. Their use in country such as that around Jhikagacha, and later in the Arakan, was very limited. However, I returned from the course full of enthusiasm, only to find that there were no carriers. For some weeks we used 15 cwt. trucks to perfect the various drills required and the signals designated for visual control on the move. Some of the men chosen as drivers had been on a short course in Calcutta, and a G.O., Jemadar Yembahadur Sahi, had also been to Saugor, so we were ready for the carriers when they arrived one morning by train at Jessore station. Drama unfolded almost immediately. As the first vehicle was driven down the ramp, the driver was unable to turn sharp right as the occasion demanded (the steering mechanism always gave trouble) and he drove straight into the station railings, which collapsed like a line of dominoes from one end to the other. Nevertheless, we drove back to camp in triumph as the first unit in the battalion to become mechanised. For a month or two, until our M.T. reached full establishment, the Carrier Platoon was something of an élite body, much admired as we roared up and down the roads, occasionally venturing on to the drier paddy fields.

Later I became Motorised Transport Officer and responsible for the training of 100 drivers prior to our receiving our full establishment of vehicles. On the whole, our Gurkhas became competent drivers from the technical point of view, but their road sense was poor. They seemed to have difficulty, at least in the early stages, in anticipating events. I have vivid memories of the long snaking convoy in which we brought back our new vehicles from the depot at Asansol some miles north west of Calcutta. They were 15 and 30 cwt. Chevrolet trucks, brand new with tight engines and stiff gear changes. They heated very quickly in the high humid temperatures and kept stopping as the petrol vapourised in the fuel pumps. The convoy became more and more attenuated and eventually ceased to be an entity. I dashed up and down in my jeep, like a sheepdog gathering errant ewes, and the M.T. Havildar, Chittrabahadur, on a motor bike, was engaged in similar rescue operations. In spite of an early start, the day was well spent before the 60 mile drive was completed and all the vehicles were safely in the fold. Standing in the lines in serried ranks, still in their Middle East khaki livery, the lorries made an impressive sight. We thought we had seen the last of mules; as it later turned out, we had not.

CHAPTER 5

BENGAL DAYS

The camp at Jhikagacha slowly took shape, with bamboo huts replacing tents, their brick floors raised above the occasional flood level and the muddy paths metalled with rolled rubble. Some of the mud huts were demolished to give space for volleyball and netball courts. In addition to these domestic improvements, urgent and expensive measures were taken to provide some sort of defence for this brigade outpost, on the assumption that the Japanese might somehow land in force and advance on Calcutta. Inside the barbed wire which ringed the camp, a huge deep anti-tank ditch was dug right round the perimeter by gangs of Bengali coolies who carried the excavated earth away in baskets balanced on their heads. It took months to complete the project, wet days often making work impossible, and it was only finished after the threat of invasion from the Bay of Bengal had long since ceased to be a possibility. Despite the low wages paid to the coolies of no more than Rs. 3 a day, it must have cost a great deal of money; a sum in no way diminished by the 'rake off' which the Sikh Staff Captain was ultimately convicted of receiving from the contractors.

Memories of life in Jhikagacha are rather vague, but certain trivial incidents come to mind. At the time of the desultory air raids on Calcutta, Divisional H.Q. got into their head the idea that the Japs might consider Jhikagacha worth bombing, and that the dire consequences of such an act might be a direct hit on the officers' mess. Accordingly, each battalion was ordered to disperse the messes and have at least four scattered over its area. As there were only 12 of us, the waste and the destruction of our already strictly limited social life was great and bordered upon the absurd. As a result, what happened was that in the evenings we tended to gather in one of the messes; it was in no way against orders but it made a fool of the dispersal. As the mess staff had also been scattered, the services and the

Subadar Manbahadur Khattri posing with a double-handed kukhri to be used for the
sacrificial beheading of a buffalo. Jhikigacha, Bengal, 1942.

Seconds before the head-cutting.

standard of cooking slumped. The mess run by Dudley Spain had allotted to it as cook a Tamil called Joseph, who in the combined mess had been the 'masulchi' or the male equivalent of a scullery maid. He was a genial old rogue with a penchant for toddy, a local 'hooch' made from the fruit of a palm tree. It was not often that he was completely sober, and he never was after 1800 hrs. Dudley, with his usual attention to any detail which could increase comfort even in the bleakest of situations, and with the help of a little Tamil waiter called Francis, had built up a mess which was always worth visiting. You could expect what he called 'little bitty things' with your gin-bitters such as olives before dinner, when everyone had assumed that olives had long since become unavailable in Bengal; you could feel sure that the usual stringy chicken would be cooked in something nice and rarely tried before; and you were sure to find that the pudding would be smothered in fresh cream (albeit from buffaloes), which no other mess had been able to keep from going sour before the daily ration of ice arrived in the afternoon. The only snag was Joseph. Would he be sufficiently sober to cook? One evening we sat round the table after our drinks and, as plates of turtle soup (tinned, from Calcutta) were carried in by the mess orderlies, Francis came rushing in shouting 'Sahibs, don't eat, Joseph spitting in the soup'. Even Dudley could find no immediate substitute for our dashed gastronomical hopes.

Recreation in the form of change of scene was very limited. There was no club in Jessore and no golf course anywhere near. An occasional snipe shoot was arranged and that was about it except for visits to Calcutta. Apart from the C.O.'s car, an ancient Ford V8 saloon, we had no comfortable transport, so we had to take advantage of duty journeys by 15 or 30 cwt. trucks going to ordnance depots near the city for stores; and that meant putting ourselves in the hands of Gurkha drivers with very little experience. The 60 or so miles of narrow road to Calcutta were fraught with hazards as it passed along raised bunds bounded by paddy fields: through avenues of rain trees, their trunks edging onto the hard surface and their canopies merging overhead; through sprawling villages and eventually to the suburbs of Calcutta and the city itself with its unspeakable congestion. On this narrow road trundled bullock carts which deviated not an inch from the middle until a blare of a horn caused the often-sleeping driver to sit up in surprise and the bullocks to panic and seek safety in the nearby paddy fields, shaking off their yokes and depositing the cumbersome cart in the roadside ditch complete with driver and his load. This spectacle always delighted the Gurkha driver, who proceeded to watch it unfold at the expense of his attention to the road, which often contained an overloaded local bus lurching round a bend just ahead with brakes totally unable to reduce its momentum. It would roar past, horns blaring, as the Gurkha shouted abuse whilst trying to keep his own vehicle on the road with the help of a terrified sahib who had already seized the steering wheel in an attempt to avoid following the bullocks into the rice field. It was all very nerve-racking, and if there was no bullock cart fiasco to amuse the driver, he would take great delight in blowing his horn when a goat, tethered by the roadside, hove in sight. This would make the wretched animal bolt in terror to be brought up sharply by its neck collar sending it flying into the air to land with a thud and lie panting. Sometimes the tether snapped, causing even more amusement and less attention to the road as the goat, free and terrified, disappeared in the distance. Driving through a village was no occasion to reduce speed, and if one had fallen asleep during a temporary lull in the drama for a few miles, and thus had failed to order a slowing down, one would wake up to the sound of blaring horns, yelling humans, yelping dogs and shrieking chickens, not to mention screaming brakes as near tragedy was averted in a melée of people, dust and confusion. On such occasions the Gurkha driver, himself at fault, would heap blame on the Bengalis in ripe Gurkhali, of which they understood not a word, although the meaning was clear enough.

Thus one progressed on the edge of one's seat until the city was reached, when, so great was the congestion, speed was reduced to walking pace, and anxiety was replaced by boredom and extreme discomfort in the clinging, clammy heat. Sadly, the traumas of the journey were scarce compensated for by the delights of Calcutta, which were few; lunch in the air-conditioned dining room of the Grand Hotel, tea at Firpos, a visit to a bookshop, and a search for tinned luxuries at the Army and Navy; and a minor chore, a search for English gin at Robbie's behest. Then came the return journey, started as dusk fell and the coconut palms stood silhouetted black against the pink western sky. At least the headlights of oncoming vehicles heralded their approach and even bullock carts became more visible as the beasts' eyes shone red in the headlights. A pie-dog lying in the dust beside the road would leap up and flee away as the driver purposely just missed it; a pack of jackals would race across the road just ahead of our truck, their eyes glinting red; a Barn Owl, white and ghost-like, would flit and weave amongst the rain tree boughs; and a civet cat might jump to the safety of a tree trunk and scramble aloft. Nightjars would be sitting in the middle of the road, pink eyes glaring, to rise only when the truck was so near as to seem sure to hit them. Yet they always dashed away safely on ghostly wings to be swallowed by the darkness.

Sometimes the truck would jerk and splutter to a halt as the engine died, with the driver murmuring, 'Areh, kya bhayo?' (Oh dear, what has happened?). A suggestion that the petrol tank might be empty often prevented the driver from probing beneath the bonnet in a pretence that he knew what he was looking for, and this was usually the reason. As the tank was refilled, the glugging noise from the mouth of the jerrycan was accompanied by sounds of the Indian night: the demoniacal howls of jackals, the staccato hoots of Spotted Owlets, the shriek of a Brainfever Bird tricked by our lights into thinking day had dawned, the sawing of crickets and the laugh of a distant hyena. By the time camp was reached, one was more than ready for the hoped-for and seldom missed summons from Robbie – 'Come in, boy, and suck the lid off a gin.'

Although facilities for recreation were few, my interest in birds and natural history in general provided me with an ever-present pastime. Extracts from letters to my parents, who shared my interest, give some idea of my growing fascination with Bengal's birds during our year-long stay in Jhikagacha.

'The commonest bird here (this was April, 1942) is, I think, the Black-naped Oriole which whistles loudly all day . . . Two species of Sunbirds, the Purple and the Purple-rumped, are often to be seen everywhere feeding on floral nectar, especially that of the silk cotton tree at this time. Bulbuls of several species are very numerous, including the White-cheeked, the Red-cheeked and the Red-vented; their fluty whistles are a delight to hear during the short cool period in the mornings. I recently saw a Pied Harrier hunting in a typical harrier fashion over the paddy fields. But I think the prize specimen so far seen, as far as beauty is concerned, is the Paradise Flycatcher. Unfortunately it was a female, but its lovely chestnut colouring and long tail made it an enchanting sight as it flitted from one mango tree to another.

'The latest copy of *The Field* which you kindly sent contains a lot of correspondence about the drumming of woodpeckers. I am surprised to see that the theory that the sound is vocal is gaining ground. I have been watching both the Golden-backed and the Maharatta species out here. They drum on a number of different trees as well as on bamboo, from which a characteristic hollow note arises which can be heard from distances of up to a mile on a still evening. I have watched a bird drumming from a distance of only 20 yards and the head was moving so quickly that it was a blurred image. The sound changes completely when the bird shifts from bamboo to another kind of tree. Furthermore, the sounds of the slow deliberate pecks of the Golden-backed when searching for food carry a great distance and are certainly caused by the beak coming into contact with wood. I also have evidence countering the theory that vultures find kills by scent. Along the road here one night three jackals and a dog were killed by cars. For the next three days they remained untouched and were finally removed by human agency. Over the road is a canopy of trees forming a perfect umbrella against aerial observation. A dead animal in the open is normally found in a matter of minutes, presumably by sight. If scent comes into it, surely putrefying jackals would quickly be discovered. King and White-backed vultures abound here.

'Snakes have become very numerous lately. The species are so many and varied that I am afraid that I behave like the misinformed at home and try to kill any snake I see. Many are, of course, quite harmless but some are extremely dangerous. I have no doubt that the large mongoose population helps to keep their numbers in check. There is a very attractive species of fox common here, its neatness and pretty russet colouration being in direct contrast to that of the vile and ubiquitous jackal, whose company it shuns. As there are no rabbits in this part of India and hares are very scarce, I imagine that the foxes live mainly on mice and rats. The rat here is not quite so unpleasant a creature as at home; its colour is much paler and its back legs tend to resemble those of the kangaroo rat. There is another species too which is definitely a jungle dweller, with a very long snout and short back legs. I have never seen it running without uttering a curious snuffling whistle which instantly betrays its presence. These rodents are a great pest here, often eating my soap at night, gnawing buttons and, on one occasion, taking a large piece out of my khaki shorts. Recently I had an even closer contact with one. In the early hours of one morning I woke suddenly as something ran across my chest. Sensing that it was a rat, I baled out of bed and the mosquito net, turned on my torch and found a rat inside the net. It raced round half way up the net like a motor cycle on the wall-of-death until I eventually managed to despatch it with my swagger cane. Talking of things being eaten, one of the Gurkhas left his boots outside overnight and in the morning only the soles were left; the uppers had been eaten, presumably by a jackal.

'Yesterday I found a dead civet cat on the road, run over during the night. It was a beautiful animal about the size of a fox terrier, but with shorter legs and a lovely long ringed tail. The countryside round here is very attractive now that the rice has ripened and is being cut (December). The tall coconut palms give a splendid background to the wide russet fields which, apart from their goodly crop of rice, support hundreds of Little and Cattle egrets stalking about singly amongst the stubble during the day or flying in white stately flocks as the sun begins to sink, and alighting in silent parties to spend the hours of darkness near a jheel or river. Today I watched some Green Bee-eaters feeding in the lower branches of the rain tree avenue. Darting away for insects with loud shrill cries, they returned to their perches only to dash off again a few seconds later, streaks of brilliant green with long curved beaks and protruding central tail feathers. Nearby an enormous flock of Swiftlets was milling round a toddy palm, performing aerobatics with matchless agility. A party of Jungle Babblers started their shrill chatter; no beauties in either dress or voice, these drab little birds, usually in parties of seven and thus called 'Sathbhai', are always friendly and faithful to their kind. They are exceedingly loquacious but unpresumptuous and retiring in their habits. One can but admire their team spirit and their ability to make so much noise about so little.

'In the current "cold" weather (November) some familiar birds have arrived, presumably on migration. Whilst fishing in the evenings, I often see Common Sandpipers calling 'kitti-needi' and reminding me of the summer riverbanks in Northumberland. Green Sandpipers are also common as well as Redshanks and Snipe. A local Bengali told me recently that there were "some fine black ducks with white foreheads" on a nearby jheel. They sound suspiciously like Coots (they were). Dabchicks I have seen frequently, often accompanied by Bronze-winged Jacanas. The Common Kingfisher is another ubiquitous link with home, to be seen near any stretch of water fishing in consort with the Pied and White-breasted species. Mongooses are very numerous. My orderly, who is quite a good naturalist, tells me that a mongoose, on finding a snake, eats the middle portion, leaving the two ends which join together and resume normal life. I am afraid that this is too much of a tall story, but on the whole Gurkhas are accurate observers and often first-rate naturalists and shikaris.

'The weather has become noticeably hotter once again (January). Various sounds denoting the approach of uncomfortable temperatures are now in evidence, pleasant in themselves but not in what they herald. The Hawk Cuckoo is calling once more; both by day and by night his aggravating and seemingly pointless screamings rend the air, to be answered by others from afar. The coming shimmering mirage of heat is vocalised by the Common Ioras with their long-drawn, wailing "we-e-e-e-tu" as they sit yellow and canary-like in the pawpaw and mango trees. The comfortable and pleasing hoots of the Spotted Owlet start when the sun goes down and have great carrying power. I can hear one now as I write, calling from a long way off, an explosive hoot mingling with the far-off bayings of jackals and the ever-present grating of crickets. The silk cotton tree is now budding and in about a month the crown will be a mass of gorgeous red flowers, dripping with nectar and a feasting place for sunbirds and that curious creature, the fruit bat or flying fox, which, as the sun goes down, will fly in silent, slow-flapping hoards to cover the tree crown in a noisy, squirming mass. The dawn chorus here is always very consistent. First of all one hears, even before it is light, the raucous calls of House Crows, accompanied by the squeaky cackle of Common Mynahs. As the light increases, the first sound which can be described as a song is heard – the pretty notes of the Magpie Robin. This is followed by the shrill song of the Purple Sunbird, very like a canary. More sunshine brings more sounds such as the contented cooing of the little Brown Dove and the rattle of the Green Barbet. But not until much later does one hear the happy chirrups of the Bee-eaters and the squeaky chatter of the Babblers, all essential sounds of the Bengal day.'

CHAPTER 6

DEHRA DUN AND KASHMIR

In August Dudley and I went on a month's leave to Kashmir, calling at our Regimental Centre in Dehra Dun en route. A through train from Calcutta took us to Delhi, where we caught the night mail to Dehra. Letters written home at the time give a more accurate picture than my somewhat hazy memory can provide:

'Dehra Dun is in the foothills of the Himalayas, about 1,500 feet above sea level. For the last 40 miles of the rail journey the scenery is enchanting as the train slowly twists its way through the Siwalik Hills, which are thickly covered with sal forest and intersected by fast-flowing streams cutting deeply into rich conglomerate soil. The sal is a lovely tree, tall and slender with, at least in this area, the lower branches high-pruned in a silvicultural operation. So slow was our progress that birds could be identified as we went along. Each stretch of the telephone wires between posts held a pair of King Crows or a Rufous-backed Shrike and nearly every bush a vociferous warbler. On many trees hung the unfinished nests of Baya Weaver-birds built, no doubt, by the unfortunate males whose fervour for construction had overtaken their ability to find mates. On one occasion a Grey Hornbill broke cover from the sal crowns. I have seldom seen a more uncouth, untidy-looking bird in flight; it seemed miraculous that its equilibrium could be maintained. The huge bill was top-heavy, the wings were seemingly set too far back and the flight feathers too widely spaced and straggly. Yet the flight was swift and it soon outpaced the train.

'Our Mess in Dehra Dun is, I believe, in one of the finest situations of any in India. It stands on the edge of a hill overlooking a deep valley beyond which are the Mussoorie Hills backed by the immense snowy peaks of the Himalayas proper. All round the building are beautiful gardens where there

60

is a profusion of all sorts of flowers. Now (August) is the time of hibiscus and cannas, both of many colours and very luxuriant. In the same setting and round about are the British Officers' bungalows, the Gurkha Officers' quarters and the mens' barracks. The whole is an ideal setting for Gurkhas and it is not surprising that our men in Bengal speak of Dehra with such affection.

'I went up to Mussoorie for a few days to stay with Cynthia Fawcett, the C.O.'s wife. The drive from Dehra was some 21 miles with a climb of 4,500 feet. To save money, I went by bus and found myself bundled in with a crowd of Indians of many races. They were all chattering in Hindustani, so I could understand something of what they were saying, mostly about the weather and minor criticisms of the driver; mine would have been major. We hurtled round corners whilst the driver turned round to add his comments to the current topic, and oft-times nearly went into the ditch when avoiding an oncoming vehicle. However, the journey was completed without mishap within the hour scheduled for it. Mussoorie is a typical hill station perched on steep hill tops between 6,000 and 7,000 feet. The houses all have corrugated iron roofs and the roads are too narrow and steep for any kind of transport other than ponies and rickshaws. Many households, including the Fawcetts', have private rickshaws staffed by four permanent rickshaw-wallahs, who stand by all day and most of the night for immediate call.

'On my first morning up there I went for a walk. The day was a typical one for a hill station in the monsoon. The rain fell in torrents, turning all the roads into little rivers. At about midday it cleared up and the Dun Valley was laid out like a map some 4,000 feet below. The vegetation was varied and lush. By far the commonest tree was a species of evergreen oak, festooned, because of the high rainfall (100" in three months), with ferns and mosses attached to the trunks and bigger branches. Other trees which grow on the fiercesome slopes are the Indian horse chestnut and the Chir pine. A very common ground plant was a species of wood sorrel, but it was not in flower. A pretty purple orchid grows in great profusion on all the slopes and red hibiscus is common in all the garden hedges. In all this mass of vegetation birds were surprisingly scarce, at least there was little sign of them. A solitary kite sat motionless on a pine, rivulets of rain dripping from its forked tail. Occasionally a yellow warbler-like bird uttered shrill notes from a thickly festooned oak and a Whistling Thrush perched on a nearby tree, raising and lowering its tail like a blackbird at home; perhaps the same bird which woke me with flutey notes early this morning. Often I saw the treetops shaking as if in a great gale, telling of a troop of langurs on the move. These long-tailed, grey monkeys, with comic black faces, are wonderfully skilled climbers and are very common in the hills.

'After a few days in Dehra, we left for Rawalpindi, arriving there the following evening and setting out for Srinagar by bus on the morrow at 0730 hrs. The first 37 miles were a slow climb to Murree, a charming hill station on the 7,000 foot contour, set amongst pines and silver firs, but misty and damp that morning. Then slowly we ran down the Jhelum valley, along slopes bearing hill rice and maize. The river was only about 100 yards wide, but a roaring torrent was sweeping with it huge logs on their way to sawmills. At Kohala we crossed the Jhelum and entered Kashmir State (it was here that my shotgun, a Holland & Holland, was confiscated by customs; I never got it back despite showing a receipt and endless correspondence over several years). From Kohala the road kept to the Jhelum valley for many miles between steep mountains covered with bright green scrub on the lower slopes, with conifer forest on the upper reaches. A few miles beyond Domeli we stopped for lunch in a shady glen of willows. More miles of rugged scenery brought us to Rampore, where we had tea in a resthouse overlooking the river. Thunder echoed round the mountains and down the conifer-clad valley. Another 30 miles brought us to the Vale of Kashmir, with the mountains on both sides receding into the background. The largely straight road passed through beautiful avenues of Lombardy poplars all the way to Srinagar, where it was refreshingly cool, 5,000 feet above sea level.'

We spent a few days in Srinagar visiting the Moghul Gardens – Shalimar and Nishat Bagh – and lazing in a shikara on the Dal Lake. Nishat Bagh, in particular, was a haven of peace where we had several picnics in the shade of the huge and venerable chenar trees bordering the terraces, which progressed in steps down to the lake's edge. The noise and bustle of Srinagar was far away; only the rustle of the chenar leaves and the ringing notes of the orioles broke the silence as the bearer unravelled the packets of sandwiches and opened the bottle of Solan beer. On the lawns around us Tickell's Thrushes ran in short dashes, stopping to listen for the sound of earthworms and occasionally pulling them up through the neatly mown grass. After lunch we snoozed fitfully in the cool shade, conscious now and again of the mewing of kites and the rhythmic splash of water as a shikara was paddled across the placid lake.

The main object of this holiday was to fish for trout. We had reserved a beat on the River Dyus, a tributary of the well-known Bringi, up in the mountains some 60 miles from Srinagar. On the day before we were due to go up there, John Beazley, my cousin who was in the 4/12th Frontier Force Regiment, suddenly and unexpectedly appeared at breakfast in Nedous Hotel where we were staying. He was also in search of fishing and gladly agreed to join our party and share in the considerable cost.

Again, I think extracts from letters written home at the time give an authentic picture:

'The fishing was approached by a good metalled road as far as a place called Achibal; from there on the road was unmetalled and subject to the vagaries of the weather. We set out at 0730 hrs in a small hired bus; the three of us and a collection of servants, together with tents, cooking pots and various provisions. All went well as far as Achibal, but there we were met by a host of tongawallahs, all declaring that the road ahead was impassable to motor traffic for at least 20 miles due to heavy rain and landslips – not a cheering thought considering that this stage included a climb of 3,000 feet. However, we had grown wise to the tricks of the Kashmiris and we considered it likely that the men were lying in order to persuade us to hire their tongas. So the driver of the bus was ordered to proceed, which he did with great reluctance. All went well for two miles when the road grew narrow, extremely muddy and obviously impassable. Thus the only thing to do was eat humble pie, call up the tongas and proceed in that way as best we could. All the kit was loaded on to five tongas, and that being all that were available, we had to walk. A 20 mile hike in thick, shiny mud was not a pleasant prospect, but on we went for five miles, the poor tonga ponies hauling with great difficulty their overloaded vehicles through the sticky morass. Later we managed to hire another tonga in which we firmly sat, relieved at last to shelter from the pelting rain. The tongawallah flicked his reins and cracked his whip but absolutely nothing happened. This went on for ten minutes when John jumped out and broke his walking stick over the pony's backside to no avail. Not an inch nearer our fishing, we dismissed the tonga and again started to walk, our tempers unimproved by the tongawallah's requests for baksheesh for "trying to start the tonga".

'Chicken sandwiches and a nondescript soup from a thermos tasted good after another five miles when fatigue was starting to creep up our limbs. But refreshed, we started off again and after a further mile a villager told us that there was a resthouse half a mile ahead. It was now 1600 hrs, raining hard and extremely muddy. So we decided to spend the night at the resthouse and wish for better weather. The half mile turned out to be four times that distance, but the resthouse appeared to be comfortable and our cook soon produced some tea and toast, to which we added a tin of baked beans and a large number of boiled eggs. After tea the clouds lifted somewhat and the rain stopped. I went for a short walk down the river, which was a rushing torrent but not muddy as had seemed likely. So my hopes were raised, as our river, the Dyus, was a tributary of this one, the Bringi, and much higher up and sure to be clearer still. Sitting on a stone in the middle of the river was a Plumbeous Redstart, the first I had seen, bluey grey all over except for a russet tail. Scolding and chivvying in a spruce tree by the river was a small party of Crested Black Tits, also an addition to my list; they resembled coal tits with black crests. Growing on the slopes were Bhutan pines while on the marshy ground grew forget-me-nots, agrimony and balsam amongst a host of other plants. The name of the place where we spent the night was Kohar Nag.

'Next morning I got up at 0400 hrs to find the day as wet as ever. After a hurried breakfast and as soon as it was light, I hired a pony and, taking my fishing tackle, set out on the last eight miles of the journey. Dudley and John, having looked out of the window, decided to stay in bed. I hoped to have caught some fish before they arrived later with the baggage. The rain had stopped by the time I reached the bottom of the beat at about 1000 hrs. My rod was assembled and, on the shikari's advice, I put on a 1X cast and a peacock lure. A nice little pool on the edge of a swift run looked like holding a fish and I cast into it. Immediately a fish took my fly and in two minutes I had a 14 oz. brown trout on the bank. Within minutes this was followed by another of similar size, but after this flash in the pan, I fished another mile of the river catching only two more fish over 10 inches. It was then time to go back to the road to see if the others were coming. They reached the agreed meeting place at the same time as I did; two tired and wet individuals with 30 coolies trailing along behind them.

'We decided, in view of the weather, not to camp but use the Forest Rest House, a building some 200 feet above the river and, according to the map, situated exactly on the 8,200 feet contour. Fires were lit, clothes were dried, a late lunch was prepared and we were ready to go and test the evening rise. It was disappointing; Dudley, a complete novice, caught two fish, I caught one and John none at all, largely because he was determined to trust his own instincts and ignore the advice of his shikari. It would be of little interest to describe each fishing day; suffice to say that our sport was to a degree spoilt by excessive rain, which was physically tiresome and chilling as well as causing occasional spates in the river. I caught 19 fish weighing a total of

15 lbs, which was disappointing considering that fish up to five lbs are plentiful in these well-stocked rivers. However, if the fishing deserves no detailed description, the place does.

'The upper part of the beat was in an extremely steep-sided valley clothed in spruce, pine and fir forest. Towering above the resthouse to the east was a peak 14,000 feet high on which some snow still lingered in a shaded chimney. The lower beat was in a somewhat wider valley, where villagers grow their maize and graze their cattle. Around the villages are walnut trees, hawthorns, wych elms and raspberry bushes. Down by the river is a luxuriance of flora, but under the conifers only grasses grow. Birdlife was disappointing. I saw only Himalayan Greenfinches, Plumbeous Redstarts, Himalayan Treecreepers and Crested Black Tits. Nutcrackers and Whistling Thrushes were there but I did not see them. English birds which I saw included Goldfinches, Jackdaws, Ravens, Starlings and, of course, House Sparrows. Bears were said to be very common in the forest, although I never saw one. Their depredations in the corn fields were plain to see and, whilst we were there, a man was killed and another badly mauled by bears in a village some two miles from the resthouse.'

Our return journey took us through the sister state of Jammu and over the Banihal Pass, with the road twisting through the 8,000 feet bare, grassy mountains to give magnificent views of the Himalayan snows to the north and the brown, dusty plains of India to the south. At Sialkot we caught the train but our journey was much impeded by disorders connected with Gandhi's 'Quit India' campaign which, like all his activities planned to be non-violent, unleashed the violence for which he always denied responsibility but for which he was actually responsible. At this time the railway lines were ripped up, passengers on halted trains were slaughtered in the name of religion and other acts of murder were perpetrated in the same cause. We did not come across any of these scenes but our trains were late because of them and we missed connections, arriving back in Jhikagacha a few days late but much refreshed by three weeks in a cooler climate and by a change of scene.

Before we left Jhikagacha for the Arakan campaign in 1943, I spent ten days leave in Dehra Dun and another ten days in Ahmednagar on an M.T. course. As on a previous rail journey to Dehra, I was enchanted by the scenes after the train left Hardwar and started the climb over the Siwaliks: the sal forests, the clear streams, the flashing colours of kingfishers, the cool morning air and the promise of restful days in the shadow of the

Himalayas. I enjoyed four days' shooting, camping out in the jungle at Jamnipur with a Gurkha Officer and a small party of men. The dawns were heralded by the crowing of Red Jungle Fowl and the 'belling' of sambhur. The sal jungle was so thick that it was difficult to shoot, but I had quite good bags of jungle fowl, which were excellent eating even when roughly dismembered by a Gurkha orderly. We saw cheetal as well as parties of rhesus monkeys and the tracks of wild boar. We were camped by the side of the River Jumna and I tried fishing for mahseer with a fly spoon, catching a few fish of two lbs. or so. Our bag during the four days was not spectacular but the enjoyment was immense. Each day I walked for miles, finding the tracks of game, hearing the harsh cries of Parakeets, the shrill whistling of Leaf Warblers and other cries and calls unidentified. Sometimes I would be startled by the sudden warning 'mee-iouw' of a peacock, which would leap into the air with surprising agility, dragging its huge tail through the sal canopy. Although peacock is excellent eating, I could never steel myself to shoot so gorgeous a bird; even a male jungle fowl is so superbly coloured that one feels guilty when picking up its limp form.

What contentment there was in sitting outside the tent in the cool darkness, refreshed by a 'chota peg' after a long day's walk, watching the fireflies twinkle like a galaxy of stars amongst the sal trees, with the river gurgling and an owlet hooting in the distance. Only the forlorn wish that the experience could be shared by those one loved at home detracted from the feeling of well-being.

I have few recollections about the M.T. course at Ahmednagar. That we lived uncomfortably, overcrowded in tents, and worked very hard for three weeks, I do remember. Endless lectures, fair copying rough notes and diagrams by the light of hissing pressure lamps abuzz with frantic insects; sessions in the garages dismantling and re-assembling ancient petrol engines; frequent tests to see if we had absorbed the Sergeant Instructor's parrot-like lectures; and last of all a 24-hour drive. In this we set out, two to a truck, after breakfast at 15 minute intervals, taking with us iron rations and a map with the prescribed route marked on it. It was an extremely useful and taxing experience, for the trucks were old and the roads and tracks on which we had to drive were rough and dusty and sometimes impassable. Tyres punctured, engines over-heated, fuel lines became blocked, radiators leaked. In fact, most of the mishaps which could befall elderly, much-used army vehicles did occur and the faults had to be rectified. True, we had the backup in the form of our Sergeant Instructor who brought up the rear and was prepared to help in cases of dire emergency, such as broken springs or wheel axles, but most of us completed the drive on our own and really felt that we would be able to cope with most M.T. emergencies when we returned to our units. The night spent beneath the stars, lying beside the truck, was a useful experience, albeit rather short, as we had to complete the drive within the specified time.

CHAPTER 7

WAR AT LAST : ARAKAN

Just before my M.T. course ended, I received news that the battalion had moved to the Arakan and I was ordered to rejoin it there. So I made my way to Chittagong, a difficult cross-country journey involving many changes. My next objective was south to Cox's Bazaar, which could only be reached by sea. A boat left Chittagong every morning at 0700 hours, the passengers being ferried out in a barge for the two-hour passage. Cox's Bazaar was a scene of considerable improvised chaos as a recently established base for the campaign to try and halt and reverse the Japanese advance north from the port of Akyab, which they had recently captured. From Cox's Bazaar to the next town, Bawli Bazaar, there was only a dirt road, which had become rutted and knee-deep in dust, with flimsy bridges threatening to collapse as hundreds of three-ton lorries plied to and fro. Later, when the rains came, only four-wheel drive vehicles could make the journey. I found a seat in a lorry and endured several hours of slow, dusty, heaving and lurching discomfort until we reached Bawli Bazaar, where I discovered that the battalion was in a forward position at a place called Gyndaw. By means of hitchhiking down the coastal road, I eventually reached Bn. H.Q. to find companies deployed at the head of a valley where a stream left the hill tracts for the narrow coastal plain under a road bridge. We were to hold this bridge until the forces to the south, which were conducting a 'planned withdrawal', had passed through with their equipment. This retreat, for that is what it was, being imminent, I was ordered to take over B Company, which I found dug in on the south bank of the Gyndaw stream in thick jungle. Fields of fire had been cleared and Danart wire erected, but the position was overlooked by the surrounding hills and hillocks, and should the Japs get on to these, our position would be untenable. The whole battalion was similarly threatened; it was a badly chosen position and everyone knew it to be so.

My first day was spent in trying to improve our defences. There was little enemy activity to hinder the withdrawal of the forward units which passed through during one afternoon, as dispirited a bunch of British troops as one could fear to see and in no way a boost to our morale. Shortly before dark, a Jap truck suddenly drove up to the bridge. It was fired on without visible effect and it made a hasty retreat, taking with it exact knowledge of our positions. We received orders to retire at a given hour after dark and, as the sun sank into the Bay of Bengal, the tense waiting started.

I shall not forget those few hours. We had eaten the evening meal early, all stores apart from sufficient ammunition had been back-loaded, and we were poised to go as soon as the signal was given. The night was moonless and pitch dark; the 'tuck-too' lizards were starting their explosive and sudden calls, now from one tree and then from another. Jackals were howling from the coastal plain. Fireflies were winking in the bushes beyond our wire. Were the lizards real? Were the flashes really fireflies? Were the jackals really what they seemed to be? We had heard that the Japs imitated jungle sounds and called out in English to deceive. Each sound, each movement by an animal, set our nerves on edge. Then, quite suddenly, human shouts came from the jungle; 'Hello Johnnie,' and even 'Ayo Gurkhali.' The men became very jittery and, when something rattled one of the tins hung on the barbed wire to give warning, a Bren gunner opened up and all hell was let loose. Every shot fired, with its attendant flash, gave a position away. The Japs moved round the perimeter, shouting, imitating animals and birds, and firing an occasional shot into our positions, while we fired thousands of rounds to no effect other than to benefit the enemy. Eventually the hubbub died down and a sinister silence ensued, all the wild creatures having been subdued by the uproar.

Would an attack take place or were the Japs just a small recce party intent upon plotting our positions? This uncertainty greatly increased the tension as we waited for the time to withdraw. One by one the startled creatures of the night re-started their usual calls, adding to the tension. As the deadline approached, I began to send back small parties with the unused boxes of ammunition, then a whole platoon followed by another, until only one was left in the foremost position. I sat in the Company H.Q. trench with Subadar Ratnabahadur Khattri, a field telephone at my side, wondering which would come first – an attack against our depleted positions or the order to withdraw. Those few minutes of extreme tension, perhaps ten at the most, seemed interminable. Suddenly the telephone buzzed, so loud it seemed that the Japs must hear it. I snatched up the phone to hear Robbie's calm and comforting voice saying, 'Scott, come.' We disconnected the phone, leaving the wire where it was, hissed orders to the forward platoon, and the men filed past us silently and unhurried. We followed, wading through the stream and stumbling over the slippery stones in the dark, half expecting an attack at any moment.

Thus did the whole battalion leave this untenable position to gather in the dark on the coastal plain. We were then ordered to move north in extended order over the dry paddy fields away from the road, keeping in visual distance of each other, behind Battalion H.Q. It was not easy, although the waning moon had come up to give a little light. We had been marching for some minutes when shots were fired, apparently from behind. We were already on edge and, spread out as we were, keeping contact was difficult. Men started to run about here and there, more shots rang out from various directions, and it was not long before the battalion was scattered in the darkness. All I could do was to collect together as many men as I could find and continue marching north. So disorganised had we become that there was no certainty that any parties appearing in the gloom were friend or foe; many were the challenges and alarms.

In this demoralised state, tired and dispirited, we pressed on north until the sky began to lighten over the Arakan Yomas and we could begin to take stock of what had happened. I was surprised to find, when daylight came, that my small party of about 20 men, which did not include Subadar Ratnabahadur, who had disappeared early on, was entirely on its own. We began to wonder if the rest had been captured, but as we approached Alythengaw and Brigade H.Q., George Bolton, the Brigade Major, came out to meet us and assure us that most of the men and Battalion H.Q. had arrived. As it turned out, only some 20 men were missing and most of these came in later after being held by the Japs and then escaping.

It should be mentioned here that no soldier of the Indian Army who had been in Jap custody even momentarily, however quickly he had escaped, was permitted to rejoin his unit or take part in any active service against the Japs. This was because of a traitor organisation called the Indian National Army (I.N.A.) which had been set up by Subhas Chandra Bose and which enrolled Indian prisoners of war or sent them back to suborn colleagues in their regiments. There is no evidence of any Nepal-born Gurkhas thus breaking faith,but we never again saw those men who had been in Jap hands during the debacle. I have not the slightest doubt that Ratnabahadur was anything but 100 per cent loyal; it was just his bad luck that no exception could be made.

As we re-assembled and took stock of what had happened, we found little to be pleased about. Every unit must have its baptism of fire and none that I know of can claim to have remain entirely steady during their first Jap night attack. It was our misfortune to have this experience immediately followed by so much confusion. But important lessons were learnt at what turned out to be very little cost. Never again did the higher command order a whole battalion in extended order to move across open ground in the dark when the enemy was known to be around, and never again were we put in a position so hopelessly impossible to defend. Morale was soon restored in minor patrol activity designed to harass the Japs and hold them roughly where they were until the monsoon made further advance well nigh impossible.

It was about this time that Robbie Fawcett left to take command of the 29th Gurkha Rifles, a hybrid training battalion incorporating both 2nd and 9th Gurkha Rifle personnel. Noel George assumed command of the 3/9th. My memories are vague about the operations following directly after our withdrawal. The Japs took Buthidaung but never advanced much further north during our time in the Arakan. Throughout the monsoon, our Division, the 26th Indian, held a line just north of this town and south westwards to the sea, including the Teknaf Peninsula. For much of the time we were in the front line at a place called Taung Bazaar, patrolling south and keeping tabs on Jap movements. There were some spectacular patrol engagements, after one of which Jim Blaker was awarded the M.C.

During this time I was adjutant and, when not otherwise engaged, I was able to enjoy the birds around us. Extracts from two letters written in pencil in my own personal dug-out, or sometimes outside when there was no enemy activity, tell of some of them:

'The birds here are an ever-present interest, but sadly I have not got my bird book with me and identification of some of them is difficult. My best friend at the moment is a little pipit which lives in the bamboo thickets and in the early morning utters a delightful song of which every note is so unexpected that the whole is a constant source of pleasure. Green Pigeons are numerous, differing from their grey relatives in their arboreal habits, feeding like large grotesque titmice in the wild fig trees. Many and beautiful are the lizards, all with harsh and strident voices. Flowers are scarce at this time of year (May) but I have noticed and admired a large, yellow bell-shaped species with a delicious morning scent. Wild elephants abound and their droppings, each a manure heap in itself, are everywhere and their immense footmarks stud the soft earth.

'During the last few days I have been watching a colony of Rose-ring Parakeet nesting in a dead tree near Battalion H.Q. They are extremely noisy; apparently nothing can be done in the parrot world unless it is accompanied by loud, piercing, tearing shrieks. The young were almost fully fledged and some emerged from the nesting holes to sit on adjacent boughs, attended by shrieking parents. These flew off to a nearby tree, had a good look around, and departed on a foraging expedition, to return in a few minutes, shrieking as they came, to pump semi-digested food into the bills of their young. The little Blossom-headed Parakeet is my favourite, but so far I have not seen a breeding colony.

'Small teak trees are dotted about in the forest here, their massive leaves drying out before falling and rattling grotesquely in the slightest breeze. It is surprising to find that these trees, giants in central Burma, are close relatives of the verbenas and such delicate herbs as common thyme. In some areas bamboo is totally dominant, no other plants, be they tree, shrub or herb, being present. It seems that nothing much favours these thickets save the pretty little swamp deer and the ubiquitous Red Jungle Fowl, which crows bantam-like at dawn.'

In early June, 1943, I was sent on a camouflage course in Shillong. I went by rail from Chittagong to Sylhet and thence by bus to Shillong. The climb up through the Khasia Hills, the air becoming cooler at every bend, it seemed, was a delight after all the heat and discomfort of Taung Bazaar. Another officer, whose name and regiment I forget, and who was assigned to the same course, accompanied me in the bus and we found that we were both to stay at the Pinewood Hotel. We were 'welcomed' by the two elderly European sister-owners who, with undisguised distaste, showed us to a double room containing two rickety wooden beds. During the few days we stayed there we felt that we had to some extent overcome the hostility; at least the two ladies began to say 'Good Morning' and even deigned to hope that we were enjoying our stay in Shillong. But when we came to paying our bills, we found on them a substantial item: 'Repairs to Beds'. As the beds were in the same rickety state when we left as they had been when we arrived, and any deterioration commensurate with the sum added to our bills would have meant that they had collapsed completely, we declined to pay, remonstrating warmly. Having deducted the sum, we wrote out cheques and left, amidst loud protestations from the two ladies against us in particular and army officers in general, suggesting that we were not the first victims of this ruse nor the first to rumble it. Indeed, I later heard that this was a regular ploy of the two sisters, known throughout Shillong, much to the amusement of the European inhabitants.

During the return journey I began to feel very ill, with diarrhoea and vomiting prostrating me in the stuffy, lurching railway carriage. By the time we reached Chittagong, my determination to get back to the battalion at all costs had evaporated. Crawling into a tonga, I told the driver to go to the Military Hospital, where I had no difficulty in persuading them that I was ill. For a day or two I could not have cared what happened to me and the doctor seemed baffled. Then quite suddenly I went bright yellow and infective hepatitis was diagnosed. I soon began to feel better and hoped for an early discharge. The doctor had other ideas and put me on a hospital train bound for the Base Hospital in Calcutta. This turned out (at least the officers' part of it) to be in the old German Consulate in Harrington Street in the centre of the city. So, when I reached the stage of being allowed out in the afternoons, I was able to go to the cinema, relieving some of the boredom. I suppose I must have been a more serious case than I thought because, after nearly a month in hospital, the doctor insisted that I should have 15 days sick leave. I tried to find accommodation in Darjeeling but failed, so I went to Dehra Dun. It so happened that Robbie Fawcett was on leave in Mussoorie and he invited me to stay for a few days. In a letter home, dated 14th July, 1943, I wrote:

'It is lovely up here; it rains heavily at night but the days are perfect. Over to the north, during the clearer moments of the day, one can see the main Himalayan range – a truly fantastic mountain mass which, although many miles away and in spite of this place being already at 7,000 feet, appears to tower over this straggling hill station. In the centre of the range, reaching even higher than the other peaks, is the famous Nanda Devi, whose summit is nearly 27,000 feet. The sight of this colossal mountain barrier is awe-inspiring; small wonder the Tibetans remain aloof. The Mussoorie hills are beautiful; last evening I climbed to a nearby summit and found spectacular views. To the north and some 2,000 feet below, was a wide, steep-sided valley where, shining a brilliant green, were the terraced cultivations of the Garwhalis, a race somewhat akin to our Gurkhas. Far to the north were the snows, tinged pink by the fast-sinking sun, and to the south was a thickly wooded valley with little coils of blue smoke rising through the trees, betraying the presence of charcoal burners converting the timber of the evergreen oaks into that essential commodity of Indian life – charcoal for cooking. Indian Grey Tits were chattering away in the stunted pines; from down in the valley came the flutey notes of a Himalayan blackbird and a faint piping suggested that a party of White-eyes was feeding high in the oaks; occasional harsh cries told of langurs in the vastness of the forest. All was beautiful and I felt that jaundice was almost worth it.'

After a few days I went down to Dehra with orders from Robbie to take another fortnight's leave. Although I was feeling much better, I did concede that a few more days in a cool climate would be a wise precaution. Life was very agreeable in the Regimental Centre and I was able to spend my time walking and enjoying the scenery and wildlife as another extract from a letter shows:

'The rains have only just started here and the flowers, shrubs and trees are not yet at their best. The sweet peas, so lovely last year, have not been sown; the only flowers are cannas. The Himalayan cypresses are very fine and heavy with cones; the peepul trees are shedding their purple figs, giving the ground squirrels an easy harvest. These little rodents are more numerous here than I have seen anywhere else. Their sharp little bird-like squeaks are a constant feature as they run along the ground in short spurts, with their straggly little tails held aloft. Sunbirds find sustenance in the flowering shrubs, trilling happily and flashing their bright colours. When heavy showers arrive, all is silent except for the roar of rain, which stops as suddenly as it began. Then, one by one, the birds start to call again. Perhaps the merry 'tonking' of the Coppersmith will be followed by the squeaky cackle of a Mynah or the guttural warble of a Green Barbet. Then a Tailorbird will whistle from a cypress, a whistle incredibly loud for so small a bird. A kite will wail and a crow will caw hoarsely; all will once again be an Indian day with its scent of once-parched earth now damp and lush with sprouting green shoots.'

Yet again my return was delayed. The M.O. refused me a discharged certificate and ordered a further three weeks' sick leave. I whiled away the time in both Dehra and Mussoorie and was finally passed fit by a medical board in Calcutta towards the end of August. I then set about organising my return to the Arakan; no easy task as the journey was very complicated.

After several days delay, I managed to get a berth on the Chittagong Mail, which left Sealdah Station of an evening at 2000 hours. Even to get near the train was a struggle, for the platform was a mass of sleeping humanity with nowhere else to go but this crowded public place, where at least they had shelter from the rain. My orderly and I, with a coolie carrying my suitcase and 'bistra', threaded our way through the prostrate forms and eventually found our carriage, I with a place in a four-berth compartment and he in the servants' compartment, of which there was one at the end of each first-class coach.

The whirr of the overhead fan was soon drowned by the clatter of the train wheels, a rhythm which, despite the heat and lurching, soon brought on sleep. The occasional stop during the night woke me but I was fairly refreshed when we arrived at Goalundo Ghat at 0600 hours, and necessarily so, for the rush and scramble for the river steamer was legendary and classless as everyone pushed and shoved towards the two gangways. I got on board in good order but Manbahadur somehow managed to find himself on the wrong boat with all my kit. Fortunately I discovered this in time to retrieve the situation and we set off down river.

This section of the journey took all day; a pleasant day on this wide, slow-flowing Ganges, now within a hundred miles or so of losing its identity in the Bay of Bengal. On both sides stretched bright green fields of paddy and jute, spotted white with egrets. Riverside villages, perched on the banks above normal flood level, slipped by in seemingly endless succession, for the area was densely populated. Other river steamers, barges, sampans and canoes swept past us going upstream as we chugged through the brown water. As evening approached, the egrets left the fields, flying overhead in little flocks, their white feathers tinged pink by the setting sun. The coconut palms stood stark and black against the roseate sky. Chandpur hove in sight and the telegraph rang loudly as we glided towards the wharf. No scrum here, for we had bookings on the metre gauge railway to take us overnight to Chittagong, but when we arrived there in the morning, we found that the boat to Cox's Bazaar had already sailed, condemning us to 24 hours in the Rest Camp, where the heat was overpowering.

The steamer left at 0700 hours the following morning and as we emerged from the river mouth, a heavy sea smote us. Many of the passengers were soon prostrated and my bedding roll, out on deck with Manbahadur, became waterlogged much to his amusement. The passage continued rough and attendance for lunch in the saloon was sparse. Transfer to barges at Cox's Bazaar harbour, too shallow for the steamer to enter, was difficult, but all went well, except that we were to learn that heavy rain had made the Tambru road impassable and another rest camp was to be our immediate destination.

The next morning dawned dry and bright and it seemed that four-wheel drive Dodge vehicles would be able to get through to Tambru. After a breakfast of fried bully beef and dehydrated chips, we set off. The road was just a ribbon of red, slimy mud, the worst stretches reinforced with small tree trunks laid crossways. We crept along through the mud at about five m.p.h., sliding one way and then the other, leaping and bouncing when we hit a timbered section, to plunge again into the morass. It was a dreadful journey which seemed endless and, added to the discomfort of the lurching truck, was the smell of the liquid mud through which we were making our laboured progress; a sickly, sickening stench which, as we were to find later, emanated from all mud in Burma through which men, mules and motor vehicles have struggled on the way. At Tambru we changed our mode of transport once again, not without relief, for the little boat which took us down the coast to Bawli Bazaar was steady on the calm sea and sleep was possible.

At Bawli Bazaar we learnt that baggage mules were not available. Without them we could not proceed as we had met up with some leave party men from the Battalion and a quantity of stores. During lunch at Brigade H.Q., I managed to persuade the Transport Officer to let us have two mules from his own pool. We set off for the Goppe Pass, a twisting, slippery, muddy track snaking up through the jungle to a pass at the top of the first range of the Kyuaktalon Hill Tracts at about 2,000 feet. Half way up Sappers were repairing the much-used path and they gave us some tea before we struggled on to reach the summit at 1700 hours. Here there were some bamboo huts and we decided to stay the night. After a supper of tinned sausages and baked beans, sleep came easily.

I woke to the mellow notes of Whistling Thrushes in the bamboo jungle and the crowing of Jungle Fowl down in the valley. The weather was clear and cloudless and the view superb; the deep blue of the Bay of Bengal contrasted with the intense green of the Teknaf Peninsula, famous for its elephant herds. Due west was Bawli Bazaar with a river steamer swinging in the tide. To the south lay the Mayu Range, clothed in thick jungle, and the coastal plain, paddy covered, stretching down to Maungdaw, then in Jap hands.

We set off again on the morrow at 0700 hours, passing a small party of Marungs, a race between the Arakanese and the Burmese, handsome and of fine stature. They were carrying great bundles of bamboo for building more huts at the summit. We asked if they had seen any Japs and they said they had not and did not want to. The downhill going was easy, if a little slippery, and we soon reached the chaung, which the path followed faithfully to Goppe Bazaar. Apart from leeches which transferred themselves from the path-side bushes to our arms and knees, but were easily removed by burning with a cigarette, the walk was uneventful. We lunched at the forward Brigade Mess whilst arrangements were made for a sampan to take us down the Kalapanzan River to Taung Bazaar. By 1400 hours we were gliding down the river, silently apart from the squeak of the rowlocks as the boatman steered his course. The river was running high and we sped along between tall banks covered with bamboo and lianas. Now and again a Pied or White-Breasted Kingfisher would fly from its riverside perch and a troop of rhesus macaque monkeys dashed noisly away as we approached, turning to show their red faces and bared teeth before disappearing into the bamboo thicket. I slept part of the way, lulled by the rhythm of the oars as the boatman found more effort necessary, for the incoming tide was stemming the river's flow. We reached Taung Bazaar, the most forward post on the Arakan's monsoon front, just as the evening rain was starting to fall. I had been away since June; it was now 26th August.

I took back my duties as adjutant from Bertie Stott to find that the job was physically undemanding in this forward position, but despite our being at the end of a very long line of communication, all the usual paperwork continued unabated. It said something of the Head Clerk, Jemadar Surrendra Mall and his staff, that they managed to cope with everything, working in a semi-underground bamboo hut with a grass roof. To hear the clacking of a typewriter amidst the sawing of cicadas and the honking of bullfrogs, and sometimes the far-distant rattle of automatic fire, all in the surroundings of bamboo jungle, tempted one to distrust reality.

A kind of monsoon truce seemed to have set in. The Japs were in Buthidaung, some ten miles south, and our job was to keep tabs on their movements and thus give warning of any general attack. This we did by regular daily patrols covering all possible paths and streams along which the enemy might approach. Now and again there were clashes as the Japs did the same thing, and a few scalps were claimed, Jim Blaker and Jacko Jackson being the most persistent performers, taking out small patrols for up to 24 hours duration, setting ambushes and generally giving the Japs some of their own medicine. These activities did much to boost the men's morale, for we suffered few casualties and certainly inflicted many on the enemy. Indeed, the battalion's standing in the Division rose steeply; we were in the most forward position, the only unit in contact with the Japs, and carrying out our allotted task with skill and determination. Jim Blaker was awarded the M.C. for his patrol work. (He was later to be awarded a posthumous V.C. in the Chindit operations).

CHAPTER 8

BETWEEN CAMPAIGNS

About a month after I returned to the battalion in Taung Bazaar, we received news of an impending relief, not without much pleasure, for the rains had been heavy and persistent. Even the Gurkhas' skill at making bamboo huts with grass and banana leaf roofs could not fully keep out the torrential downpours; and despite our raised positions on little hills above the often-flooding river, our dugouts often took in water. Nothing really got dry or remained so for any length of time. Our mess cook, a redoubtable Punjabi Mussalman, who regarded active service as an exciting duty, did wonders with mostly tinned food and the occasional piece of fresh beef brought over the pass on mules. 'Soya links', a kind of 'square' tinned sausage, and bully beef provide poor material for even the most imaginative of cooks, and sitting round the table, our feet on improvised duckboards above the liquid mud, faced with a well known repetitious culinary theme, meant that this fare soon began to pall. The Gurkhas fared little better; curried bully mutton and rice were the usual items on their menu. Eaten out of mess tins, topped with a generous portion of dhal, it smelt most appetising; indeed, one was often tempted to forego the mess fare and order up a portion from the cookhouse.

In early October the eagerly awaited change-over took place. The 8/8th Punjab Regiment struggled across the pass and took over our positions. We made our way to Goppe, crossing the swollen Kalapanzin River with difficulty; a mule, carrying two boxes of three-inch mortar bombs, fell into deep water and sank without trace. Praying for a dry day on the morrow, we camped at Goppe Bazaar. The dawn broke bright and clear and we scaled the pass without much difficulty and, with only minor repairs to the path to help the heavily loaded mules, we reached Bawli Bazaar in good order and spent the night there, the most taxing part of the journey completed.

In two river steamers and a 'flat' we arrived in Tambru the following evening, but it took four more days to reach Dohazari, sometimes marching, occasionally in transport; days of intense fatigue with many men falling out with heat stroke. At Dohazari we entrained for Comilla. Much of the organisation involved in moving some 800 men by various modes of transport fell upon me and my staff; I did not get heat stroke but I was on the verge of exhaustion when we arrived at our new camp. The final stage was a seven-mile march in the dark from Comilla to this camp at Mynamatti. A full moon lit the dusty road as our long column wended its weary but expectant way through the night. But I sensed a light-hearted mood amongst the men; many of them were due for leave and they had seen a job well done.

Thus began our rest period lasting a month or so. We despatched more than 100 men on leave to Nepal, while the rest of us started training for an as yet unknown role. We now knew that we could match the Japs in the jungle, and we were further encouraged by the appointment of Lord Louis Mountbatten as Supreme Commander of the new South East Asia Command (S.E.A.C.). Indeed, he paid us a visit during which he gathered the men round whilst standing on a crate, and addressed them in a carefully learnt and much appreciated little speech in Gurkhali. That the King's cousin could do this greatly impressed the Gurkhas, as indeed it did the British officers.

The rains had ceased and something approaching cold weather had set in. The camp site was on undulating ground, dry and open to any breeze which happened to be blowing. Although we were in tents, most of the administrative buildings, such as cookhouses, latrines, showers etc., were in bashas with concrete floors, so keeping them clean was easy. The main problem was the difficulty of obtaining water. Again, we had double-acting pumps, which fell ready prey to the heavy-handed Gurkhas and were often out of order. I remember one occasion, when water from the pumps was scarce, my orderly drew some water from a pond for my evening ablutions. When I stepped into my canvas bath, I found I was sharing it with a number of frogs which were floating dead on their backs. They had succumbed to the hot water poured in from a kerosene tin which had been boiling over a wood fire. My orderly expressed much amused surprise, but I think he must have known they were there and thought it a good joke to let me find them.

The camp was a pleasant place and, as Christmas approached, the weather became delightful; warm and sunny during the day and cool at night, with dew forming on the grass before dawn. The men were happy, regaining their health and training hard in jungle warfare and on the field-firing ranges. Evening parades, at which each man was seen by his Section Commander to swallow a Mepacrine pill, cut down the incidence of malaria to negligible proportions, and prickly heat vanished in the cooler, drier air. Working as adjutant and at the hub of things, as it were, I found extremely interesting and, after two years service in a Gurkha regiment, I felt more than ever privileged to serve with these splendid men, as a letter I wrote home at the time shows:

'I write by the light of a small hurricane lamp on a warm, rather sticky evening. It is 7.00 p.m. and the sun set an hour ago. All round the camp the men are singing and beating rhythms on their "madals". Their songs are about their homes in the hills, homes where they have left their wives and children or their parents to serve a King whose country is in peril and to give that country service such as no other race has so consistently given for a century and more. Intensely loyal to those of us who are privileged to lead them, magnificently brave in the face of great odds and endlessly cheerful in conditions of heat, filth and fatigue. Well and rightly may one praise the Desert Army and its victories in Sicily and Italy, but out here a ruthless and cruel enemy has been kept at bay in the disease-ridden, swampy, steamy jungles for over a year by a comparatively small number of men (very many of them Gurkhas). It is in these conditions that the qualities of loyalty, courage and cheerfulness, so strong in our men, have been sorely tried, and never once have they been found wanting.'

I also found time for walks in the countryside and my general interest in natural history made my life more interesting than that of my colleagues. In the evenings I used to watch the Eastern Nightjars out on their vesper hawking expeditions. Their flight was entirely silent and as irregular as that of butterflies. In and out and over the mango trees they would flit as I sat outside my tent removing my sticky feet from boots. And the nuptial flight of the termites also took place as the sun was setting; many thousands of them emerged from their underground termitry to spiral upwards towards the darkening sky, later to be attracted by the brilliance of my petrolmax lamp and fall wingless on the floor. Even before the sun went down, the crickets started to sing from their little burrows round the tent, the stridency of the cacophony increasing with the darkness and altogether disproportionate to the size of the insects.

At this time a circular came from 14th Army encouraging us to be more expansive in our letters home, informing our relatives about our living conditions and so on. As a result I wrote:

'I live in a tent 10 ft x 8 ft. The furniture consists of a camp bed, a chair (collapsible, made in Bengal, and living up to its name), my tin trunk which has things in it as well as on it, and a small table. The floor is carpeted with bamboo matting, now rapidly being eaten by white ants. My mosquito net is suspended by tapes sewn on to the inside of the tent. My bathroom consists of a roofless pen of bamboo matting tied on to bamboo poles, with a flimsy door which often falls open at the wrong moment. Inside is a small bamboo table on which sit such things as soap, toothpaste, sponges etc. The centre piece is a tub (a great acquisition in these parts) to fit into which one has to adopt an immediate pre-natal pose. The water for the bath is heated in an old four-gallon kerosene tin and I have a hot bath every night under the dome of the stars; after the accidental inclusion of soap in my eyes I find it reassuring to catch a glimpse of Orion's Belt or even of the Pleiades. The bathroom is rigorously "flitted" before my entry, and when it bears some resemblance to a gas chamber, I rush in to enjoy the brief mosquito-free respite which this atmosphere ensures. As I have previously mentioned, I sometimes find frogs in the bath and, on one occasion, a drowning rat, much to my orderly's amusement.'

In mid-November, 1943, Dudley and I went to Darjeeling on ten days' leave. I had not been there before and I was instantly enchanted with the place, as extracts from letters written home show:

'Of all the pretty hill stations I have seen, this is the prettiest and what is extra nice about it is that the inhabitants are so cheerful and welcoming, being Gurkhas and other hill tribes. The railway up here from Siliguri is most enthralling. It climbs about 7,000 feet in 50 miles through the most beautiful wooded mountains. For the first five miles along the flat, the train consists of 12 coaches and one engine, but at the last station before the climb it is split into three trains of four coaches, with one engine to each. One man sits on the "cowcatcher" of each engine and sprinkles sand on the line to increase friction, another on the top of the boiler breaks up coal with a hammer, another drives, and a fourth walks about on the coach inspecting the couplings. Curves in the line are such that in a few hundred yards the train crosses over the line just passed over, in so tight a curve that should it be of normal length, the engine would be on the bridge above the last few coaches.

'How you would enjoy the constant spectacle here of a 28,000 foot mountain (Kanchenjunga) above you; the tinted evergreen oaks in the early morning sun, which colours the whole Himalayan range a roseate hue; the view of East Nepal where a hundred Gurkha villages cling dangerously to the steep, grassy slopes, here stepped with little fields, there left to their virgin selves as grazing grounds for goats, cattle and little ponies. The people would amuse you too. A dozen Himalayan races are gathered here to buy and sell, barter and gamble. Bhutias pull the rickshaws; Tibetans, in all their finery, come in from their vast, lofty plateau bearing wool, yak skins and semi-precious stones; Lepchas, quaint little people with three-cornered fur caps and streaming noses, bring loads of furs and nick-nacks for the tourist trade. Sherpas, famous as porters on Everest expeditions, make their way here at this time of year – 18,000 foot passes are too hot in summer, they say – to exchange the goods of their beautiful, rugged country for luxuries from the plains of India. Many are the tongues heard, a veritable babel, but the "lingua franca" is Nepali, which I can now speak with fair fluency, adding to the pleasure of being here.'

We stayed in the Planters Club in Darjeeling. When we arrived there we were almost turned away as all the rooms were occupied. But the Secretary took pity on us, poor pallid officers from Bengal's steamy heat. He had two camp beds put in a bay in the library, where we were very comfortable, surrounded by leather-bound volumes, the masks of long-since bagged tigers, the antlers of sambhur and the tusks of wild boars set in silver mountings.

Walks up to the recruiting depot at Jalapahar, visits to the Lebong races, where little ponies galloped round a tight circular track urged on by a yelling crowd of hillmen, and shopping filled our days. In the evenings we went to one or other of the cinemas, or 'flea pits', as they were called by the retired planters who lived in the club. Each day in the cool, crisp air, we found ourselves feeling fitter and fell more in love with this enchanting place. On the morning of my 24th birthday I climbed Tiger Hill and described the scene in a letter home:

'This morning I climbed an 8,500 foot hill south of Darjeeling to see the famous view. It was about 10.30 a.m. and the clouds were few, giving me a marvellous panoramic view. To the N.N.W., just peeping over a mass of foothills, was Mount Everest – a magnificent white block sticking 29,000 feet into the heavens; due north, much nearer and more impressive, lay

Kanchenjunga (this is the Tibetan name meaning "Seven Little Storehouses of Snow") and its subsidiary peaks. Looking through the binoculars at these peaks, I could see great masses of snow being hurled into the blue sky by the continuous gales which blow up there, five miles above sea level. I could see the glaciers on the slopes, cracked and compressed and for ever flowing downwards. I could pick out monasteries on the lower slopes in Sikkim and I could follow with my glasses the whole range of the Eastern Himalayas from Mount Everest in Nepal right across the Sikkim crags to the snowy peaks of Bhutan; in fact it must be one of the finest views in the world. Behind, to the south, were the plains of Bengal, their sluggish rivers shining a dirty silver and barely above sea level.

'I wandered down in the hot sun, passing clumps of bamboo, stopping to pick a blackberry from a straggly bush, or stooping to taste a wild strawberry. Occasionally, amongst the mosses, I saw a flaming bunch of arum lily berries or the upturned leaf of silverweed glistening in the sun. I saw viburnums and whitebeams, which indicated a calcareous soil, confirmed by the absence of rhododendrons, so common elsewhere in these mountains. And I watched a Red-headed Tit searching magnolia flowers for insects and the flight of kites and crows circling high in the rarefied air. The morning was lovely; how I wish you could have shared it.'

We returned to Mynamatti, much refreshed, to find that our new role had been decided. We were to join Wingate's Special Force, which was to be expanded from the Brigade strength in which it had operated in Burma behind Jap lines in 1943, to a Division of three brigades, each with two Battalions of British troops and one of Gurkhas. We were designated to be the Gurkha Battalion which would defend the airfield to be built in the middle of Burma behind enemy lines. Training for this new role had already started.

Just before Christmas, 1943 the Regimental Pipe Band came down from Dehra Dun, looking very smart in their white uniforms and tartan plaids. That this visit took place was entirely due to Lord Louis, who fully realised the value to morale that military bands could be. He had pressed G.H.Q. in Delhi to authorise these visits to units in the forward areas. The men were delighted to see and hear the pipes and drums, which certainly reinforced morale and the regimental spirit. As did a ceremony held about the same time when the General gave the insignia of the Order of British India (O.B.I.) to our Subadar Major, Bhimbahadur Khattri. As adjutant, I had to hand the insignia to the General, who was so flustered that he nearly gave it to me. After staring at me for a few seconds, he asked me what he should do. I told him and he eventually managed to put the ribbon round the Subadar Major's neck. I gave Bhimbahadur a bottle of whisky by way of congratulations, which he finished in one evening with the help of two brother officers.

From the social point of view, Christmas was a tame affair. We could not get a turkey but we managed to find two Chinese geese which were really very good eating. For drinks we had Indian-made gin, rum and whisky; all very sub-standard but much better than nothing. After lunch, there was the usual football match between the British and Gurkha officers which, to our surprise, we won. Otherwise the day was much like any other, with the temperature reaching 85°F.

As the year turned, we continued with training for our new role and moved further north into Assam, where, in the hill tracts and further from civilisation, the jungles were more akin to those we were likely to encounter in N. Burma. It was then early January and the weather was fairly cool. In fact every prospect pleased; the jungle-clad hills with cultivated valley-bottoms, the villages shaded by mango trees, each little mud-walled and grass-roofed house with its banana and papaya trees, and the people apparently well-fed and content. Our arrival was, of course, an event of great significance to them, bringing a few weeks of increased prosperity, for much of our fresh rations were bought from them and they provided services on payment. We spent most of our time on jungle training and accustoming our mules to the heavy loads which they were destined to carry. These mules had all been de-voiced by some sort of operation on their vocal chords to prevent them from betraying our presence to the enemy by the sickening cries of which normal mules so frequently deliver themselves for no apparent reason.

This remote, unspoilt area was an enchanting place for wildlife, and in order to satisfy the censor, my letters home contained little else than notes about the wild things around me.

'We have just settled into another place even more remote than previously, but the country is very pretty and although on the same latitude, has a more temperate appearance. I saw a new bird yesterday, a Jerdon's Chloropsis. It was bright green with a small black bib and longish beak. It was about the size of a starling and was sitting on a silk cotton tree calling loudly in mellow tones. The bird is by no means rare and I wonder why I have not seen one before. Teak trees are very abundant; my orderly tells me that in

Nepal they give the leaves to milch buffaloes and increase their milk yield by 50% by so doing. This may or may not be true. Barking deer are everywhere with their inevitable companions, the Red Jungle Fowl. I saw a Greater Snipe in a paddyfield; it was surprisingly tame and I had to throw mud at it to make it fly. Red ants are a menace. Three officers have so far been driven out of their tents by these insects, which attack in hordes, coming down tree trunks. The only way to stop them is to make a barrier of dry leaves and set fire to them. They bite with incredible vigour but do not seem to inject any formic acid.'

In addition to the mules, we had a number of horses, one of which was allotted to me as adjutant. I remember particularly one morning when I had some business to do with a village headman concerning field exercises in his area. I went on horseback and my letter home brings it all back:-

'I went for a nice ride this morning, combining business with pleasure. The country here is undulating and heavily wooded with Indian teak, jack fruit and many other trees. The clear skies all 24 hours of the day are conducive to large-scale radiation at night, causing very heavy dew which drips audibly from the trees and gives beautifully cool mornings. By 0800 hours the sun is deliciously warm and at 1000 hours it is not unpleasantly hot. It was at this latter time that I set out, with the sun well up in a completely clear sky. We squelched through a boggy field, and tiny fish fled away in terror to hide in the straggly, rotting roots of the already cut paddy. Two Cattle Egrets, stalking some 50 yards away, raised their heads in mild curiosity as my pony dragged his hooves out of the sticky mud and scrambled on to firmer ground. Lizards rustled in the dry leaves along the edge of the old bullock-cart track, and a Magpie Robin suddenly poured forth one of India's few pleasing bird songs from the tangled shrubbery; the pony jumped sideways. I trotted on glancing about me. I noticed a huge "paper" nest of a colony of red ants hanging precariously in the topmost fork of a tall, slim tree. A monkey saw me and bounced up and down on his perch, rattling the leaves with such fury that some fell off and floated down to the ground. A noisy crowd of Pied Mynahs were chasing grasshoppers on the crisp, dry turf, and two Sirkeers called shrilly as they wheeled overhead. These hawks are odd birds, for their wings are so light that they appear translucent and strangely fragile, yet the birds glide and circle for hours on end with effortless ease.

'The path led through open teak jungle and a flock of Rose-ring Parakeets was screaming in the canopy, whilst showers of seed "keys" were twisting their way down to the ground. A Crow Pheasant, clumsy but resplendent in chestnut and black, flapped across my path and dived into the undergrowth. I emerged from this wood to find a vast expanse of paddyfields, reaped and brown and dull. Emaciated, humped cattle were wandering here and there, and villagers in gaudy rags went slowly about their daily chores. I took a raised path passing through a small village; naked brown children stood and gaped; women, flattering themselves, covered their faces and ran to their huts, while the men sat and spat, talking and smoking. A herd of domestic water buffaloes came ambling down the path, their enormous horns waving aloft as they lurched along. The leading animal carried a huge wooden bell round its neck and a small boy belaboured the hind quarters of the last animal with a cracked bamboo which sounded like a whip. A few pie-dogs, in advanced stages of mange, scratched themselves savagely as they lay in several inches of filthy dust.

'A little further on I inspected what I had come to see and started back. I retraced my steps exactly as I had come as there was no other way across the many streams and muddy fields. Some Barbets were calling loudly as they fed on peepul figs, and a Choropsis whistled shrilly as he extracted nectar from a bunch of loranthus flowers. It was now 12.40 p.m.; the heat was great but not unbearable, a soft breeze blew and the air was full of sounds. Men urged their ploughing cattle with loud cries, children shrieked at play, dogs barked at nothing much, vultures cackled in the heavens, kites mewed from midday roosts and a galaxy of other bird sounds told their several tales. I felt that the only thing which could make me feel more euphoric would have been a May day in England, but that seemed far off.'

A few days later, I wrote:

'Work is very hard and I feel I earn my pay. As I write now, 2.30 p.m. on a Sunday, all is hot and sleepy. Doves are coo-ing in a gudgeon tree, and a Tailorbird is "ticking" furiously in a bush near my office (a large tent). I can hear the distant shouts of the Gurkhas playing football and, nearer, the sharp commands of the Quarterguard Commander as an officer drives past in a jeep. My clerk taps incessantly on his typewriter, producing more and more letters for me to sign. Thus does a Sunday afternoon carry on, a holiday for some but not for me.'

CHAPTER 9

BROADWAY : THE CHINDITS

Towards the end of February, 1944, we moved to Hailakandi in Assam and were camped near a grass airstrip, in bivouacs on the jungle-clad hills. Battalion H.Q. had been reduced to a mere operational office. Bertie Stott had become Commander of the Rear Party which would administer the Battalion while we were in Burma and respond to our requests for air-drops during operations. So I found myself with just one clerk and my duties were concerned solely with operations and keeping the war diary. We spent much of our time practising emplaning into Dakotas and gliders, as well as doing route marches carrying our heavy packs, which contained up to five days' rations, mess tins, clothes, blankets etc., the whole weighing some 65 lb. After an hour's march carrying these loads, as well as personal arms and ammunition, the ten-minute halt was exceedingly welcome. As you took off your pack, your shoulders seemed to rise involuntarily and the relief was enormous. Of course the Gurkhas, well practiced at carrying heavy loads long distances at home, seemed hardly to notice their packs and appeared tireless on these long marches.

We had seen very little of the senior officers who were to command us on the coming operations, but one morning I received a signal informing us that General Wingate would be visiting us on the following morning at 1000 hours. I was to arrange the digging of a 30 foot square sand pit which was to be marked by one foot grid squares by tapes stretched across both ways. I chose a spot for the pit below a gentle curving mound so that the officers could sit above the pit and see clearly what the General intended to show us. Much digging in the hot sun by a fatigue party resulted in a very neat job such as Gurkhas are so adept at doing. The much-depleted Quartermaster's store had, by good fortune, a large roll of somewhat loosely-bound string, and with this we were able to make the grid lines. That evening, when all was finished, the Jemadar Adjutant and I were able to look upon this handiwork with some pride. Five minutes before the appointed hour on the morrow we were all seated above the pit in the warm sunshine, confident that the General would have no cause for complaint about our execution of his orders. After a considerable wait, a small cloud of dust appeared at the far end of the airstrip, from which emerged two ponies galloping '*ventre à terre*' in our direction. They bore down upon us and it seemed that they must flash past. But all of a sudden they reined in, the ponies rearing up like a scene in a cowboy film, and came trotting towards us. We could then see that the leading pony, which from its blotchy appearance seemed to be basically white but in most places dyed khaki, carried the General. He sported a beard, in contravention of King's Regulations, and on his head was an old and battered Wolsey solar topi. The rest of his uniform, bush shirt and slacks, was far from clean and much creased. On the pony was his A.D.C., immaculately dressed. The General leapt from his mount, handing the reins to the A.D.C., and strode over to our Commanding Officer, Noel George, whose salute he acknowledged without taking his cane from his hand. He then turned and gazed at us with his piercing blue eyes. Having thus taken us all in, as it were, he ordered us to sit in the sand pit while he stood where we expected to sit, and gave us a short pep-talk. Despite my disappointment, even annoyance, with his peremptory disregard of all our hard work on his express orders, I found myself greatly impressed with him and what he had to say. He exuded confidence in what he and we were about to do, and I received the impression that he would rightly guess what the Japs' reaction would be to any situation brought about by his tactics, and he would thus be able to press home any advantage gained. Having wished us luck and assured us that we were in for a hard but rewarding time, he leapt on to his pony and disappeared in a cloud of dust similar to that which had heralded his arrival, leaving us astonished but somehow more confident.

D Day was to be during the first week in March and we continued to practice emplaning and, more important, de-planing, which might easily have to take place under fire. Manifests had to be prepared so that the authorities would know who was in what plane or glider, in case of mishaps. We were now shown maps and were given the exact location of two areas deemed suitable for the airstrips: one in the Shweli bend of that river, a tributary of the Irrawaddy, code-named 'Broadway', the other some miles further south to be named 'Piccadilly'. The former was preferred, but 24 hours before we were due to fly in, aerial photos showed what appeared to be large logs lying across the proposed airstrip. It seemed that the Japs had somehow got wind of our intentions and that Piccadilly might have to be our destination. D Day was put back whilst further aerial reconnaissance took place. No more logs appeared and those which were there were not deemed likely to prevent the first wave of gliders from landing safely. Yet another day showed no more activity and it seemed probable that the logs had been put there by fellers during ordinary forestry operations and that the Japs had had no hand in it. So Broadway it was to be.

The plan, as far as 3/9th G. R. was concerned, was that Noel George and Bill Towill, the Intelligence Officer, would go in by glider on the first night, flying in company with other gliders containing Sappers and mini-bulldozers, as well as troops to protect them. The Sappers' job was to clear the strip of logs and generally make it suitable for Dakotas to land on the following night. Noel's glider also carried a bulldozer and a pony, as well as Bill and a section from H.Q. Company.

It was a tense and frenzied scene which gripped Hailakandi Airstrip that evening. Since daybreak the Dakotas had been flying in to be lined up with their gliders behind them, attached by long nylon ropes. As the sun sank, troops seemed to appear from nowhere, marching in single file to their allotted gliders. Flares were lit along both sides of the strip, aircraft engines coughed into life to be test-run at maximum revolutions, rendering the night air hideous with noise and fumes, before lapsing into comparative silence and awaiting the signal which would start the long-planned operation. When it came, one after another the planes trundled down the runway, the gliders behind them becoming airborne before the parent aircraft made their belaboured break with gravity.

Once airborne, the planes and their gliders (some were towing two) circled round and round gaining the height necessary to overfly the mountains. Like skeins of geese, black against the fast-darkening roseate sky, they wheeled in widening circles until they all set course due east and the natural sounds of the night broke through the fading hum of the planes.

Although we never saw it happen, Noel's glider failed to get airborne and came to a somewhat ignominious end on the edge of the runway. Neither he nor Bill was any the worse for this alarming experience; the horse was undamaged but considerably shocked, and the bulldozer disappeared out through the front of the glider to lie on its back with its tracks in the air. On the following morning we heard that some of the gliders had crash-landed at Broadway, resulting in considerable casualties, but the strip was reported ready for us. We were doubly relieved that we were not to go in by glider and glad that Noel and Bill had got no further than Hailakandi airstrip.

It is odd how little I recollect of that fateful night on which we went into Burma. We were taking part in a very risky enterprise; we might be shot down or career into mountains in bad weather; we might crash on landing, for putting an aircraft down on an improvised strip must be very hazardous; and we might be engaged by the enemy before we had time to deploy. Yet I never thought for one moment that any of these calamities would overtake us. We emplaned full of confidence and were airborne without any real apprehension.

I remember very little about the flight, except that we sat on hard benches along each side of the aircraft, with our bulky packs between our knees, each, no doubt, with his own thoughts becoming blurred and rambling as fitful dozing overcame the initial wakeful excitement. As we slowly gained height, the engines in full-throated roar, to cross the mountain range which topped, in many places, more than 7,000 feet, the clammy heat which we took with us from Hailakandi gave way to a dry chill, at first welcome but later such that many of the Gurkhas unstrapped their blankets and wrapped themselves up.

After an hour or so, the silver line of the Chindwin River could be seen snaking its way towards the Irrawaddy. The roar of the engines changed to a less urgent note and our ears began to pop as we lost height. Then, in the even blackness of the jungle below, yellow lights appeared, marking out the landing strip at Broadway. Slowly we circled, and by peering through the windows, I could see other planes making their final run with landing lights ablaze. It was an astonishing scene. In a jungle clearing – a few days earlier nothing more than that – were scores of transport planes, alighting briefly to disgorge their loads of 30 or more men and roaring off again into the night to let others take their place. Our turn to land came and we sank swiftly towards the jungle, the engines cutting back and coughing as we bumped and bounced along the rough grassy strip. The door opened and we jumped out on to Burmese soil. Guided by the advance party, we marched in single file along the edge of the airstrip, the smoky smell of paraffin flares assailing our nostrils and the roar of aircraft battering our ears. Soon the grim evidence of the glider mishaps could be seen in the flickering light; upturned machines, their wings shattered by the dense-growing trees, their flimsy fuselages ripped and torn by the force of their loads breaking free in the headlong rush to destruction; and most poignant of all, the sickly stench of death so quickly generated in the humid heat – a smell which was to accompany us throughout the next few weeks.

Once in amongst the trees, we bivouacked as best we could, spending what was left of the night in insect-plagued discomfort. But at least we were safely on the ground and intelligence reports suggested that the Japs were unaware of what was happening in their midst.

During the next few days we were busy making the Stronghold, as this defensive position was to be known. Each man dug his own foxhole, keyhole-shaped with the round portion open and the long section roofed with tree trunks and earth. It was astonishing to see the speed and skill with which the Gurkhas worked. Small trees were felled with kukhris, cut into lengths and shaped to cover the foxholes. As adjutant I had a bigger bunker, also roofed with logs, in which the bare minimum of an office was installed and into which Noel and I could retreat during air raids, and from which we could direct operations if an attack occurred. It was connected to Company bunkers by field telephones. Miles of Danart wire were stretched round the stronghold and lines of fire were cut out of the jungle to give fields of view along likely enemy approaches. In a matter of days we felt very secure, both from air and ground attack; and our water supply was assured by a stream of cool, clear water flowing right through the middle of the stronghold. As far as food and ammunition were concerned, we anticipated no difficulty, as planes came in nightly and we received all we asked for.

Broadway soon became what it was planned to be – an important strategic airfield. R.A.F. Hurricanes used it as a re-fuelling station, giving them greater range in their support of the army on the Assam border and for attacks on Jap positions in Burma. The US Airforce B25 bombers (Mitchells) frequently came in to re-fuel during sorties in support of General Stillwell's advance down the Burma road; and light planes flew in casualties from the mobile columns and from White City, the position held by the rest of 77 Indian Infantry Brigade, commanded by Mike Calvert, astride the railway corridor near Indaw. So it was an increasingly busy place and, as the days passed and no Japs appeared, we began to become a little complacent.

Then, one day about a month after our arrival, the hand-operated siren on the airstrip began to wail and the distant hum of aircraft could be heard. For some unexplained reason, the Hurricanes did not take off; their pilots too, perhaps, had been lulled into a false sense of security and were not sufficiently alert. The hum increased and, unless a high level attack was the Japs' intention, it seemed likely that they would pass us by. But, suddenly, there was a noise like an express train dashing through a station and sticks of bombs crashed across the airstrip and along the edge of our positions. The planes wheeled and made another run with more bombs bursting in the jungle with subdued roars and on the airfield with reverberating thuds. No fighters strafed the strip and no bombers made low-level attacks; they just dropped their bombs from a great height and were gone. There was some damage to the Hurricanes and a few fuel barrels were set alight. One or two of our men sustained shrapnel wounds, none serious, and there was no damage to our positions. Only Philip Keilly's dignity suffered. As second-in-command he had no specific job, so he had taken it upon himself to train some snipers. The Japs used them to good effect, often operating singly from treetops. When the warning sounded, Philip was in the top of a tall tree where, like the Japs, he had strapped himself to a major upright branch to give himself security when using both hands. Feeling that the warning might well be a false alarm, he had not started to come down. Suddenly he heard the whoosh of bombs and in his agitation to get down, he could not get the strap undone. So, there he was, in the tree-tops with bombs falling all round him. Before the bombers' second run, he managed to extricate himself and came down to earth in a manner reminiscent of a Hoolock's gibbon rather than a portly major.

As part of our defence strategy, one rifle company, known as the 'Floating Company', remained outside the perimeter for a week at a time patrolling many miles in all directions to give warning of enemy approach. Not long after the air raid, a suspicious band of Shans (hillmen from beyond the Irrawaddy, who tended to work for the Japs) was encountered by the floating company and brought in for questioning. They all denied any knowledge of Jap movements, but as they had all seen our positions we could not let them go free and be potential guides for the enemy. Some were kept prisoner, others were flown out and one was shot. That they were acting as scouts for the Japs we felt certain and expected an attack. Sure enough, it came one night without any warning from the floating company. As in the Arakan, the first we knew of the enemy's proximity was cat-calls, stray shots and shouts of 'Hello Johnnie'. But the Gurkhas were now wise to these tricks and held their fire. The Japs cruised around the perimeter wire, trying to draw our fire, but to no avail. In the meantime, the floating company, hearing the commotion, closed in and, much to the Japs' surprise, pounced on them from behind. Hand-to-hand fighting raged and kukhries were wielded to good effect. By dawn the Japs had retreated and were later reported by loyal Kachins to have been seen carrying many wounded through the jungle. Certainly they never bothered us again. But this victory was not won without loss; Irwin Pickett, O.C. D Company, was killed, together with a Gurkha Officer and a number of men, whom we buried just outside the perimeter. The wounded were flown out the same day and none suffered any lasting disabilities.

On that very day, 2nd April, 1944, I wrote home:

'You will probably have guessed what we are up to, but don't worry. In spite of all that is going on, I find time to notice the birds and beasts; as usual, this letter will concern them mainly. One of the most interesting birds which I have seen here is the Greater Hornbill, a bird about twice the size of a heron. In flight above the trees its wings make an astonishingly loud whining noise which carries several hundred yards. Other birds which I have seen recently include River Terns, Laughing Thrushes, White Wagtails, Barbets and Parakeets. But perhaps the nicest thing about these jungles is the butterflies. All the heaps of elephant dung, and they are everywhere, are covered with literally scores of these insects, many a brilliant blue in colour and some with wing spans of up to six inches. The woodpecker family is well represented and from observations I am sure their drumming is mechanical. Many happy returns of the 28th (my mother's birthday); it was rather hair-raising here, but I thought a lot about you.'

It was about this time that we had a visit from General Wingate. He was, as usual, affecting his pose of unshaven scruffiness, one which we in the Battalion firmly opposed by allowing no beards, while our orderlies ensured that we never looked scruffy. Despite his appearance, the General radiated confidence and made us all feel that we had struck a decisive blow at ridding Burma of the invader. He told us that Broadway had been a great success and that the activities of the Chindits had helped to relieve pressure on the troops in the vital Imphal area on the Assam front. It now seemed certain that the Japs, their line of communication greatly extended, would not be able to invade India. It was simply a question of holding them on the frontier until supply difficulties obliged them to withdraw, and it was we who were making these difficulties greater every day. He told us that Broadway would soon have outlived its usefulness and that we would have to leave it and march north to join another brigade in the Force, with the eventual object of meeting up with the Americans under General Stillwell who were approaching Mogaung from the north.

Shortly before dusk on that day, I walked out to Wingate's plane, an American B25, with his party. They all climbed in and I handed the latest instalment of the Battalion's war diary to the A.D.C. for him to give to Bertie Stott. The plane's engines coughed into life, spurting blue smoke and blowing dust and leaves in a cloud along the edge of the jungle. A crew member started to close the door, when two American war correspondents came running up, shouting, 'Say, General, can you give us a lift?' The crew remonstrated, maintaining that the payload was already too great. But Wingate ignored them and helped to haul the Americans into the plane, which took off without any apparent difficulty, disappearing into a threatening black sky. Later that night we had a wireless message reporting that the General's plane was overdue and feared lost. Some days later, the wreckage was found high up on the mountain range; there were no survivors. It seemed that the weather got the better of the plane but no one really knows what happened or, indeed, if the apparent over-loading had any bearing on the disaster. For some years I assumed that the crash happened soon after the plane left Broadway, but in Derek Tulloch's book, *Wingate in Peace and War*, it is confirmed that the plane landed safely at Imphal that evening, and it was only after the plane took off again that the disaster occurred. It is interesting to note that Colonel Claude Rome, the overall commander at Broadway, who had also gone out to the plane with Wingate, was quoted in that book as saying that the pilot was worried about one of the plane's engines being faulty and he had suggested that Wingate should ask for a relief plane. The General was in a hurry to complete other engagements and would not agree to any delay. Colonel Rome, unlike me, did think that the take-off was unusual, being laboured and with one wing slightly dropped. Whether engine trouble or overloading or even both had any bearing on the crash will never be known, but the loss of our leader was certain and came as a great blow to us all. Our war diaries were also lost.

Wingate was replaced by one of the brigade commanders, Joe Lentaigne, formerly 4th Gurkha Rifles, but in everything except strict factual terms, Wingate was irreplaceable and much of the steam went out of the operations. Without his inspired leadership morale suffered more quickly in the severe conditions in which we operated than would otherwise have been the case. As the weather deteriorated with the coming of the monsoon, making air drops less frequent and privation more persistent, inspired leadership was that much more vital; we were not conscious of its continued existence.

Shortly before we left Broadway, Noel George was taken ill and evacuated to India by air. Later we heard that he had contracted poliomyelitis, an almost unheard of occurrence in someone in his early forties, and we knew we had lost him for ever. Philip Keilly had already been posted elsewhere and we had thus lost both our senior officers. Somewhat to our surprise, and initially to our dismay, Alec Harper of the Deccan Horse was posted to us as C.O. He knew no Gurkhali, but we soon realised that we had someone who would lead us with skill and determination during the next difficult phase of the operations. He was an inspired reader of our often-inaccurate maps and, despite being trained as a cavalryman, he had experience of jungle warfare as he came to us from the 4/9th G.R., fellow Chindits operating further east.

In anticipation of leaving Broadway, the Battalion was reorganised into two columns, designated 39 and 93, each with two rifle companies and assorted support such as mortars and mules. This was to bring us into line with the other battalions in the Force whose columns operated independently. In the event, we always remained together as a battalion. Reggie was one Column Commander and Alec the other. I had handed over the adjutancy to Bill Towill after Irwin Pickett's death, and took over D Company.

Gradually all the stores – the aircraft fuel and other equipment connected with a temporary airbase and our own stores which could not be carried by man or mule – were back-loaded to India. By the middle of May, 1944, nothing remained but our defensive position, which we left early one morning to the mercy of the encroaching jungle.

CHAPTER 10

MARCH THROUGH NORTH BURMA : BLACKPOOL

We left Broadway as dawn broke, heading north-west in a long, snaking column, with Alec and his compass at its head. Our destination was another stronghold called Blackpool, which had been established across the railway and road south of Mogaung. We had a march of about 100 miles ahead of us, keeping ourselves hidden all the way. This meant that we could not use open country (not that there was much of it) but must keep to the jungle all the time. And we could not light fires during the day, lest smoke should attract the attention of enemy aircraft. All our cooking had to be done before dawn or after dark. We carried with us, each in his pack, five days supply of K rations – three packs for each day marked 'Breakfast', 'Dinner' and 'Supper'. Breakfast contained instant coffee, powdered milk, a tin of cheese flecked with small ham pieces, biscuits, sugar and a date bar; dinner consisted of lemonade powder, tinned spam, biscuits, chocolate and a fruit bar of indeterminate composition; and supper was much the same with soup powder replacing the lemonade. All the packets contained four American cigarettes. Cooking, such as was necessary, was done individually in mess tins, and the Gurkhas quickly devised recipes which consisted largely of mixing the meat, cheese, soup powder and biscuits together with water and heating the whole lot until it formed a thick stew. My orderly concocted variations on this theme, including fried spam garnished with fern fronds which he collected in the jungle. Some tea was left over from Broadway for which I traded my coffee. I also swapped my American cigarettes for chocolate. Sometimes, the Gurkhas, well versed in jungle lore, found Jungle Fowl nests and we would then have an omelette for breakfast. But taken by and large, we lived on K rations which, despite their monotony, kept us in good health. Drinking water was a problem and there were occasions when strict water discipline had to be enforced. Water was plentiful in the jungle

streams and it rained most days to keep them flowing, but we often spent
many hot and sweaty hours crossing hills where no water was available.

It was a gruelling march for both men and animals. Sometimes we found
game tracks which were going in the right direction, but never for long; after
a mile or two of fairly easy progress, our compass line of march would
dictate leaving the track and once again the forward section, armed with
kukhries and dahs, would re-start their wearisome task of hacking down
bamboo, lianas and small trees to give space enough for the heavily laden
mules to struggle along. Often the tracks led up steep slopes where each
step forward was followed by half a pace slip back, as one clutched the
path-side bushes to haul oneself and the 60 lb pack upwards and drag one's
feet from the sucking mud. As hundreds of men passed the same way, the
track became progressively more difficult for the poor mules, weighed down
as they were by mortar bombs, rifle ammunition and radio batteries, not to
mention a charging engine and its fuel. They lurched and staggered up the
slopes, their handlers pulling at their heads and whacking the posterior of
the beast in front to encourage it to greater efforts. Progress was painfully
slow and very exhausting. Some impression of a day on the march can be
gained from a letter I wrote from hospital a few weeks later:

'The day starts at first light, about 0500 hours, when Jungle Fowls are
crowing and Koels are calling loudly. At this time fires are allowed in the
bivouac for up to half an hour. At 0530 hours my orderly brings me a mug
of tea and powdered milk, with some biscuits and a heated tin of ham and
eggs. The meal finished, mules and men must be loaded and ready to march
at 0600 hours when we set out, possibly along some well-defined track or
game path, but usually just cutting our way through the jungle. At all
events, progress is slow as the mules keep throwing their loads or falling
down. A swamp deer barks close at hand and the Gurkhas smile at one
another, knowing what a welcome addition to their rations it would be. We
halt occasionally, flinging off our packs with relief, to lie prone and resting
for ten minutes, listening to the sounds of the jungle. Some doves coo softly
in a giant teak tree, a pair of Greater Hornbills fly noisily overhead on
whining pinions and a party of gibbons calls jackal-like from the fastness of
the bush. Nearer and nearer comes the drone of an aeroplane – Our's or
Their's? – anyhow we are well hidden and care little. On we go again,
plodding wearily along, sweating profusely, until midday when, near a
stream, we halt for lunch of synthetic cheese and lemonade. This longer-
than-usual halt goes all too quickly and we are soon on the march again.

Perhaps we may pass a Kachin village where the ravages of Jap rule are only too clear. The villagers rush to greet us, poor half-starved creatures, amidst a flurry of fowls and squeaking pigs, to tell us that the Japs have stolen all their rice and have butchered their cattle and most of their pigs. When are the British coming back? they ask. Their welcome is pathetically genuine and it is hard to leave them, for the Japs might return at any time to demand information about our movements and threaten their lives if they fail to give it.

We move on and as evening approaches we start thinking about choosing a place for a night bivouac; somewhere in thick jungle near a stream. As darkness falls, we light fires, cook our soup powder and eat it with spam and biscuits. Then, with fresh leaves cut as mattresses and half a blanket pulled over our heads to keep off the mosquitoes, we are glad to rest after a 14-mile march, heavily laden and with the ever-present possibility of clashing with the enemy.'

We had one air-drop during our march, for which we had to pin-point our position very accurately. We chose a clearing near a stream, where we had a 24-hour halt after signalling the map reference and the time at which we wanted the drop. It was a bit of a gamble because of the weather, as low cloud would make it impossible for the aircraft to find the drop zone. Luckily it was fine and, at the appointed hour, we heard the drone of the Dakota which circled the area once while we gave the recognition signal – firing a red Verey light. Then the plane made a straight run over us and a cascade of parachutes emerged from the door to float gently down towards us, most of them landing in the open but some going astray to become caught in branches of trees. It required skilful climbing to get them down. Somehow, during the airdrop, I felt for a few minutes less cut off from the rest of the world; but as the drone of the plane faded into the distance, the tenuous link with civilisation stretched and snapped, leaving us isolated in this seemingly limitless jungle.

It was fine for the airdrop, but it rained at some time on most days or nights; trying to sleep during a nocturnal downpour often proved unprofitable. The ground was already damp, if not sodden, so rain cascading through the canopy soon formed little pools. In order to keep even slightly dry, one was obliged to have the groundsheet on top rather than underneath where it should have been, with the result that one ended up lying in a pool. I found it best to remain as still as possible, with a minimum of turning over, because any movement stirred up the water and made it feel cooler. Waking up after such a night was a depressing experience and, although a mug of hot tea cheered one up somewhat, it was drunk whilst trying to decide whether to seek out the drier clothes in one's pack, change into them and carry the wet garments for the rest of the day, or simply endure the chill of starting the march in soaking clothes and let them gradually dry out. Often it was wiser to change because it gave an opportunity to see if any leeches had attached themselves to one's person during the night; they usually had.

On dry nights, after the efforts of the day, it was not unpleasant to lie there alone with one's thoughts, listening to the nocturnal sounds; the shrilling of crickets, the distant trumpeting of elephants, the sleepy cheeps of roosting birds and, nearer at hand, the snoring of the Gurkhas. One night I particularly remember, when all hell was let loose as yells from one man were taken up by others, suddenly awakened. Thinking that the Japs had found us, a sentry stupidly opened fire, adding to the commotion. A Gurkha Officer's loudly shouted orders soon restored silence and the original culprit was found. It transpired that a small nocturnal animal, probably a lemur, had dropped from a tree on to his face as he slept and he had awakened in terror, yelling to high heaven. I lay down again listening to the men's laughter as they chided their comrade; he took a long time to live it down.

At about midday on the tenth day of our march, we arrived at the edge of the jungle which fringed the railway corridor. We could see Blackpool in the distance across the open paddyfields and we could hear the occasional crump of mortar fire. Somehow we had to cross the open space during daylight, for to do so at night would almost certainly involve us with roving Jap patrols and confuse our own side in the stronghold. As the enemy clearly did not expect us, Alec decided that we should go across straightaway. So in extended order we did just that, all 800 of us with scores of mules, and not a shot was fired. We could scarcely believe our luck; but the situation in which we found ourselves when once inside the perimeter wire made us wish we had never come.

The morale of the hard-pressed defenders was at rock bottom. For days they had been pounded by artillery and mortars. Constant night attacks all round the perimeter had allowed them no sleep and enemy pressure had eventually forced them to give up an important hill feature which had given the Japs a vantage point whence they could observe everything which the defenders did. On the day we arrived an attempt to re-take this hillock had been made and failed. It was quite clear that the stronghold was rapidly becoming untenable; indeed it was no longer necessary to prolong the sacrifice of lives, as Stillwell's force was already nearing Mogaung and the

Chindit's role of harassing the Japs to the south of this town had proved successful. Instead of trying to defend the indefensible, it seemed that we should move north and meet up with the Americans. In fact, orders to this effect came a day or two after our arrival in Blackpool.

Of those few awful days I have rather limited but vivid memories. One of our companies joined the British Battalion in an attempt to re-take the infamous hillock; it failed and they suffered a number of killed and wounded. My company took over the defence of part of the perimeter, and I remember sleepless nights as the Japs probed the positions with their usual noisy tactics. Occasionally we opened fire and at dawn had the macabre satisfaction of finding a few corpses lying by the wire. During the day we were constantly harassed by mortar fire and the occasional artillery shell. Most of the vegetation had long since been blasted away; there was no shade, and the consequent heat increased the discomfort, with water rationing an additional burden. Altogether it was the worst place I have ever been in; the stench of death hung like a cloud over the blasted hillocks in which we had our foxholes, mixed with the acrid fumes of cordite and the foetid stink of latrines. When we took over the positions from the British Battalion, I found a soldier sitting in his slit-trench looking out over the valley. He took no notice of me when I jumped into the trench beside him, and when I asked him what he was doing he still failed to reply. I then tapped him on the shoulder and he rolled over sideways, stiff with *rigor mortis*. There were no signs of wounds and I never discovered how he died. But finding him like that, with none of his officers or comrades having even noticed his absence, was a chilling experience and one which typified the atmosphere in that ghastly place.

The order to withdraw was greeted with general relief, tempered by the knowledge that to extricate ourselves under the eyes of the Japs and march, as we had to, over a range of mountains to the Indawggi Lake, was going to be a hazardous operation. We started to vacate our positions in the early afternoon, taking with us the walking wounded and as many mules as we needed to carry essential ammunition. The rest of these faithful animals we had to abandon, something about which the Gurkhas felt strongly, and many more mules started out with us than we had planned. Much to our surprise, the Japs made no attempt to follow us, being content, perhaps, merely to take over Blackpool, which they had so long been striving to achieve.

So the first part of our journey was accomplished without much difficulty, except for the wounded men, who were either helped by their comrades or were propped up on mules. It was only when we reached the mountains that the real problems began. There were several ranges to be crossed, each of 300 or 400 feet and almost sheer on both sides. In places steps had to be cut and it soon became clear that to coax even one or two mules over the hills would be well nigh impossible. Many had to be abandoned with the stores they carried, and the wounded had a terrible time as they were hauled up and down the slopes. At the final summit, which we reached in the morning after an all-night struggle, we were pleased to meet a battalion of the West African Frontier Force, who had cut a path for us on the last leg down to the lake. The Gurkhas' amused surprise at meeting these 'Habshis' was followed by raised eyebrows when we saw that most of them were stark naked; at least their clothes must have kept clean for longer than ours did.

Our withdrawal over the mountains had resulted in considerable loss of equipment and mules, which had perforce been abandoned because of the extremely difficult terrain and the absence of defined paths, let alone roads. We lost our mortars and their bombs, as well as all our small arms ammunition; in fact, practically everything which could not be carried by the men was left behind. So when we reached the area immediately east of the Indawggi Lake, we had to set about urgent re-equipping by daily airdrops. These included rations, clothing, ammunition, mortars, medical supplies and, eagerly anticipated, mail from home. During one drop, a free-falling sack of boots struck and instantly killed one of the Gurkhas.

The week or so during which this re-organisation took place was a period of comparative tranquillity. Units already in the area were responsible for our security, so we had no worries about the Japs. There was time for the men to build little shelters of bamboo, and we were thus able to sleep soundly at night even in rain storms. As usual, I found solace in the wildlife and it was on one evening, when I was out by myself, that I saw a herd of elephants. I was sitting on the side of a hill where a small clearing gave me a western view over to the Indawggi Lake. Between me and the lake was a stretch of open ground, marshy with pampas grass and rushes. The sun had sunk behind the mountains and thin wisps of mist were starting to form over the marsh. Suddenly, from the jungle to the north a black object appeared, followed by others in a long line and through my binoculars I could see that they were elephants – some 20 or more, large and small, wading up to their bellies through the rushes. I watched them making their slow progress until failing light absorbed them into the jungle background. I counted myself lucky to have seen them; although it was obvious that elephants were numerous in Northern Burma at that time from the evidence of spore and droppings seen everywhere, I had never actually seen them until then, and I returned to my shelter well-pleased with my walk, anxious to tell my colleagues what I had seen. But they rated their news much more important, for while I was away a message had been received to say that the Second Front had been opened and our troops had landed successfully in Normandy. Nevertheless, my orderly and I had a long discussion about elephants when he brought me my soup and bully beef stew, accompanied by boiled potatoes and some white bread spread with margarine and jam, these luxuries being part of a recent airdrop. He at least found the elephants more exciting than the Normandy beaches.

Gradually, as other units which had been operating in the railway corridor came over the mountains along the path we had pioneered, a very considerable number of wounded accumulated in the temporary 'hospital'. They lay on stretchers on the ground, with groundsheets and other makeshift roofing held over them on bamboo poles. There must eventually have been about 100 of them, some in a very bad way and in great pain. Most of them were British soldiers, with some Gurkhas and a few Burmese from Intelligence Units. It was a pathetic sight to see these men, bearded, pale and drawn, lying there and wondering how on earth they would ever receive the further treatment vital for their survival. We wondered too, but one day we suddenly heard that the R.A.F. had decided to land a Sunderland flying boat on the lake and take away 20 to 30 wounded on each trip. Sure enough, on the following morning the usual aircraft drone revealed one of these huge planes dropping steeply from the high altitude needed to cross the mountains, making a run over the lake, and then alighting gently on to the calm, blue water. The boost to morale was enormous, and the Gurkhas' pleasure was matched by incredulity; a flying boat landing in the middle of Burma was difficult to believe. Local sampans quickly ferried the most serious cases out to the plane, which took off immediately, hauling its dumpy bulk slowly off the lake surface and leaving a line of foam and wavelets never seen there before. On several successive days the flights were repeated until all the poor suffering men had been taken to base hospitals. It was a relief to see the make-shift hospital become nothing more than a patch of well-trodden ground, ready to revert once more to jungle.

All too soon this rest period came to an end and we were ordered to move north towards Mogaung. Running out of the Indawggi Lake, north towards this town, was a sluggish river which the Japs had used as a line of communication and which we intended to use for the same purpose. Intelligence reports suggested that the Japs were still occupying a village called Lakhren, a few miles down the river from the lake, and I was ordered to take D Company, find out if they were still there and, if so, flush them out. It was about a day's march from our base, through thick jungle and we set out early in the morning, intending to get within a short distance of the village, lie up for the night, and attack it at dawn. When some distance away, we halted for our evening meal which we ate cold and uncomfortably and with as little noise as possible. Then, very slowly and stealthily, we edged towards the village, disposing ourselves in a semi-circle about 200 yards from the nearest huts and the river. I can't say that I slept very well; the constant ping of mosquitoes and anxiety about the outcome of the morrow, combined with Subadar Indrabahadur's snoring (he seemed to have no worries), made anything more than fitful naps impossible.

The sentries woke us before dawn when it was pitch dark in the thick jungle, and we put on our equipment (our packs etc. we had left behind with a small rear party where we had our evening meal) ready to move towards the village. Very slowly we edged forward, even the sound of our clothes scraping against bamboos seeming enough to wake the Japs. The grass-roofed huts began to appear in the misty twilight, looming larger than life, but not a sound was to be heard nor was any sign of life to be seen. As planned, the central platoon charged into the village whilst the other two went right and left to block any escape routes. Still no sound nor any sign of the enemy. I was in the middle of the village with the assault platoon when suddenly firing broke out from the right hand platoon, both rifle and automatic fire, but only for a few seconds, followed by a deathly hush. I went to investigate and found that a small party of Japs had apparently been approaching the village at the same time as our attack, and both sides had opened fire simultaneously. The Japs had fled but our Section Commander had been mortally wounded and he died as I bent over him to try and discover the extent of his wounds. Giving orders for the platoon to position itself on the track in case of a counter attack, I went back to the centre of the village and joined Indrabahadur to plan our next move. I was standing next to him, looking over the river, when a shot rang out to my left and I felt a tremendous jolt to my left arm. I looked down and saw my forearm hanging at right angles with bits of bone sticking our here and there and a rapidly swelling pool of blood on the ground. I heard a scuffle as a Gurkha charged into the jungle from where the shot had come (he shot and wounded the Jap and finished him off with a kukhri) but gave little thought to it; I just did not believe what had happened, for immediately I felt no pain, just a deep, shattering numbness. Indrabahadur, who himself was bleeding from his chest (it transpired that his wound was caused by a piece of my left ulna becoming lodged between his ribs) came and supported me, as I had already begun to feel very groggy. He laid me down on a stretcher and very carefully applied a tourniquet and a field dressing. He told me not to worry; he would take complete charge and the men would carry me back to base.

My memories of what happened later that day are blurred. Sometimes I was conscious, often I was not. Morphia, injected by my orderly, helped to dull the very considerable pain but the unavoidable lurching was no help to it. Occasionally, I heard firing (I subsequently heard that the Japs were met several times during this slow procession through the thick jungle, when I was gently put down on the ground under a bush whilst my carriers and escort took aggressive action). How long the journey took, I knew not; all sorts of fantasies flitted across my mind. At times I felt I was being a burden and adding danger to the Company by the slow progress; at others I feared being left behind, although, goodness knows, this was totally irrational; the Gurkhas would never have done that even if I had died. I hovered between unconsciousness and a vague realisation that something very odd was happening to me, when suddenly I awoke to find Reggie Twelvetrees kneeling beside me. He and A Company had been sent to look for us. He took charge of both companies and sent me on my way with the escort. Next time I awoke was to find our M.O., Doc Wright, holding out my arm and sprinkling it with sulphonamide powder. He gently assured me that I would be alright, but soon the sound of his voice and the urgent chatter of the sick orderlies faded and then came back again in waves as I found myself asking for water. Other officers came to commiserate and I felt sure that I was safe, if I felt anything at all.

CHAPTER 11

AT THE MERCY OF THE MEDICS

The day after I was wounded the Battalion moved on north, leaving a small defence party to guard me and a number of other casualties until such time as we could be flown out. The flying boat airlift had ceased as the number of sick and wounded was too small to justify the risks to the aircraft. As far as I was concerned, there followed several very confused days. My orderly, Bombahadur, took complete charge. He built me a shelter, with a bamboo bed raised off the ground and a little table beside it. There he attended to my every need; he gave me morphine injections on a schedule ordered by Doc Wright, he made a bed-pan out of an old kerosene tin, he made powdered milk drinks and other concoctions out of K rations, he sat and talked to me and gave me encouragement. His devotion was deeply touching and never to be forgotten. I can see him now, never more than a few yards away, sometimes squatting by a little fire over which he would be cooking something that he hoped would stimulate my wretched appetite; at other times just sitting nearby waiting to give me my next injection or ready to give me the nursing help I needed in my desperately weak condition. If it rained at night, he would be there in an instant to make sure that I was keeping dry. He never failed and seemed to know instinctively exactly what I needed; and all this in the back of beyond with minimum facilities. How can such loyal devotion ever be matched?

Although I was not feeling better, I began to have longer periods of consciousness and became able to make limited efforts to do things for myself; not that Bombahadur encouraged them. One morning he seemed even more cheerful than usual; he told me that the defence party had been ordered to make a small landing strip on nearby paddy fields. He thought it could easily be done because the work only involved cutting gaps in the bunds between the fields, which in any case were quite dry. He was right;

next morning I heard the sound of a light plane and shortly after I was carried out on a stretcher to the strip, Bombahadur constantly ordering the carriers to be careful and not jolt me. The American pilot of the plane helped the orderlies to put me on the stretcher into the plane, behind his seat with my legs pointing towards the tail; Bombahadur, to the last moment, ensured that I was lying comfortably. As the plane's engine roared and we started to move, he raised his arm in salute and I mine in grateful acknowledgement. We met again 18 months later in Java.

We bumped and hopped along the rough strip, the tail rose and I found myself lying flat as we became air-borne and the tree tops flashed past. As we flew just above the jungle canopy, the plane dipped and rose in the air currents and the pilot chatted cheerfully, shouting loudly against the roar of the engine which eventually lulled me into fitful dozes. I am not sure how long the flight lasted nor where we landed, but it was at an American airbase from which the light planes operated with such skill and dedication. Flying in these flimsy little planes, landing on make-shift strips often enveloped by trees and presenting sitting targets for enemy aircraft, required courage of a high order. Those of us whose lives, in many cases, were saved by this splendid American service owe the airmen a great deal.

At the airbase I was quickly transferred to a Dakota in which I lay on the floor with many other stretcher cases, and the only thing I remember about that particular part of the journey was that we were all given fresh white bread which, despite not being hungry, somehow tasted especially good. How I got to the comfortable bed in the base hospital at Panatola in Assam I cannot remember, but I woke to find myself between sheets and dressed in army pyjamas, with new bandages on my arm. The Q.A. sister came and told me that I was to have an operation in the morning and assured me that all was well. Next morning, I was wheeled off to the theatre and later woke to find my arm in plaster from wrist to armpit, the resulting rigidity easing the pain. But I was alarmed to find that I could not move my fingers and had no feeling whatever in my hand. When I told the surgeon this and expressed my worry, he said he was not surprised; I was lucky to have an arm at all and I would probably get the feeling back, as well as some movement.

In the next bed on one side was the brother of the surgeon, by the name of Kelly, who had been shot through the ankle. He had been operated on by his brother, who paid frequent visits, and the three of us became quite good friends. On the other side was the Viceroy's son, Capt. Wavell, who had lost his right hand in a grenade explosion. Very soon the Viceroy came to see him and the fuss and bother which preceded the visit had us all much amused. Carpets were hastily placed between the beds, the faded red blankets were replaced by new ones, and we were all spruced up and almost made to dress by the right. Lord and Lady Wavell stayed but a few minutes and their son was whisked away next day, presumably to be cared for by the viceregal doctors in New Delhi.

In the meantime, unknown to me, a telegram, followed by a letter from the India Office, had been received at home. The letter confirmed the telegram in telling that I had been wounded in action on 11th June and added that the nature of the wound and the hospital to which I had been admitted were not known. It went on in effect to say that no further news would be good news from which it could be assumed 'that your son is making normal progress, and in this event you will, no doubt, receive a communication from the officer himself in due course regarding his wound and progress'. This, indeed, they did receive; I asked Sister to send a telegram on 24th. June which read, 'Wound not serious comfortable love Scott', and on the same day I managed to write a letter explaining what had happened.

I suppose I must have been at this Advanced Base Hospital for about a week, waiting for the next hospital train to move everyone fit to travel to hospitals in Northern India. By the time we were due to move, I was up and about, albeit feeling very weak and unsteady on my pins. So I was able to walk to the ambulance which took us down to the station and clamber into one of the ward carriages. These had bunks along both sides, with a loo and wash basins at each end. I was pleased to find another officer from 3/9th. G.R., G.D. England, in the bunk opposite. He had been evacuated from Burma before me, suffering from recurrent fever. Although I tried to talk to him and tell him about our fortunes since he left, he seemed disinterested and soon lay down with his face to the wall. It was evening and I too went to bed and soon to sleep, drugged by the sleeping pill given to me by the carriage orderly. When I woke up it was already light and, from the generally built-up scenery, I assumed we were somewhere near Calcutta. I noticed that England was not in his bunk and when I got up and went to the loo, I saw that the anti-insect gauze which covered the window had been torn and was hanging in tatters. It looked as though someone had jumped through it. I found the orderly and told him that England was not in his bunk and that the loo window was broken. A hasty search of the train was made but England was nowhere to be found. When we reached the next station, the Station Master informed the O.C.Train that an officer's body had been found on the line about 100 miles north. Sad to say, it turned out to be England's body. Apparently he had cerebral malaria and obviously did not know what he was doing. It was a sad end to a diligent and conscientious officer who had been with us since Gardai days.

I was delighted when I discovered that we were bound for the hospital in Dehra Dun, a wartime establishment which was quartered in the Forest Research Institute building – a magnificent edifice, built in the same grand style as New Delhi. The journey took several days and once again I enjoyed the delightful views as the train climbed through the Siwhaliks towards the Himalayas. As dawn broke over the sal forests and flooded the gorgeous panorama with golden light, I felt that I was coming to the next best thing to home.

As was the case in all the Indian hospitals in which I found myself, the welcome and the constant kind and caring treatment I received in Dehra Dun was something I shall long remember. After an X-ray, the surgeon operated on my arm and his prognosis was very reassuring; I shared his optimism because I had begun to have some feeling in my hand and I had a little movement in some of the fingers. A new plaster was put on and I was told that it would become very smelly, but as everyone else in the surgical ward was similarly afflicted no one would notice. The forecast proved correct; each day when I held my arm above my head, a quantity of suppurating liquid ran out, giving temporary relief from the painful pressure which built up inside the plaster. Friends who came to visit me from our nearby Regimental Centre never flinched, and later when I was up and about and visited the Centre myself, I must have trailed a very unsociable scent after me, but no one ever said anything. The Matron even asked me to tea and never batted an eyelid.

After I had been in the Dehra hospital for about a fortnight, Cynthia Fawcett, ever mindful of the welfare of her husband's officers, came to see me and decided that I would fare better in the cool climate of Mussourie where she was living. Without further ado, she went straight to the C.O. of the hospital and extracted his consent. She also wrote a very kind letter to my mother. The Fawcetts' bungalow in Mussourie had in its compound a little bothy with a bedroom and bathroom, so I was not constantly in their bungalow, smelling the place out. How they put up with me at meals I do not know; but I was made wonderfully welcome, and this warm friendship, combined with the cool air and the excellent food, soon made me feel very much better.

Unfortunately, my stay in Mussourie was very short. After a week or so, I was recalled to Dehra Dun and transferred to the British Military Hospital in Bareilly, about 200 miles east of Delhi. I had no sooner arrived there than

I was smitten by a severe recurrent fever which the doctors at first failed to diagnose. It eventually turned out to be malaria, but the evidence, usually found in blood samples, had been suppressed by the mepacrine which I had been taking in Burma. I was put on a course of quinine which was itself no mean ordeal, for the intense bitterness lingered after each of the four doses per day for almost as long as the interval between them, and I became quite deaf with a singing in my ears. However, I was soon cured, but the week of wracking fever took a lot out of me and I felt like the proverbial chewed string for many days. As always, I found solace in the birds which I could see and hear from the ward, as a letter I wrote home shows:-

'It is a lovely sunny morning during a break in the rains and everything is green and fresh – unusual for the plains. Crows are calling loudly from the fastness of the mango trees. Red-vented Bulbuls are whistling shrilly as they clumsily catch insects in the tall grass. A Tailor bird's explosive chatter may indicate a snake near its nest, for there are said to be many cobras in this area. Kites are wheeling in the sky, strangely silent; I have not heard their cries at all this morning. Here and there a butterfly flits among the grass stems, aimlessly and rather sadly, for the rains have come and its day is done. Rivalling the noisy crows are the cackling Mynahs, waddling erratically on the lawn in search of grasshoppers. These are such dull observations, but they do make life in bed more bearable. I recently came across this little verse:-

> The wonder of the world, the beauty,
> The power, the shape of things, their colours,
> Lights and shades; these things I saw,
> Look ye also while life lasts.'

We were a very mixed bag in the officers' ward at Bareilly. In the next bed to me was an Indian major who had been promoted from V.C.O. rank and was thus much older than the rest of us and with a great deal more service. He had been blinded, had lost a leg and both hands, yet he was the most cheerful patient in the ward. He had a wheelchair which he managed to propel with his forearms and, although he could not see where he was going, he had learnt by trial and error how to avoid most obstacles in the ward and out on the verandah. If he collided with anything, it was simply an occasion for laughter. His running commentaries in his poor but quaint English, although incessant and thus, by evening, somewhat tedious, livened up the whole ward. He eventually left us for St Dunstan's, depriving us of an inspiration and making many of us realise how relatively lucky we had been. But the Bareilly hospital was a depressing place; whether it was the patients who depressed the nursing staff or vice versa it was difficult to say, but there was a general lack of good cheer about the place, compounded by an occasional death in the ward, and I was delighted when I heard that I was to be transferred to the hospital in the hill station of Ranikhet.

On 17th August 1944, I went up to Ranikhet and was glad to see the last of Bareilly. A letter written home on the following day describes the journey, amongst other things:-

'I arrived here yesterday after a drive of 130 miles, sitting in the front of an ambulance. The scenery was spectacular; I will tell you about it later. The Ranikhet hospital is very nice and the climate absolutely lovely. It is cloudy this morning and the view is limited; but when clear, from the ward window one will be able to see the Himalayan snows. I am now allowed to wear mufti, which is a pleasant change. Many officers are being sent home from here but what happens to me depends upon what the surgical specialist has to say. I am hopeful, having seen some of the cases due for repatriation.

'As I said, the journey up here was delightful. It started with about 60 miles of flat country of no great interest, except one long jheel which we passed fairly slowly. There I saw and identified the following as we went by: Sarus Cranes, Pheasant-tailed Jacanas, Dabchicks and Paddy birds, and nearby we overtook an elephant carrying seven persons. Eventually we reached the foothills which rise suddenly from the Gangetic Plain. Here vegetation is dense tropical evergreen forest which seemed to be swarming with rhesus monkeys and Grey Hornbills, for I saw hundreds of the former and dozens of the latter. A recent light shower had caused a steamy atmosphere which carried with it a wonderful jungle fragrance – a mixture of sandalwood and the heady scent of many jungle blooms around which, no doubt, sunbirds would be hovering. The climb started up a river valley, a tributary of the Ramgunga, itself flowing into the Ganges. Twisting and turning, we gradually climbed up to 5,000 ft., where the vegetation changed to open grassy slopes, studded here and there with small trees. Many of the slopes were terraced, supporting grain crops and little villages seemingly clinging to the precipitous slopes, their white houses shining through the purple Himalayan haze. A further thousand feet up brought us to the coniferous belt where Chir pines and deodars grow in mixture. Ranikhet is in this belt and the air has a clear resinous fragrance.

'Ethnologically, these Kumaon Hills are interesting. The Kumaonis who live here, are a Gurkha-like race who are enlisted into the Hyderabad Regiment. They seem to be transitional between the Garhwalis to the west and the Gurkhas to the east. I can't understand their language (I tried yesterday), nor can they understand Gurkhali. I have just engaged a Kumaoni bearer; we shall have to struggle along in Hindustani, the native tongue of neither of us.

'I have had the plaster changed. The radius is now quite firm and seems to be doing all right. The wound is far from healed and the specialist says he is going to cut a window in the plaster and do a skin graft to speed things up. The fingers are about the same as before – a fairly useful grip between thumb and fingers but no opening movement. This may be due to nerve lesions or lack of muscle. The sensory nerves are intact in the hand.'

If one had to be in hospital, then Ranikhet was the place to be. The climate was ideal, the club and other facilities were available free to officer patients; the views and the countryside were superb. On 25th. August I wrote home:-

'It is such a lovely morning and I have just had such a marvellous view of the snows that I felt I must write and tell you about it. Immediately after breakfast I went down to the club where, from the verandah, one gets an unimpeded view. In the foreground was the huge glacial valley which carries a relatively small river, the Gagus, which was a deep purple colour from the indirect rays of the sun, then not high enough in the sky to tint the valley bottom. Some 80 miles away, in vivid contrast, was the vast Himalayan mass, sparkling white. To the left was the three-stepped Nanda Ghunti, to its right the gigantic hogsback, Trissul, and behind it, reaching higher still, the dome-like peak of Nanda Devi, the celebrity of the mass. To the right of Nanda Devi, at the end of one of her spurs, as if in attendance, sits Nanda Kot – a sparkling snowy point. I don't think it is possible for anyone to comprehend the splendour of these Himalayan scenes unless he has actually seen them. This one today was something I shall never forget, although in my opinion it does not quite equal that of Kanchenjunga from Darjeeling. After I had enjoyed the panorama as a whole, I looked at the peaks separately through a powerful telescope. I could see great cracks in the glaciers with the black volcanic rock showing through the white blanket of snow where it had not completely adhered to the precipitous slopes.'

An examination by a senior surgical specialist, followed by a medical board which confirmed his recommendations, led to my being put on the list for repatriation and transfer to a holding hospital in Poona. This did not take place immediately; I had three more weeks in Ranikhet, for which I was very grateful. One of the most enjoyable weekends of these latter days was when Bertie Stott, Reggie Twelvetrees and John Thorpe came up to see me. The Battalion had come out of Burma and all the men had been sent on two months' leave in Nepal. They had had a pretty tough time after I left and many men had been killed and wounded, including Jim Blaker who had been awarded a posthumous V.C. The Battalion had acquitted itself magnificently and morale was very high.

We spent much of the weekend going for walks and visiting the club in the evenings. I was very touched by the trouble my friends had taken to come all the way from Dehra Dun to see me. Just before they left, they presented me with an inscribed silver cigarette case as a parting gift from the Battalion. Pleased as I was to receive it, it seemed to set the final seal on my service with Gurkhas, for discharge from the army appeared to be certain. When they left, I wondered if I would ever see them again or, indeed, if I would ever again speak Gurkhali or hear it spoken. Only the thought that I might soon be home buoyed me up. That evening I went to the cinema to cheer myself up. The film was not particularly good but the antics of a troop of monkeys which jumped about on the tin roof for some minutes, making it impossible to hear the soundtrack, caused laughs all round; and by the time I went to bed, after a meal at a Chinese restaurant, I felt more cheerful. The following morning I received a letter from Subadar Indrabahadur, thanking me for the Rs. 100 which I had sent D Company for a nautch. He said they would not have one until I came back. I then felt that they would never have one, but as it happened they did and I was there, 18 months later in Malaya.

CHAPTER 12

HOME AND AWAY

The rail journey to Poona was very comfortable as we had an air-conditioned coach and thus avoided all the smuts and sweating. I found the climb up the Western Ghats after Bombay just as fascinating as when we had travelling on the same line en route for Bangalore in 1941. The recent monsoon had turned everything the brightest green and in many places huge waterfalls were cascading down the sandstone cliffs. Soon after our arrival there, I wrote home about Poona:-

'This hospital (3 B.M.H.) is a very good one, the chief asset being very good food. The waiters are Italian prisoners of war who seem to enjoy their work. Poona itself is a cheerful spot with many amenities, including four cinemas. I went to one last night and in the interval had a strawberry ice-cream soda – a very poor example of the real thing, bright scarlet and exuding a sort of ashes-of-roses vapour. In the afternoon I crept into the Poona Club and made myself a temporary member. The place is nice and quiet and it has a fine library-cum-reading room. The proverbial Poona diehards were not in evidence. A story is told of one of them who was dining there during the last war when a temporary member came in dressed in khaki drill instead of mess kit. Thereupon the old stager ordered a screen to be put round the miscreant's table.'

We were free to do what we liked after the M.O. had completed his morning rounds and we had finished our physiotherapy sessions. My arm was still in plaster but I went daily to these sessions, when my fingers were stretched and pulled by an English Lance-Corporal of the R.A.M.C. who gave no cause for confidence in his professional competence; a doubt further compounded when he came to remove my plaster. His knife slipped and cut

114

the base of my thumb, leaving a scar which is there to this day. I usually went out in the afternoon and, although we did not have to be back in the ward until 2200 hrs., I normally returned in time for supper, which, after all, was free and always very good. After a visit to the races on 29th. Sept., I wrote home:-

'I won Rs. 100 at the races last Saturday, by dint of paying my bearer a small commission to go and find out the likely winner from the jockeys before each race. Racing out here is very crooked. What I really enjoy about a meeting is watching the people. Every meeting is an oriental pageant. In the first class enclosure there is sure to be a collection of British officers, the seriousness with which they take the racing being directly proportional to the size and power of their binoculars. Their wives lounge in chairs, waving fans and dressed like strange mutations of rare birds of paradise. Then there is the inevitable gathering of Parsees from Bombay, wearing the most expensive European clothes and flinging money about with embarrassing abandon. Outside the enclosure is a choice assembly of humanity, clamouring and sweating in the crush. The renegade Pathans are lending money at crippling rates, the Marwaris are borrowing it with no thought for the future; Sikhs stand and chatter in shrill voices, punctuated by penetrating giggles; pick-pockets make sure that money changes hands as they swiftly disappear into the crowd.'

Often in the afternoons I used to go over to the Indian Military Hospital and visit the Gurkhas in the surgical ward. They were pathetically grateful for such attention but it grieved me to see so many amputations, for life in Nepal without a leg or even an arm would be very hard. Needless to say, they were all very cheerful despite their injuries and seemed to enjoy telling me about their experiences, however horrific. Once again I realised how lucky I had been to serve with these indomitable men, whose steadfast loyalty and courage had overcome the greatest of trials and whose misfortunes were lost in a cheerful and boundless optimism. There were several men from 1/9th.G.R. who spoke with affection about my relatives, Mike and Paddy Radcliffe, both of whom had been killed in action in North Africa and Italy respectively; and one of them even remembered my brother visiting the Battalion and taking some of the Gurkha officers up in his Beaufighter.

The Poona hospital was really like a hotel. All temperature-taking and charts at the ends of beds had been done away with in the walking surgical ward, and provided one got up before bed-making started and was in bed again by 2200 hrs., there were virtually no rules. But, for one brief period, things were different. Bubonic plague broke out in the Poona bazaar and we all had to be inoculated against it. Within an hour or two of the 'jabs' we were all smitten with high fevers which raged for about 24 hours and few of us rose from our beds on the following day. The Sister in charge, who subsequently married one of her patients, Dickie Barber of 6th. G.R., did not seem at all surprised or particularly sympathetic; doubtless, she had seen it all before. She ran a very well-regulated ward and we were all very fond of her. I continued to go out on most days and described one of them in a letter home of 16th October:-

'I seem to have had a very social week one way and another. Yesterday, I went to a tea party for Burma wounded given by an Indian cotton millionaire. The food was all Indian and at one time I had six different things on my plate at once. The edibles consisted mainly of extremely hot curry puffs and sickly-sweet sweetmeats made of sugar and ghee. The teapots were all silver partridges which spewed tea into cups from their beaks. The ladies in the party were all Indian, the wives of rich merchants, most of them recently released from purdah and largely illiterate. I found it very hard to understand my very kind hostess's valiant efforts to speak English. I might have been able to have a reasonable conversation in Hindustani but she, like the rest of the hostesses, was extremely touchy about her English, or lack of it, and it would never have done to have uttered a word in the vernacular. After this huge tea, I went to dinner with the Conservator of Forests, Bombay Presidency. He and his wife were very kind. He is retiring and going home after 25 years in the Indian Forest Service.'

Another piece of very kind hospitality which I enjoyed was provided by Brigadier and Mrs Hungerford. He had been our Brigade Commander in Gardai and somehow or other (probably from Mrs Fawcett) he had heard that I was in Poona. They invited me to dinner at the Turf Club one evening and very kindly offered me the free run of their bungalow, saying that I could come and sit in the garden or go inside and listen to the wireless whenever I liked. This I did on several occasions and was deeply grateful to them.

Rumours were rife, almost daily predicting our imminent departure for home but always turning out to be false. The chief speculation was whether or not we would be home for Christmas, but as November came and went, this became unlikely and eventually impossible. The waiting certainly became very tedious, but a few days after my 25th birthday my plaster was finally removed. The doctors were amazed at the amount of movement I had, considering the fairly extensive damage, and I temporarily forgot about the waiting. In my optimism about the eventual usefulness of my arm I suppose I was less bored than many in the ward, for at least I could enjoy the wildlife which, even in the town, was always to be seen or heard. Extracts from letters mention some of the creatures which interested me:-

'There is nothing attractive about jackals, either in their appearance or their habits. Often they are mangy and always cringing and cowardly. Offal is their staple food, the older the better. Their cries at night are one of the commonest sounds of India – a sound eerie and almost terrifying as hundreds of them take up the call and pass it on across the plains until it fades away into the black warmth of the night, leaving the grating calls of the crickets and the honking of the frogs to continue the tropical cacophony.

'The weather here is perfectly lovely at present (5th. Nov.). Bright sunny days, not too hot, with gorgeous misty mornings full of Indian bird chatter – Mynahs, Crows and Green Barbets – and when the sun is up and slightly warmer, the shrill cries of Sunbirds as they hover over the flowering magnolias.

'I went to the Queen's Gardens the other day. It is one of the largest botanic gardens in the Bombay Presidency and is a wonderful place. A splendid tropical aroma – a mixture of nutmeg, cloves and frangipani – pervades the air, which is saturated with water vapour transpired by the vast mass of evergreen vegetation. Giant bamboos, such as I saw in Burma, surround the gateway and a huge banyan tree spreads over the lawn where Mynahs waddle in search of insects. A Coppersmith tonks loudly from a peepul tree and tall areca palms stir gently in the breeze. A golden mohur, struggling into new leaf, is tinted a delicate green seen only in leaves fresh from their bud prisons.'

On 26th. November, 1944, we received definite sailing orders, and we embarked on *S.S. Almanzora* in early December. By a stroke of good fortune, Bertie Stott was also on board, going on two months' leave prior to being demobbed. He had not been home for eight years and the prospect of doing so made him even more cheerful than usual. I shared a cabin, normally intended for two, with three other officers, two of whom were a Lt. Col. and a Major in the R.A.M.C. From their conversation it was quite obvious that they had 'fixed' their repatriation by some bogus medical board. I was glad that I saw little of them during the voyage, for I despised their deception; there must have been many thousands of deserving cases who had been fraudulently by-passed by these very people who should have helped them.

The ship was old and slow, the slowest in the convoy. Indeed, one wag, whilst playing horse racing, named his steed 'Almanzora : By Degrees, Out Of Bombay', much to the amusement of the passengers and some of the crew. The weather, after Suez, was cold and the Mediterranean very rough with the ship rolling like a barrel. We spent a rather cheerless Christmas on board, made the more so by news of setbacks to our forces in the Ardennes, which made any very early end to the war in Europe unlikely. In early January, 1945, we sailed into the Clyde and disembarked at almost the same place in Gourock where I had embarked on the *Highland Chieftain* almost exactly four years before. The surrounding mountains were, as before, flecked with snow which, after so many years of uncomfortable heat, we were all delighted to see.

Those of us from the Indian Army who had been in hospitals in India were taken to civilian hospitals in Glasgow for check-ups and an overnight stay, before being given rail warrants to travel home. I put through a trunk call, which took over an hour to connect, and spoke to my parents for the first time for four years. They sounded older, I thought, and indeed they looked older when they met me at Liverpool's Lime Street Station the following evening. My mother in particular seemed to have aged considerably, which was not surprising, for she must have worried constantly about my elder brother and me. Apart from this, she had previously led a very sheltered life, with servants and nannies to relieve her of chores, until they left to work in factories or take on other war work, leaving her to do the cooking and housework. My father too, now in his 70th year, looked thin and strained from his vocation as an E.N.T. surgeon who also gave his services free to several local hospitals. He must have found his work that much more difficult in conditions of wartime scarcity and stress. But to be home again amongst all the familiar things of childhood after such an eventful four years was at once very agreeable and slightly unreal. And when I found that, apart from my parents, who had learnt about my feelings and whereabouts from my letters, no one really cared much about where I had been or what I had done, I soon gave up trying to tell them; and it was not long before I began to consider how I might get back to India and the Battalion.

Being Indian Army, I was not ordered to a military hospital but was told to make arrangements with a local hospital which had a surgical department. This was easy, as my father had a colleague who was Professor of Surgery at Liverpool University and he took me under his wing. He invented a contraption which was strapped to my forearm from which five springs protruded, each with a finger stall at one end. These held out my fingers and thumb under tension, the aim being to straighten them. Daily I travelled by tram and underground from Birkenhead to Liverpool with this strange-looking appliance on my arm, which my fellow-passengers found intriguing and I profoundly embarrassing. Wearing it was extremely painful and I found that I could not bear to have my fingers under tension for more than an hour or so at a time. Eventually, it was abandoned and a medical board pronounced me fit enough to cease treatment.

During the next few months my father retired and we moved to Northumberland, the war in Europe came to an end and VE Day was celebrated. I pestered the India Office to let me go back, for the war in the Far East seemed far from over and I longed to be back with my regiment. In early July a final medical board designated me Category C, which gave me a better chance of persuading the India Office to send me back. I was further helped by Noel George being posted to that Office, and towards the end of July I was ordered to report to R.A.F. Lyneham for a flight to India.

We set out in a Dakota at about 1000 hrs. and crossed the French coast about an hour later. During the next two hours, the green of the country below us gradually turned to brown, contrasting with the bright blue of the Mediterranean as we approached Marseilles, where we landed for lunch. The next stage was to Sardinia and we flew over many ragged mountains and a myriad of little cultivated fields in deep valleys before landing for tea and refuelling at an old Italian Air Base right on the southern tip of the island. As the sun dipped into the Mediterranean, we were heading for Malta and passed over Pantelleria as darkness was closing in. We landed in Malta in the dark, after circling over the Grand Harbour at Valetta, which was a mass of twinkling lights. After a two-hour stop, we set out for North Africa but were ordered back when no more than an hour out because of low cloud at Tobruk, our next destination. In Malta again, we were glad to get some sleep at R.A.F. Luqa, but in the morning, just before our scheduled take-off time, the plane was pronounced unserviceable and thus began a week's enforced stay on the island.

Bubonic plague in Malta restricted our movements because, officially, we were not allowed to leave Luqa. However, a vehicle was put at our disposal to take us to a recognised bathing place at St Paul's Bay at the entrance of which is St Paul's Island where the apostle was shipwrecked at night after the crew of his ship had 'cast seven anchors out of the stern and wished for the dawn'. The bathing site was an R.A.F. Rest Camp, with several terraces leading down to the sea, along which palms had been planted to give shade. The sea, absolutely clear and bright blue, washed against the bottom terrace and was immediately very deep. The temperature of the water was 75°F and I bathed without ever feeling in the least cold.

An odd thing about Malta was the almost complete absence of birds. I saw a few House Sparrows and one warbler, otherwise nothing, not even a seagull. Vegetation was very sparse, olive groves and prickly pears predominating.

After a week on the island there was still no sign of the plane being repaired, so three of us decided to make our own way. We found seats (we actually sat on the floor) on a cargo plane – a Dakota of course – leaving for Cairo that afternoon. Three hours of flying over the sea brought us to the African coast, bleak and barren but with a lovely sandy shore on which white surf was breaking. After crossing some mountains, we came to the desert, where there were still signs of war such as tracks of tanks, burnt out vehicles and wrecked aeroplanes. We landed at El Adam, near Tobruk where we had supper, before taking off again in the dark; two hours later we were circling over Cairo. It was a marvellous sight to see below a whole city lit up, with trains creeping along and coloured neon lights flashing. How our pilot found the airfield amongst the myriad of winking lights I do not know, but he set us down perfectly and we were whisked off to a magnificent hotel in Heliopolis. In the morning (it was Sunday) we went to the B.O.A.C. offices and managed to obtain seats on a Sutherland flying boat, recently arrived from E. Africa and leaving for Karachi the following morning. Meanwhile we toured Cairo, which we found a disappointing place, almost as dirty as Calcutta, with shops full of cameras, watches, etc., all at fantastically high prices. Even the famous Shepheards Hotel, where we had a glass of expensive beer, failed to live up to our expectations.

Early next morning we took off from the Nile in the middle of the city, just missing one of the big bridges as we banked over highrise flats, and were soon over the Suez Canal. After some bumpy flying over desert country, we crossed the Dead Sea, shimmering in the sunlight, with the River Jordan a thin silver ribbon running away to the north. An afternoon nap passed the time away and in the evening we landed on the lake at Habbaniya, an R.A.F. base in Iraq, where we spent a very hot night.

At 0500 hrs. next morning, we took off again and flew down the Euphrates to the Persian Gulf, landing at Bahrain in time for breakfast. I had been in some very hot places during the previous four years, but none so hot as this. The relative humidity was 98% and the temperature 95°F, so there was virtually no evaporation of sweat and within half an hour we all looked as if we had been bathing fully clad. We had just finished a most uncomfortable breakfast and were preparing to go back to the aircraft, when news came that the weather in Karachi was too bad to land and we would not be able to leave until the following morning. The only accommodation available was in tents, with no fans. So, our stay in Bahrain was, to say the least, extremely unpleasant; it was really too hot to look round and see the place.

We left early the next morning and were soon in the cool air at 6,000 ft. above the Gulf. Some hours of dull flying above the clouds brought us to Baluchistan and its barren, rocky coast, where we came down to 100 ft. above the sea to avoid a bank of cloud. We circled twice over Karachi and landed in the harbour. It was great to be back in India; that evening I took the train to Dehra Dun.

I still remember vividly my arrival there. I took a tonga from the station out to Birpur and I can see now the road down to the nullah beyond which were the 9th. G.R. barracks. The pony took the slope slowly, slipping now and again as the tongawallah twisted its tail and tugged on the reins. Beyond the barracks were the purple foothills shimmering in the heat, with the snows above them sparkling white. I could hear the sound of shots fired on the rifle ranges, and some Gurkhas, dressed in neat mufti, passed us, smiling cheerfully and saluting. Down in the nullah, villagers were washing their clothes and children were bathing in a pool. Kites were wheeling in the sky and I could hear a Coppersmith tonking in a tree near the entrance to the lines. We trotted past the quarterguard and the sentry shouldered arms and saluted with impassive face but welcoming eyes. I somehow felt that I had come home. At the Mess, the butler greeted me as though I was the only person he ever wanted to see, calling for an orderly to take my baggage to my bungalow and for another to bring me a 'nimbo pani'. I sat on the verandah gazing at the wonderful mountains. How could anyone want to be anywhere else? It was a moment of unalloyed happiness.

CHAPTER THIRTEEN

KHATMANDU, 1945

Shortly after I arrived in Dehra Dun I found that Dudley Spain was also serving at the Regimental Centre. He and I were lucky enough to be selected as the first officers to go to Nepal as guests of the British Minister. This came about because Col. Alan Duncan, Commandant of the Centre, had written to Lt. Col. George Falconer, the British Envoy to the Court of Nepal, suggesting that it would be helpful if British officers serving with Gurkha regiments could visit Nepal, then a jealously guarded closed independent state, and learn first-hand something about the country where their men lived. To this Col. Falconer agreed and offered to put up the officers in the Legation providing he was not subjected to any great personal expense. Thus it was that we were able to go on an historic and fascinating visit, and join, albeit briefly, the eight Europeans living in Nepal at that time. They were the Minister and wife, the First Secretary, Col. Sandy Macleod and wife, the Head of the Hydro-Electric System, Mr Kilburn and wife, and the Chief Forestry Officer, Mr Smythies and wife.

Before describing the visit, it might be appropriate to give a short account of the historical events which led to the somewhat Gilbertian regime which held sway in Nepal at the time of our visit and which was responsible for the isolation which we were lucky enough to penetrate.

During the Mohammedan invasion of India, many Hindu Rajputs fled into the Himalayas for safety and to escape persecution; there they intermarried with the indigenous population. Gradually this new blood spread into the hill villages throughout Western Nepal and eventually 24 small kingdoms evolved, ruled over by the more dominant of those with Rajput blood in their veins. The strongest of these was the Kingdom of Gorkha from which hailed the Shah kings of Nepal who, by treaty and conquest, united all the small kingdoms. Further conquests added the Newar

Malla kingdoms, centred in the Khatmandu Valley, as well as the Kiratis of Eastern Nepal whose kings, in ages past, had themselves ruled in Khatmandu. The present-day martial tribes of the east, the Rais and the Limbus, are now included, together with their fellow subjects of the west, the Thakurs, Chettris, Gurungs and others, in the generic term Gurkha, originating from the town of that name.

The great king, Prithai Narayan, the ancestor of the present king, ruled over a formidable domain stretching at its greatest from the River Sutlej in the west to the River Teesta in the east. He was accepted, as was the custom, as an avatar of the God Vishnu, exercising the Divine Right of Kings. But eventually from such supreme power was born intrigue and massacre which resulted in the royal powers being taken over and wielded by hereditary Prime Ministers or Maharajahs. The first of these was the famous Jung Bahadur Rana who ruled from 1846 to 1877. His direct descendant, Joodha Shamsher Jung Bahadur Rana, ruled supreme at the time of our visit, in the name of the King, the nominal sovereign who was then presumed divine with no executive power. The King was known as 'Panch Sirkar' (Five Government) and the Prime Minister as 'Tin Sirkar' (Three Government), the former being entitled to five of the honorific prefixes 'Sri' and the latter to three.

We left Dehra Dun by train one evening at the end of August, 1945, arriving in Lucknow the following morning. We spent the whole day there awaiting a connecting train which took another two nights and a day to reach Raxaul in North Bihar. There we stayed a night in the Legation Rest House, where the accommodation was good but lacked electric light and fans. On the morrow we travelled from Raxaul to Amlekgunj by the Nepal Government Railway in four-wheeled, narrow gauge coaches with polished panelling, a silver vase on the table containing a drooping rose and antimacassars on the seat-backs. This little train, which would delight the modern railway buff, chugged 28 miles through Terai jungle and up steep gradients, taking three hours to reach its Nepal terminus. The jungle, noted at that time for its large numbers of tigers, elephants and rhinos, also harboured a particularly virulent form of malaria, known locally as 'awal'. So savage was the disease, that no people were allowed to spend the night in the jungle except the indigenous inhabitants, the Tharus, who had developed an immunity. The dominant trees were sal, many of them festooned with lianas and parasitic orchids. In the clearings were large areas of beautiful tall elephant grass.

At Amlekhgunj we were met by the Station Master in formal dress, who ushered us into an upper room at the station and gave us lunch. Then our kit was piled into the mail lorry and we, sitting in front, were driven at a furious pace for about 25 miles up a hill road, unmetalled throughout, to a small village called Bhainsi, where the road petered out, turning into a footpath and horse track. Here we were met by Nepalese officials, who had coolies ready to carry our luggage and ponies for us to ride; all provided free by Maharajah Joodha Shamsher.

During the lorry journey we went through a crude tunnel, the same which British troops reached during the Gurkha Wars in 1815 when the Nepalese, fearing lest the British should penetrate the Khatmandu Valley, sued for peace. There followed the Treaty of Segauli by which the Maharajah agreed, amongst other things, to allow recruitment of Gurkhas into the Indian Army, provided they were led by British officers.

From Bhainsi we rode and walked about 10 miles, via Bhimphedi, to Chiso Pani Ghari (Cold Water Fort), within which a small bungalow had been made ready for us, the same which was also used by the 'Bara Sahib', as the British Minister was called. This place was an 18th-century star-shaped fort with a drawbridge, built to protect the road to Khatmandu; it was never taken by the British. In keeping with past times, our rooms had old fashioned hand-pulled punkahs and vast mosquito nets.

Next morning after a large breakfast, we set out at about 0730 hrs. on our ponies, escorted for the first mile by a band of minstrels – drummers, fiddlers and flautists, all creating a considerable noise and a very merry atmosphere. Over about three miles we gradually lost some 3,000 ft. of our previous day's 4,000 ft. climb, and at the foot of the descent we came to Kulikhane, mainly a collection of barrack-type buildings in which coolies, carrying stores to Khatmandu, could rest. Here we were met at the inn in true 'Pilgrimage to Canterbury' style by ostlers who took away our ponies to feed them, whilst we were given an excellent lunch in an upper room. (Now, alas, Kulikhane lies beneath the waters of a lake formed for hydro-electric generation).

After lunch we rode for nine miles through flat country, followed by sundry ups and downs, culminating in a final climb of 3,000 ft. to 7,000 ft. and the top of the Chandragiri Pass. Much fatigued, for the final climb was far too steep for the ponies, we sat down to rest in the shade on a carpet of dried leaves. Gradually we became conscious of a sinister rustling which grew in intensity. Our porters had wisely sat elsewhere and, amidst some laughter, they shouted 'Jhuka Ayo' (leeches have come). Indeed they had; from every direction their brown looping forms were advancing towards us, rustling the leaves as they came. Others, creeping along the overhanging branches of trees and shrubs, started to drop onto us. So great were the numbers and so relentless their approach, that it was really rather frightening. But as soon as we realised what was happening, it was easy enough to take evasive action. Never before or since have I seen leeches in such numbers and in such a hungry mood.

From the top of the pass we had a view of the Khatmandu Valley. Although low cloud partially obscured the scene, this irregular bowl lying between Himalayan foothills was strikingly beautiful, with the sinking sun tinting the snow-clad mountains in the background and the electric lights in the city twinkling in the dusk. Khatmandu had electricity before Chester, we were told.

At the bottom of the pass we were met by the British Minister's car, which took us to the Legation, a distance of about seven miles. We were amazed to see so many cars in the valley, to which no roads led. We later learnt that they were carried up the same track along which we had walked. The wheels of a vehicle were removed and it was then lifted up on long poles and borne aloft by as many as 200 men. Much of the other produce not grown or made in Nepal was also carried in by coolies, but heavy things, apart from motor cars, were transported by an electric cableway.

As we drove through the streets of Khatmandu, the first thing that we noticed was how extraordinarily un-Indian was the architecture and how great an affinity it bore to the Chinese. Tibetan and Chinese traders had left their mark almost to the exclusion of Aryan influence from India, although the pagoda style of the buildings was one which the Newars, the majority inhabitants of the valley, claim to have invented. For centuries these people had ruled in the valley and beyond, eventually to fight amongst themselves and suffer conquest by the Gorkha King Prithi Narayan Shah. Nevertheless, about their origin there seems to be some doubt. Some say they hailed from Southern India, others maintain that they were Himalayan aboriginals. Their language and that of the Tibetans, Gurungs and Magars all show a certain affinity; consequently, the second opinion about their origin seems to be the more likely. Furthermore, their features are decidedly mongolian and their skins the light browny yellow typical of Himalayan tribes; as, indeed, we noticed as we drove along the streets.

On our arrival at the Legation Residence, we were given a friendly welcome by Mrs (later Lady) Falconer, who probably yearned for fresh faces. Col. (later Sir George) Falconer was more formal and gave the impression that we were one of the crosses he was obliged to bear; another and much greater, so we later felt, was the Himalayan isolation in which he found himself. He was not a diplomat but a member of the Indian Political Service, of which he held one of the plum appointments. The Residence, which was quite new when we stayed there, is now occupied by the Indian Ambassador.

We spent several days sight-seeing in the valley, where there are three other towns apart from Khatmandu: Patan, Bhatgaon and Kirtipur (also called Naskatipur because, for resisting the Gorkha conquest of the valley, men had their noses cut off). We visited them all and were ourselves 'sights' for the inhabitants, who had rarely seen Europeans. Our ability to speak their language increased their wonderment and our enjoyment.

At the old Palace of Hunuman Dhoka, where the grotesque statue of Kala Bhairab stands on guard, we saw the King's Throne Room, an 18th century salon, with portraits of George V and Queen Mary flanking the throne. Here the King received the credentials of new ambassadors with the Prime Minister acting as 'interpreter'. Then on to see the sweet-faced god lying prostrate in the clear stream which gushed from the hills at Balaji; the all-seeing eyes which gazed upon the pilgrims turning the prayer-wheels at Swayambunath; and the great Hindu shrine on the banks of the Baghmatti River. All these things we saw and more but none so poignant as the latter place, Pashupattinath, where many thousands of pilgrims came annually, some to breath their last and have their ashes cast upon the waters of the sacred river. Where the huge golden-roofed temple stood the river passed through a small gorge, flowing swiftly without a ripple beside the burning ghats. Behind lay a wooded hill where a troop of sacred rhesus monkeys lived, emerging in little groups to scamper about the temple and snatch tit-bits from the pilgrims' offerings of food. In the still damp air on the evening of our visit, blue smoke curled upwards from the funeral pyres of those who had died in peace, their feet gently lapped by the sacred waters. Into the fast flowing river priests were casting the ashes to be borne away, perhaps to a nearby sandbank, perhaps even to the confluence with the Ganges and along the doubly sacred waters of that mighty river. Lying hidden by screens were other pilgrims waiting patiently for death to overtake them, for anyone who could afford to be carried there on his deathbed would never wish to die at home. Such was this place of death which, at that time, few Europeans had ever seen – a place of infinite sadness amongst the whispering pines.

We first saw Joodha Shamshere on the Tundikhel, a vast open space in the centre of Khatmandu, where he was taking the salute at a parade in honour of four Nepalese regiments returning from the war. He was seated in

Gurkha Girls

an ornate chair on a plinth surrounding the Kari ko Bhot, where traitors were wont to be hanged in olden times. Each Commanding Officer threw down golden ashrafis at the Maharajah's feet as a homage and a sign of loyalty. His only acknowledgement was to shout tersely 'Pick them up'. We left the parade in General Bahadur Shamshere's car, the Minister having offered his to the Maharajah, whose own vehicle was stuck in the mud. A Colonel rushed forward to close the door of the General's car in which we were sitting, and just as it was pulled shut the Colonel's fingers got squashed. The General's sympathy extended to a shouted remark: 'If you hadn't put your finger there, it wouldn't have been crushed'.

Our first meeting with Jooda Shamshere was at his Palace, the Singha Durbar. We drove there with the Minister in his car and were ushered into the huge audience hall, where the Maharajah was seated on a throne surrounded by courtiers. He motioned us to sit down on two ornate chairs placed before him. He asked us if we spoke Nepali and, on hearing that we did, he dismissed Col. Falconer, somewhat to our embarrassment, with the words 'You may go, I will send your guests back later'. The Minister's eyebrows rose, but he said nothing and left.

The conversation was entirely in Nepali, and very jovial was the Maharajah, quite unaffected by his position of supreme power. The subjects ranged from conditions in wartime Burma to the exchange rate between the Nepali and Indian rupees (then much to the disadvantage of Nepal) and finally to his great interest, tiger and rhino shooting. He told us that he had shot over 450 tigers and 60 rhinos; oddly enough he seemed proud of it. There followed an effusion from Dudley extolling the natural beauties of the country. The Maharajah held up his hand and said 'You have seen England, Europe, India and many other large countries. How can you say that my small country is so beautiful?' To which Dudley replied, 'But, Your Highness, a diamond is small.' This delighted the old man who turned to his courtiers and said 'Did you hear that? Did you hear that?' again and again, adding 'He has intelligence.' On this happy note the audience ended, after an A.D.C. bearing a large velvet cushion had been called. Upon it were two ceremonial kukhries and two photographs of Joodha Shamshere framed in carved sandalwood; especially memorable gifts considering how rarely, at that time, Europeans had ever been to Nepal and how even less often they had met the Maharajah. On our return to the Legation, the Minister asked how we had managed to get two presents; most people only got one, he said.

When we left the Singha Durbar after that first visit, the Maharaja said that we must come again and he would show us various things. He promised to send his car for us. He was as good as his word several days later when an open car arrived at the Legation. As we drove through the streets, the Maharajah's car was recognised and the general public did obeisance until they saw the undeserving occupants, but I think we both enjoyed our brief moments of glory. At the Singha Durbar again, the Maharajah proudly showed us the fountain in front of the main facade. Controlled by electricity, it displayed a programme of continually changing patterns of water jets floodlit in ever-changing colours. It was acquired from France after the 'Grande Exposition' at the turn of the century. Strange to say, it still works almost a century later. The pictures, of which the Maharajah was inordinately proud, were in the 'Gadi Baitok' or Throne Room (now the Parliament Building), mostly of a sporting nature, one of them showing King George V shooting from a howdah and another of a tiger clawing at an elephant's head.

On our way back to Thankot at the end of our visit, we came upon a palaquin being carried by four bearers, and we stopped to take a photograph. It was preceded by a Mukhiya with a staff and a silver moon of office on his headdress. He was crying 'Make way, make way for the daughter of a great lord.' The procession stopped as we approached, and a high-pitched voice from within the palaquin asked why it had halted. 'It is only some spare Englishmen' was the literal translation of the Mukiya's reply, and the procession moved on.

We left a Nepal which, in 1951, suffered a revolution. The King, Tribhuban, abolished the hereditary principle of the premiership, changed the constitution and, after a period of direct rule, appointed the then leader of the Nepali Congress Party as Prime Minister. This arrangement did not last long; he tried out a number of other parties, the abilities of which did not satisfy him, but he died before he could proceed further. He was succeeded by his son, King Mahendra, who organised a general election for a parliament under a new constitution devised by a British constitutional expert. The Congress again won this election and B.P. Koirala became prime minister. After a year, the King dismissed the P.M. and put him in gaol, before promulgating a new constitution and introducing the 'Partyless Panchayat System' – universal suffrage but no parties. This was intended to prevent various corrupt practices but was only partially successful, for the Panchayat system, although potentially a good one, was misused. Another revolution and another election, won again by the Congress, resulted in G.P. Koirala, brother of B.P., becoming prime minister. All these changes and the reasons for them bring to mind what Joodha Shamshere said to us: 'I don't know whether all the peoples' petitions reach me or whether all my commands reach the people. Those in between twist everything around to their own advantage. This is not to the advantage of Nepal'. Plus ça change, plus c'est la même chose!

We returned to Dehra Dun by the same route by which we came. As we walked through Thankot a very attractive little puppy came running after me, and I went back to the shop whence it came and bought it for Rs.10. It was fawn coloured with white paws and mask, and a slightly squashed nose like a Pekinese. My orderly, Dhanbahadur, who incidentally had come with us, greatly approved of this purchase (although he thought the price exorbitant) and promptly named the little creature 'Tilaki' because of the small white spot on her forehead. She was to accompany me to Malaya, Singapore, Java and Sumatra. She was always a great favourite with the Gurkhas, not only because she was engagingly pretty and sweet-tempered, but also because she was recognised as a genuine Nepali 'Moti Kukur' and a link with their well-loved country.

CHAPTER 14

DEHRA INTERLUDE

When I arrived in Dehra Dun from home in early August, 1945, I was appointed O.C. No.3 Training Battalion with the acting rank of Major. Both my company commanders were younger than I and neither had seen any active service, but the senior Subadar, Gaganbahadur Khattri, had, losing an eye in the process. As we had both suffered personally from enemy action, we felt we had a common bond shared by no other officer in the Battalion. This made for a happy partnership and an enjoyable few months before I eventually got back to 3/9th. G.R.

It was but a few days after I took over the Training Battalion that the atomic bombs were dropped on Hiroshima and Nagasaki, followed by the Japanese surrender. Suddenly all the talk was about release, disbandment and the political future of India. But a reminder of what the last five years had all been about was soon given when men of the 2nd. Battalion returned from Singapore where they had been prisoners of the Japs for more than three horrendous years. We all went to the station to meet them and found them looking rather thin but very cheerful, considering what they had been through. Each man was lost in a jungle of garlands round his neck and the strains of the Pipes and Drums scarcely competed with the joyful shouts of recognition and greeting. In a matter of days all had departed on long-overdue leave in Nepal. The officers came about a week later and had sorry tales to tell.

I found the job of O.C. No. 3 Training Battalion an absolute dead end. The Indian Army was bound to be greatly reduced in numbers and the British Labour Party had recently been returned to power and was committed to giving India independence. It therefore seemed that the Regimental Centre was going to be a place of demobilisation and contraction, whereas the still active battalions overseas, although their lives might be limited, would at

No. 3 Training Battalion, 9th. G.R. Regimental Centre, Dehra Dun, 1945.

least have a constructive, and perhaps exciting, role to play. Not that living in Dehra Dun was anything but pleasant.

The Mess was superbly run and delightfully situated. The lawns, lined by canna beds, stretched down to the Tons Nullah, with the mountains forming a backdrop to the intervening flat jungle-clad country. High on the first ridge hung the hill station of Mussouri and beyond, the eternal snows. Sitting out in the shade before lunch, one was regaled by the sounds and sights of cantonment India; a distant bugle call, the popping of rifle fire on the range, the harsh cawing of the House Crows, the squeaky cries of Mynahs, the yapping of pie dogs and the sleepy murmur of the Spotted Doves. The eye would catch the yellow flash of Sunbirds amongst the scarlet hibiscus flowers, the wheeling kites and above them the black specks of soaring vultures. A ground squirrel, scuttling across the lawn, would scamper up a tree trunk and chitter with unprovoked rage from a low branch at the squatting malee, who would be cutting grass with a curved knife and bundling it into a sack whilst his colleague would be sprinkling water on the canna beds. All was peace in contrast with the recent strains and stresses.

At evening time too, the peace was just as real. From the velvety sky the stars shone and twinkled in apparent competition with the myriad of fireflies in the tree canopies. Even the distant howls of jackals seemed to blend with the throb of madals in the barracks and the clink of glasses in the orderlies' pantry. The scent of frangipani struggled to overcome the harsh smell of cow-dung smoke, providing a nasal cocktail which was uniquely Indian. In such surroundings the day's frustrations evaporated. Why did I want to leave this heavenly place? The call of friendships forged in danger and adversity was greater than the feel of ease and comfort.

It was not only the lifestyle and living conditions which gave so much content. The shooting and fishing trips were pure delight. On Friday evenings, we would set out with a dozen or so volunteer riflemen and a Gurkha officer in a 30 cwt. truck, complete with tents and rations and a cook from the mess. The destination was usually Kulhal, where the River Jumna cut through the sal jungle, flowing blue-grey over large, white rounded stones. On flat ground near the jungle edge the tents would be pitched and the cook would start to prepare dinner. In the short time before darkness fell we would take our guns and, accompanied by our orderlies, walk along the jungle edge. A kakar would bark a warning and a cheetal might let us know that our presence had been detected. With a sudden whir of wings, a Jungle Fowl would leap from cover and plane towards the river, to be dropped, perhaps, by one of us before it reached the water's edge. The sound of the shot would reverberate amongst the trees setting off all manner of jungle cries; the mass twitterings of Munias, flushed in little flocks from riverside grass, the crowing of Jungle Fowl, the strident 'meowing' of Peafowl and the harsh cawing of Jungle Crows. Then silence, broken only by the rush of the river, the distant hammering of tent pegs and the clatter of cooking pots being moved into the kitchen tent. Perhaps we would return with two jungle fowl and a few green pigeons, as well as with a feeling of profound well-being and very ready for the hot bath to be taken in a tub with water heated by a bearer in a 4-gallon kerosene tin. Then drinks beneath the stars with nothing more to worry us than the 'ping' of mosquitoes. Against the background hiss of the pressure lamps, the chatter of the orderlies and the sawing of countless cicadas, came the night sounds of the jungle: the devilish howling of the jackals passing from one group to another with decreasing intensity, the 'belling' of a sambhur, the hoot of an owl and occasionally the 'cough' of a leopard.

Before dawn broke, the camp would be astir. The throat-clearing 'hoicking' of the staff, the clatter of pans, the clink of crockery and the cries of 'Chae Sahib' would herald a new day, no part of which was to be wasted abed. Orderlies with guns were outside the tents as the sun's rays tipped the treetops with yellow, and we were soon walking in single file to the place of a drive, the heavy dew on the shrubs and long grass soaking our shorts. The Gurkha officer in charge, a veteran of shikar in those parts, would place us and then take the beaters to start the drive. A whistle would signal that all was ready and the shouting would commence. At first nothing much would appear. Some Tree Pies would hop from tree to tree crying harshly at the disturbance and raising their long tails in defiance, and a Black-naped Oriole might show his indifference by a few liquid musical notes. Then shouting by the beaters would increase and cries of 'sungur' would precede the sound of a creature crashing through the jungle. Suddenly, if one was in the right place, a black form would come hurtling through the undergrowth and a wild boar would be within range to come to a somersaulting end and lie kicking from a barrel-load of S.G. Giving little time for reloading, a Jungle Fowl would come whirring down the line to be picked off by someone more ready for him. One or two cheetal or perhaps a barking deer might come dashing through the trees but they could not be shot with shotguns; we always allowed peafowl to pass in safety, both because Hindus revere them and because they are such beautiful birds, albeit excellent eating. Some Green Pigeon, a few Jungle Fowl and a pig would be a good bag, and we would come back to camp hot and hungry to a breakfast of mulligatawny soup and scrambled eggs.

Fishing for mahseer occupied part of the rest of the day; not for the monsters of up to 100 lb. but for the small fish of two or three pounds, using a light trout rod and a fly spoon. Casting into the edges of pools at the end of swift runs usually produced a rise and often a well-hooked fish, which fought very vigorously for its size. But it was hot work during the day, and it was pleasant to take frequent rests in the shade of a sal tree and watch the jungle world go by. A White-breasted Kingfisher, rusty brown and iridescent blue, would be sitting on a drooping branch over the river, occasionally plopping into the water to catch a little fish. A Red-rumped Swallow would skim over the river dipping into the water now and again to pick up an insect. A Black-naped Oriole would call 'whee-oo' and flash golden in dipping flight across the river. Some langurs would come swinging through the treetops to stop briefly and raise their eyebrows up and down in anxious curiosity before uttering warning 'coughs' and moving on. The penetrating call of a Peacock would temporarily drown the constant singing of cicadas, and the 'cheel' of Black Kites would interrupt the strident shrieks of the Hawk-cuckoo. It was a magic place where man, so numerous and noisy elsewhere, seemed far away; a place where the Almighty must surely have been close at hand.

Shortly before Christmas, 1945, my re-posting order to 3/9th.G.R. came through and I received a letter from Alec Harper telling me that I was to be his adjutant and asking me to escort a returning leave party and bring with them the Battalion chowdhadri and his stores. Fortunately, Bertie Stott had just returned from home leave and was on his way back to the Battalion, so we travelled together. In a special coach attached to the Calcutta express were loaded the leave party, and a mountain of boxes and crates containing cigarettes, cloth, stores for the sunwar and the mochi and, no doubt, many private items for men in Java who would have heard of the chowdhari's return. After a few days of uncomfortable travel, we reached the Transit Camp at Barrackpore to find that those who were to arrange our onward journey to Singapore were unaware of our existence and in no way inclined to be helpful. Air travel was out of the question because of all the stores, and shipping was apparently in short supply. After a week or two, when it had become clear that we could expect no help from those who should have helped us, we took matters into our own hands and went down to the docks in search of a ship bound for Singapore. Eventually we found one; it was a 'Liberty Ship' called the *Carlton*, painted black on the outside and coated black inside with coal dust from a recent cargo. The captain agreed to take us provided we obtained the necessary papers. These the transit authorities readily gave us, being only too glad to get rid of us. We embarked a few days before Christmas, delighted to leave behind the squalor of Calcutta.

The *Carlton* had no cabin accommodation for Bertie and me, so we had our camp beds put up in the same hold as the men, screened off by a tent flap. The hold was filthy, coated with layers of coal dust, and there were no portholes; just the ship's ventilation blower which merely helped to distribute the dust more evenly. We messed with the ship's officers, who put up with us mainly because we had some whisky, which was in very short supply at that time. They were a dour lot of Scots, particularly the chief engineer, who when offered a drink merely said, 'I'm not particular'.

If we were uncomfortable, the men were doubly so. All the most basic amenities were in short supply or non-existent. Salt water only was available for washing, cooking took place on deck where there was little enough space as it was, but we never had a single complaint; the men were as keen as we were to return to the Battalion and, as was always the case with Gurkhas, they improvised to a remarkable degree. After about ten days, we arrived in Singapore without mishap.

We were a scruffy-looking lot when we arrived at the Race Course Transit Camp early one hot and sticky morning, to find that our accommodation was to be in the grandstand. Various sections had been screened off for officers, British troops and Indian troops. There was no furniture, just stepped stages on which officers put their camp beds in serried ranks and the men their bedding rolls, with mosquito nets rigged up as best could be managed. The mess was in one of the large storerooms beneath the stand, and the quality of messing was deplorable. There were two menus, if one could give such edible travesties such a name; one called 'Indian' and the other 'British'. The former was basically vegetable curry and the latter, when hot, soya links (a kind of synthetic sausage, square in section extracted from a tin) and when cold, bully beef of an extremely inferior brand with bits of skin and fur boosting its bulk, both accompanied by fried sweet potatoes. So revolting were the 'British' meals that everyone went for the curry, which was really quite good. But, of course, there was never enough and we all tried to get to the mess early with resulting long, temper-destroying queues. Eventually a sort of apartheid system was introduced whereby, if your face was white, you willy-nilly got soya links and, if brown, curry. Consequently, Bertie and I ate out whenever we could, which was not often because transport was hard to come by; and even when we did, the meals were nothing to write home about, for the Japs had raped the countryside and everything was in short supply.

It was surprising to find how docile were the Jap prisoners of war. Everywhere parties of them were marching about without escorts under their own officers to carry out fatigue duties, to repair damaged buildings and generally help to get things going again. Their discipline was excellent and there were never any reports of trouble caused by them. We employed them to unload our stores from the ship. When one net-load of boxes was being swung ashore, a carton of cigarettes burst open and a Jap fatigue man quickly stuffed some into his pocket. Unfortunately for him, his officer saw what happened, walked up to him, knocked him down, picked him up and knocked him down again and kicked him. This sort of behaviour, which would have resulted in an officer in the British or Indian armies being court marshalled, was part of the Japanese army code; small wonder British prisoners of war suffered so much brutality in Jap hands.

After the dismal squalor of Calcutta, Singapore seemed so clean and green and lush. Even after three years of Japanese occupation, the roads were in very tolerable order and most of the public buildings were in fairly good repair. The inhabitants, be they Chinese, Malay or Indian, were obviously pleased to see the British back again. At least we were the devil they knew and despite our humiliation in 1942, we were still recognised as fair and humane, unlike the cruel and repressive Japanese. The whole atmosphere was quite different from that in India – friendly and relaxed with much evidence of a determination to get things back to normal as quickly as possible. Had it not been for the discomfort of the Transit Camp and our wish to return to the Battalion as soon as possible, we would not have been so keen to leave. But to find a ship sailing to Java was difficult indeed. Almost daily we went to see the transport authorities and equally often we visited the docks to try and make a private arrangement. This went on for a fortnight or more, interspersed with signals to the Battalion, to 5th. Indian Division in Sourabaya, not to mention personal calls at Singapore District H.Q. at Fort Canning and at Army H.Q. at Tanglin. It was a dispiriting exercise and I cannot remember how long it was before we finally found a freighter bound for Sourabaya on to which we embarked our men and stores, while Bertie and I obtained seats on a D.C.3 of R.A.F. Transport Command which took us to Sourabaya via Palembang and Batavia. I remember the great impression which the mountains of Java made upon me. As we approached the coast near Batavia, they appeared cone-shaped and rich purple, changing to a fertile green near their bases, this green gradually taking shape as a mosaic of paddyfields, square and half-flooded on the flat, but narrow and irregular on the contoured slopes of the mountain, the whole scene giving the impression of extraordinary fecundity. Along the whole length of the island between Batavia and Sourabaya this tropical lushness spread as far as the eye could see from our fine vantage point 10,000 ft. above the sea, the purple mountains on one side and the intensely blue sea on the other. The picture remains with me to this day.

CHAPTER FIFTEEN

JAVA AND MALAYA

The sudden end to the war in the Far East in August, 1945 left a power vacuum in the Netherlands East Indies (Indonesia) and other countries not recovered by the Allies. In Indonesia the Japanese XVI Army failed to obey orders to maintain law and order. Indeed, some Japanese army units actively encouraged the Nationalists, particularly the more extreme elements, to fill the vacuum. Anarchy prevailed and Dutch internees and prisoners of war were in mortal danger.

Thus it fell to the weary British forces, predominantly Indian Army including no less than seven Gurkha Battalions, to obtain the release of Dutch personnel and protect them; to guard and evacuate the Japanese prisoners of war and capture those still at large, and to secure the key towns, including their lines of communication, until the Dutch Forces could take over.

The situation in Java, where the Nationalists were particularly strong and of murderous intent, posed the greatest threat. In late October, The Rajputana Rifles, Mahrattas and a Field Regt., R.A., comprising 49 Indian Infantry Brigade of 23rd Indian Division landed in Sourabaya to be greeted by an atmosphere of explosive nationalist suspicion. Leaflets were dropped from aircraft stating Brigadier Mallaby's intention to disarm both the disaffected colonial forces and the armed rabble which supported them. The city erupted with little warning; units and sub-units of the Brigade were surrounded, suffering grievous casualties; the Brigadier was treacherously murdered whilst parleying with the Nationalists. The Brigade extricated itself only after some 400 men had been killed or wounded.

A few days later 3/9th. G.R. and Dogras and Punjabis of 123 Brigade 5th. Indian Division with revenge in their hearts, landed in Sourabaya with supporting naval guns and armour. Fierce street fighting gradually subdued the insurgents (as they were called), but it was not until early December that the Brigade secured the town and established itself in perimeter positions. The main insurgent forces withdrew some ten miles beyond this perimeter, but for the next two months they continued to probe the Brigade's forward positions in platoon and company strength.

In Central Java the same suspicion and distrust of the British forces, thought by the insurgents to be bent upon bolstering the hated Dutch, prevailed. The 37th. Gurkha Brigade (3/3rd/G.R., 3/5th. R.G.R., 3/10th. G.R.) both in Batavia and later further south in Bandoeng, suffered severe casualties as they successfully took over detention camps and saved Dutch civilians from certain massacre. As elsewhere, here also the cheerful, courageous and determined way in which the Gurkhas carried out their distasteful task gained the profound respect and gratitude of both the Dutch and the Javanese, most of whom found the insurgents' murderous tactics to be well beyond the bounds of reasonable Nationalist dissent.

In the outer islands of Indonesia, and in the largest island of all, Sumatra, Gurkha units, including 3/9th.G.R. were also deployed in late 1946 and found themselves in the same repugnant role which, although the insurgents were less extreme, put the Gurkhas in a very invidious position. The Dutch wished them to regain control on their behalf (they had no forces of their own capable of achieving this) and the insurgents were set upon destroying those things which they eventually wished to own, especially the oil wells. It was, as the modern saying goes, a 'no-win' situation.

Inevitably, in such bitter fighting, there were scenes of heroism, poignancy and even farce. In the first few days of operations in Sourabaya 3/9th. G.R., reached the Kali Sosok gaol where a large number of Dutch civilians were held prisoner by the insurgents.[1] Our orders were to obtain their release. Snipers had set themselves up over the main gate and any approach by the

---

[1] In May, 1995 a chance contact was made with Mr B.F. de Baat Doelman, who, now aged 86 and living in London, was one of the prisoners released from the Kali Sosok Gaol. Part of his report on this rescue is given below:

'On the 10th. of November, 1945 a whole division of Gurkhas landed. They reached our jail about noon and towards 4 p.m. we were liberated and transferred to Perak (Tanjongperak) by truck. There had been brisk fighting in the jail before we left, but the Gurkhas made short work of all the personnel. They arrived just in time, as the Indonesians intended to burn us alive in our cells on that day. That morning, a short time before the fighting started, a truck loaded with kerosene and petrol for this purpose had come to the jail under escort of some soldiers of the Republican Army.'

This report of the planned killing of the prisoners is corroborated by a Dutch history of events which states that an Ambonese warder from the gaol had escaped from his fellows on 9th. November, and had told an Intelligence Officer of the 5th. Indian Division that all the prisoners would be killed by the Indonesians on the following morning.

Gurkhas was met by heavy fire. An armoured car was driven at the huge iron gate in the hope that it would burst open. Unfortunately, it was one which slid sideways to open and it merely became hopelessly jammed. Reggie Twelvetrees, the Company Commander, then decided to blow a hole in the wall with a 'Bangalore Torpedo'. When the Gurkhas crawled through the hole they discovered that there was yet another wall inside, but by moving along between the walls towards the gate, they found a way into the gaol, and the defenders, sensing that the game was up, fled into what turned out to be the mortuary, which the Gurkhas found to be empty apart from some corpses lying on slabs under shrouds. But one of the Gurkhas, rightly conscious of the insurgents' guile, prodded a corpse with his bayonet. Immediately, all four 'corpses' came to life and tried to escape, but duly met their deserts. Meanwhile, the cells were opened and Dutch men, women and children, the sexes segregated during three years of barbarous treatment, and each loved one unaware of the fate of the other, ran out into the forecourt. The scenes of extreme emotion which followed, especially amongst those who sought for relatives in vain, and the pathetic gratitude shown to their liberators by these sorely persecuted Dutch, were such that the Gurkhas and their officers were moved nearly to tears. As the united families came out of the gaol through the hole in the wall (the gate was still jammed), all wished to shake hands with their Gurkha liberators and, as Reggie Twelvetrees wrote, 'We all finished the day with very tired hands and arms'. They also felt that on this occasion at least, their task had not been as thankless as on so many previous days and, as it turned out, it was to be during so many future weeks.

Another objective in the town was the zoo, where a measure of comedy was injected into the generally grim scene. The keepers had all fled, leaving the animals unattended for many days. The smaller birds had perished as had some of the smaller mammals. A decision was made to release all those creatures which were not dangerous. Those which were, such as lions and tigers, were fed on shot pie-dogs which were roaming the streets in great numbers. The only real problem was a very large male orang-utan which occupied a huge cage in the centre of the zoo. The Gurkhas were fascinated by this enormous anthropoidal ape or 'Ban Manchhe' as they called it, the like of which they had never seen before; they were determined to see that it survived. Most of the day it attracted an admiring audience and its chief party trick was to pull into the cage a pole with one arm, resisted by four or five Gurkhas hanging on to the other end. This it did with ease, much to the delight of the men, and it remained a favourite until we left the island, enjoying boiled rice from the cookhouse as a staple diet, supplemented by bananas, papayas and such other fruit as came in the mens' rations. The animals which had been released quickly dispersed, but for weeks afterwards an emu strutting down the main street or a little herd of cheetal rushing panic-stricken from a noisy skirmish near the perimeter added a touch of farce to an otherwise grim scene.

We held a portion of the defensive perimeter round the city of Sourabaya for several weeks while the Dutch and the insurgents parlied. Occasionally, patrols went out to ensure that there was no build-up of potential attackers, and a few harmless skirmishes occurred but for the most part it was unmitigated boredom and not easy to keep the men gainfully occupied. One sad incident resulting from this boredom was to do with local 'hooch'. It was devilish stuff and a number of men who drank it went blind, mostly only temporarily. The saddest case was that of the well-liked and much respected Havildar Dhakalbahadur, who had been in charge of the mules throughout the Chindit campaign; he drank the stuff and never regained his sight. Another consequence of this tedium, accentuated by the knowledge that we were engaged in the thankless task of propping up a totally discredited Dutch colonial administration, was a great increase in V.D. throughout the Division. The men had no difficulty in buying the favours of the local ladies; a day's issue of cigarettes sufficed. Even the riflemen were quite well-off, for in addition to their pay, each received a 'ration' of Japanese paper dollars, which were still the local legal tender. It was a frustrating and soul-destroying time, and when we heard that the Battalion had been chosen to garrison the island of Bali, there was general rejoicing. There had been no insurrection there and the Balinese were Hindus like the Gurkhas. But it was not to be; a few days later we heard that the Australians were to provide the garrison and we were to return to Malaya.

I think an extract from the 3rd. G.R. Regimental History summed up our thoughts as well as theirs:-

'There was not a man who was not glad to see the last of this unhappy land and what, to them at least, had seemed its so unnecessary war.'

H.E. the Viceroy, Earl Wavell, wrote of the campaign:-

'Our soldiers went out there on an errand of duty and an errand of mercy. Their tasks have been rendered difficult by the action of extremists and lawless elements instigated by our Japanese enemies. It is these extremists which our troops have had to fight. The courage and discipline of Indian troops (mostly Gurkhas), attacked without provocation whilst rescuing defenseless women and children, and murdered while protecting peaceful citizens against mob rule, has been worthy of the highest standards.'

Kota Bharu in the state of Kelantan in N.E. Malaya was our destination. We sailed from Sourabaya in a tank-landing ship, the men en masse in the hold where tanks were normally housed, and the officers in tolerable comfort, several to a cabin. On arrival in Singapore, we disembarked at Keppel Harbour and went straight to the railway station and on to a troop train. The transfer took several hours and it was evening before we were ready to move. There was no chance to enjoy the delights of Singapore. A letter dated 26th. March, 1945, written home after we had arrived in Kota Bharu, describes the journey:-

'We eventually left Singapore railway station at 8.00 p.m. To say that the trains in Malaya are uncomfortable is to indulge in a considerable understatement. The Japs had, during the occupation, removed nearly all the rolling stock to Siam, leaving only the oldest of the old; it was into these latter that we squashed ourselves and left the island. It was a bright moonlight night and the temperature was perfect as I sat by an open window in pyjamas watching the scenery of Singapore, I won't say flashing by, but moving past at a sedate rate. The lights of Johore Bharu, as seen from the southern end of the causeway, looked magnificent. On we went through endless jungle until I eventually fell asleep. In the morning, having extricated ourselves from piles of coal dust which covered our bunks, we found ourselves in Kuala Lumpur (before the war, an east coast line had branched off at Gemas and made its way to Kota Bharu, but the Japs had taken up the rails to use on their infamous Siam railway). In K.L., a beautiful town and the seat of the British Military Administration, we changed trains and waited all day; but we were able to wash away the grime and sweat in hot baths at the Majestic Hotel. In the evening we set off in an equally frightful 'new' train, reaching Prai (opposite Penang) at about 9.30 a.m., where we again changed trains – a laborious business when you have 800 men and 20 tons of baggage. At midday we moved off, arriving at the Siamese border at about 9.00 p.m. Here, the Siamese driver and engine which was supposed to haul us through southern Siam had not turned up; so we had to wait for three hours until he did. And then the engine proved unable to pull us up the initial slope. So the train had to be split into two sections, which took an interminable age. By the following morning we were still in the depths of Siam, travelling very slowly along a permanent way, the lines of which were only approximately parallel with occasional switchbacks to liven the proceedings. We eventually reached the Malayan border, again on the east side of the peninsula, to find that the bridge, which the British had blown up in 1942, had not been made strong enough to carry our engine. So we had to languish in the boiling sun until an engine light enough to cross the bridge in safety had been found. Needless to say, this engine, being small, could only just pull the train and the remaining 30 miles of the journey was completed at a snail's pace, and we arrived at Palekbang, on the north bank of the Kelantan river, 12 hours late to find that we had to unload everything on to rafts to cross the river; and having done so, go seven miles in lorries to our barracks. So, as you can imagine, we were mighty glad to arrive. The journey from Sourabaya had taken six days, travelling all of every day and night.'

The barracks were wooden huts erected as temporary accommodation after the 1914/18 war, but they were infinitely better than anything the men had lived in for years and they were delighted. The officers were housed very comfortably in a large bungalow in the town.

Although at the time of the Japanese surrender the leaders of the Malayan Communist Party had come out of hiding, they soon realised that they were not going to get any vestige of official influence or power. So many of them, the leaders nearly all Chinese who had fought with Spencer Chapman, went back into the jungle; others took refuge in the comparative safety of Southern Thailand. Our reason for being in Kota Bharu was to keep an eye on their activities and prevent them from gaining any influence or control over any part of the State of Kelantan. Thus we had a company stationed at Yala in southern Thailand and another with platoon detachments at strategic points up the Kelantan River; and two in reserve which were able to do some much needed training.

The all-too-short three months we spent in Kota Bharu were some of the most enjoyable of my service. It was a delightful place and the east coast Malays were some of the most attractive of a truly charming people. The Kelantan royal family made us most welcome and many were the parties in the Mess and in the houses of the Mentri Besar (Chief Minister) and other relatives of the Sultan. The coastline of sandy beaches shaded by coconut palms, and the blue-green sea with its offshore jungle-clad islets, presented a picture of tropical paradise, especially vivid to those of us who had for so long seen so many dark and hellish scenes. We were sufficiently cut-off for Brigade and Division H.Q.'s to leave us alone. Our line of communication was a daily plane from Butterworth which brought us mail and an occasional senior officer, using his visit as an excuse to inspect the Beach of Passionate Love – a prototype complex of attap-roofed huts for holiday makers, the brainchild of one of the Sultan's brothers, and soon to be copied in many other places throughout the tropical world.

After a few weeks, we received news that this daily plane would no longer visit us as it was to be handed back to the Americans. I went to Penang on its last trip, describing my journey in a letter home:-

'We took off at 0800 hrs and flew a few degrees south of west. Stretching up to the north-west as far as the eye could see was the west coast of Malaya, and to the south the silver ribbon of the Kelantan River twisted its way through the rich green of the paddyfields and coconut groves, after emerging from the jungle-clad hills round Kuala Krai. Ahead was the dorsal range of the Malayan Peninsula, made strangely aloof from the rest of the countryside by billowing white clouds filling the valleys. At 6,000 ft. we flew steadily on as the clouds lifted to reveal the fantastic thickness of this tropical rain forest, which covers the mountains like a multi-green blanket and is the home of the aboriginal Sakai; here and there we could see their jungle clearings and little bamboo huts – oases with no apparent contact with one another.

'After about 40 minutes flying, we began to lose height and soon Penang Island – a green mountain in the blue Malacca Straits – loomed ahead. We sped across the stretch of water dividing the island from the mainland and then banked steeply to the left, dropping to a perfect landing on the Butterworth airstrip. After a breakfast, I caught the mail lorry to Sungei Patani, some 25 miles to the north, where a Battalion of 5th. R.G.R. was stationed.

'On the following morning I went to Penang to complete the business for which I had come (after all these years, I cannot remember what it was, but it was probably to do with our pending move to Sumatra). After returning to Sungei Patani in the afternoon, I had to decide how to get back to Kota Bharu, the choice being either by the Siamese railway – a ghastly prospect – or by road over the mountain track through Betong to Yala. I chose the latter and 5th. R.G.R. lent me a jeep and a driver.

'I set off at 1100 hrs. on the first stage of the journey, mostly through rubber plantations as far as Baling where the road turned abruptly east and started to climb towards the Siamese border about seven miles away. It was marked by the usual dilapidated raising gate with a small and equally antiquated customs house nearby. Geographically and ethnologically this area is, of course, Malayan but it has the misfortune to be under the jurisdiction of a corrupt administration in Bangkok. Here and there you are reminded of this by the appearance of some petty official wearing a German-style peaked cap supporting a badge, the size and magnificence of which is out of all proportion to the importance of the wearer.

'At Kroh we turned north again, heading for Betong along a steep and rapidly worsening road. I lunched in Betong with another Gurkha Battalion and there changed from the jeep to a 15 cwt. truck, which was far more uncomfortable, especially as it had started to rain in true equatorial earnest and the roof leaked. Some 35 miles of very hilly and rough driving brought us to Kampong, where a Gurkha company was stationed. I knew the Company Commander, as I had come out to India on the same ship in 1941, so I stayed the night there. Although he was living in a very remote place, he had an excellent bungalow belonging to a nearby tin mine, which at one time was managed by a European. Lying in bed at night in the middle of this vast expanse of jungle, listening to a myriad of sounds, was a pleasing experience. Most of the sounds were made by lizards and crickets, with the booming of bullfrogs as a frequent accompaniment. Occasionally there was a loud and eerie shriek of unidentified origin, perhaps a lemur or some such creature. At dawn the beautiful and haunting cries of green pigeons were a delightful alarm clock, accompanied by Bulbuls, Tailor-birds and Magpie Robins.

'At midday I set off again heading for Yala. En route we had a ferry to enable us to cross where the river cut through steep rocky hills. Lofty limestone crags jutted out from bamboo brakes in welcome contrast to the greenness of all else.

'We reached Yala at about 5.00 p.m. and I stayed the night there in the mess of a British Parachute Battalion. These Siamese towns like Yala bear a distinct resemblance to an 'away out west' ranching town in the U.S.A.; straight and dusty street, the houses on either side all built of wood and painted white. Gangsterism also prevails, although temporarily subdued by the presence of the British Army.

'After waiting a whole day in Yala, I eventually got away in a jeep fitted with railway wheels which ran on the ordinary narrow gauge track all the way to Palekbang. It was a strange experience speeding along in a jeep and not having to bother about steering. Sudden acceleration caused wheel-spin on the rails, and I had to hand in a key on a bamboo stick at signal boxes to ensure that I did not meet an oncoming train, but otherwise it was a trouble-free and exhilarating journey.'

As adjutant, I occasionally visited the companies stationed up the Kelantan River. For transport we had an ancient motor launch crewed by Malays, which chugged up the sluggish river at a very sedate pace, giving me ample time to observe the creatures of the jungle and to marvel at the enormous trees with their buttressed trunks clinging to the very banks and their huge branches dipping into the brown water. Over the chug of the engines, the 'whoops' of the gibbons could often be heard, reaching a gradual crescendo and then tailing off to be lost in the vast green canopy. White-breasted and Pied Kingfishers seemed to line the banks, perched on overhanging branches and plopping into the water to seize little fish. A loud whine of pinions would herald a pair of Great Hornbills flying just above the canopy, their heavy horned bills held clumsily on their long outstretched necks; and incessant above all other sounds was the whirring of cicadas. Little birds too flitted about; iridescent Sunbirds, Yellow Ioras, Spectacled White-eyes and Paradise Flycatchers, all in a restless quest for food.

Of an evening, sitting out on the verandah of a Company H.Q. bungalow on a bluff high above the river, as the sun sank below the distant purple trees, was an experience in itself. Small flocks of green pigeons would be flighting to their roosts from the fig trees where they had gorged themselves, and winging their clumsy way to the same trees would be hosts of flying foxes (fruit bats) uttering raucous cries. As the velvety darkness enveloped the jungle and the rising moon shone in reflection on the river, fireflies would twinkle like stars round the garden trees and the sweet scent of the frangipani would mingle with the cookhouse smells from behind the bungalow, where some 30 Gurkhas lived in outhouses and tents. House lizards, attracted by the light from pressure lamps, would scuttle up the walls and across the ceiling, snapping up moths and fighting one another for the choicest morsels; often, indeed, falling to the floor unharmed and dashing up the wall again to resume their quest. Weird and often unidentified calls would come from the encircling jungle: eerie shrieks, owl-like hoots, the constant din of cicadas and the winding up of the explosive 'tuck-too' of a lizard which we first heard in the jungles in Burma. As the night wore on, the Nightjars would start their monotonous tonking, never the same number of 'tonks' in each series, sometimes seven or more, often less, the irregularity being so constant that the Chinese use these calls as another mode of gambling.

Life for the men and the Company Commander was primitive but he was at least his own master and almost completely out of touch on any more immediate basis than a minimum of three days. Radio communication was most unreliable, for the jungle-clad mountains intercepted the waves and the ancient charging motors for the batteries could rarely be coaxed into more than a few minutes of gainful revolutions. Not that he had much to communicate; the country was virtually uninhabited, the few centres of population being timber camps manned exclusively by Chinese workers. It was these camps which supplied and gave succour to those members of the Malayan Communist Party who either had never emerged from, or else had returned to, the jungle. The Company's job was to keep an eye on the camps and try to find out about the movements of these subversive groups. It was not an easy task; patrols would visit the camps and talk to the workers through interpreters of doubtful loyalty and perhaps pick up a few scraps of information. But who would betray another of his race unprotected from the retribution which was sure to follow? For the patrol might only stay a night, to move on in the morning and not be seen again for many days.

Supplying these outpost platoons was no easy matter; days would elapse before rations reached the farthest flung, so fresh meat could not be sent. Live chickens went on their last uncomfortable journey, cabbages and brinjals reached the cooking pots somewhat shrivelled up, and even the rice often suffered a wetting from the torrential rain which cascaded upon the launch, adding to its leaking bilges. But the Gurkhas were not without resource when rations were scarce or of unavoidably poor quality; unfolding jungle fern fronds made excellent vegetables, jungle fowl eggs could be found by those who knew where to look, and the little mouse deer, no bigger than a hare, could be snared and curried better than goat. A month out in the jungle was no great hardship to men reared in the rigours of the Himalayan mountains. We never had any complaints.

I tried to improve the communications by using locally bought homing pigeons, much to the amusement and, as it turned out, the justified scepticism of my brother officers. Not one pigeon ever returned to my loft in Kota Bharu and I could not make out why. Trials from short distances were successful, but birds released from companies far up the Kelantan River were never seen again. Perhaps they were caught by raptors or just got disorientated amongst the jungle-clad mountains. At least the Gurkhas thought it was a good idea and were just as disappointed as I was when it failed.

CHAPTER 16

SUMATRA AND MALAYA

Life in Kota Bharu was too good to last. One Sunday, after we had been there for about three months, we were all down on the Beach of Passionate Love, lazing away the afternoon beneath the palms. Occasionally I opened my eyes to see Black-naped Terns plunging into the waves and rising again with little fish in their beaks. The flutey notes of Orioles rang out above the swish of the cool breeze in the casuarina trees. It was time for tea. A jeep drew up and an orderly brought me a message. We were to move to Sumatra in a matter of days. Forty-seven years were to elapse before I saw this beach again.

The same tiresome slow journey through Siam brought us eventually to Port Swettenham, where we embarked on H.M. Troopship *Dunera* for an overnight passage to the mouth of the Palembang River. There we transferred to barges which towed us several miles up to the jetties. Motor transport took us to Palembang, where we found ourselves within a wired perimeter encircling the main European section of the town. Our Battalion area included a lake and a huge Chinese graveyard, well shaded with mature trees. We were all, including the men, quartered in modern bungalows, with running water and electricity, the latter, however, of very uncertain reliability. But there was a claustrophobic feeling about the place, for no one was allowed outside the perimeter or more than 50 yards either side of the laterite road which ran out to the airfield, our chief line of communication.

We were sent there because the Japanese, who had been guarding the oil wells since their surrender, were due for repatriation; we were to take their place and, together with 3/4th. G.R. and a British Battalion, ensure the safety of the oil wells, which were threatened with destruction by the insurgents. It was the same old story as in Java; the myopic Indonesians were bent upon destroying their own precious assets and we, as disinterested

149

but increasingly 'fed up' parties, were there to stop them from doing so. I cannot recollect what our specific duties were, except that they were boring and seemingly pointless. But, as ever, the Gurkhas remained cheerful and well-disciplined.

In a house of one of the Japanese officers from whom we took over, I found a .410 shotgun and a box of dust shot. This find was greatly to relieve the boredom for Terence Phillips and me; we decided to make a collection of bird skins. I remembered the technique of skinning from pre-war days and I managed to persuade our M.O. to let me have an old scalpel and some surgical scissors, as well as some alum. The graveyard proved a fruitful hunting ground for the tree-loving species, and the road out to the airfield provided species which inhabited more open country. During the two or three months we spent in Palembang, we collected over 100 species, the smallest being an Orange-bellied Flower-pecker and the largest a Great Hornbill. This latter I shot one evening but had no time to skin it before other duties intervened. So in haste I pushed it into the mess fridge. Before breakfast the next morning, the mess orderly came to me, as Mess Secretary, carrying a pat of butter which was totally encased in reddish-brown avian mites which, as the carcass cooled, forsook the sinking ship, as it were, and made for the butter pat as a more attractive proposition. This mistake on my part refuelled the argument amongst some of my brother officers about the morality of our skin collecting. In retrospect, I suppose it was rather reprehensible, but in those days there was no apparent threat to any species and a bird in the hand was much easier to identify than one in the bush. Some of the more colourful skins I took home and gave to my brother for tying fishing flies (the male Jungle Fowl was a real prize for this) and for the others I had a cabinet made in which I kept them for several years until, when I was on leave, mice got in and destroyed them.

Eventually, as the Nationalist Government in Batavia or Jakarta, as it had then been renamed, gained control, the Indonesians were able to guard what had become their own oil well and our Brigade was able to leave. The troopship *Dunera* returned to take us back to Malaya. One of the companies had somehow managed to collect a litter of wild piglets – delightful little creatures which, although ultimately destined for the pot, were held in great affection by the Gurkhas, who were determined not to leave them behind. There had been strict orders banning any kind of livestock being taken aboard troopships, and the piglets' fate seemed sealed. But large cooking pots draped with sacks can contain more than rice and the eagle eye of the O.C. Troops, as he watched the cookhouse equipment being put aboard from a barge, saw nothing untoward. Next day, during troopdeck inspection, a little squeak from a life jacket locker revealed a piglet, but only one of a number. Our C.O. was ordered to search for others. However, to O.C. Troops' surprise, but to that of nobody else, none was found.

Our destination was Taiping, a delightful little town in the state of Perak. The Mess was in the old club on the edge of the main padang, and the men were housed in good barrack blocks. I had recently taken over command of D Company and I found myself on detachment at a place called Parit, not far from Ipoh. Our task there was to give aid to the civil power, invested in those days in the District Officer, a young man of about my age with the name of Staples, a scion of the family which started the spring mattress firm, and recently appointed to the Malayan Civil Service. I do not recollect that I had much contact with him, for there was little happening which the Police, the D.O.'s immediate support, could not cope with. We did occasional patrols in the remoter areas where the M.C.P. might be expected to exert some influence, but for the most part we tried to do some training with the newer weapons we were beginning to receive. Most evenings we went out shooting. Subadar Indrabahadur Khattri, my second-in-command, was an inveterate shikari and an excellent shot with his ancient 12 bore, taken from the Japs on some occasion or other. I had found a 16 bore as part of my 'loot' in Java, and we had both managed to collect a good store of cartridges of a variety of shot sizes, including S.G. and S.S.G. Indrabahadur needed no encouragement to organise shooting parties and I was always delighted to join them. Sometimes we went in search of Green Pigeons, whose evening flight path had previously been determined during patrols or training exercises. For these we required no beaters, but would go out in my jeep with one or two other Gurkha officers and some orderlies to 'pick up' in a following 15 cwt. truck. We then stationed ourselves across the flight line and waited. At first, as the sun started to sink, the pigeons came in ones and twos, and few got past the guns. Gradually, the numbers increased until there were often so many that scores flew past while we were reloading. We always came back with a good bag. At first I had difficulty in preventing the G.O.s from shooting sitting birds, for Green Pigeons were not the only quarry in their sights. Blue-breasted Button Quails were very common and it must have seemed only sensible to the Gurkhas, in the interest of cartridge economy, to bag as many as possible of the bevy on the ground with one shot. Likewise, if a pigeon sat on a tree within range, why not make sure of bagging it *in situ*? They were also inclined to shoot what one might call non-gamebirds such as Crow-pheasants and Slatey-breasted Rails, both of which are very common. But they soon learnt not to, at least when I was present.

Other more exciting shoots were the pig hunts. During the Japanese occupation, firearms control had been very strict; to carry an unauthorised weapon was a capital offence. In consequence, wild pigs had multiplied exceedingly and it only needed beaters to flush large sounders out of the lallang grass and lantana scrub. We used to set out with a platoon of Gurkhas and a 30 cwt. truck, again to places discovered during patrols, and divide the beaters into two parties; one each side of the selected area to meet and line up at the far end. At a given signal, usually a loud note blown through the barrel of a shotgun like a trumpet, the beaters would start to shout and strike the undergrowth with their sticks. A crescendo of excited yells would denote that a pig had been seen and we guns would release our safety catches. Soon a crashing amongst the bushes would bring excitement to a fever pitch and quite suddenly a grey form would come hurtling out of the undergrowth and cross the narrow path, giving but a split second for a shot. Many pigs escaped but we always came home with up to half a dozen. On one evening, which I still remember with pleasure, I bagged two with a right and a left. Although we were using S.G., some animals were, regretfully, only wounded and had to be followed up by blood trails. In the case of old boars it was sometimes dangerous and on one occasion a rifleman had the flesh between his thumb and forefinger torn by a boar's tusk.

Back at camp, the carcasses, following the removal of the entrails and edible offal, were put over fires to singe off all the bristles. They were then dismembered and roasted. The resulting meat was delicious, whether curried or not, although I never really appreciated the special 'delicacies' which my orderly brought me; fried stomach lining, burnt pieces of skin and other morsels spiced and salted beyond recognition.

It was during our stay at Parit that I became covered from head to foot in ringworm. The little local hospital took me in, quite unofficially, and first of all covered me with a purple dye. When that had no effect, they tried a yellow one which did enough to enable me to return to duty, although still acutely uncomfortable. Fortunately, we received orders to move to Lumut, a coastal town on the Straits of Malacca some 50 miles south of Penang. Opposite the town and a few miles from the coast was the island of Pankor, an idyllic place with sandy beaches, on which I was ordered to place a detachment. I included myself in the party and after a week or so of sea bathing and cool sea breezes, I began to recover my health and my morale. To look and feel so awful was an unnerving experience.

At that time Lumut was not more than a large fishing village with a few brick-built houses, but it is now a naval base and a very different place from where I had my headquarters in 1947. We occupied a building in the main street with a view to the river estuary, and we worked in close liaison with the local police and customs. The population was predominantly Chinese, and our designated task was to watch out for smuggling and subversion by the M.C.P. Perhaps we had a slight deterrent effect which may have helped in the process of getting things back to normal after the trauma of the Japanese occupation; certainly, the place remained orderly and peaceful all the time we were there.

Shortly after I recovered, our three most senior officers, Alec Harper, Reggie Twelvetrees and Terence Phillips, were all posted to the Staff College at Quetta, leaving me as acting C.O. for a period of a month or so. The Brigadier, De Burgh Morris, ex 8th. G.R., and the elder brother of Nigel Morris, later to be Commissioner of Police, Singapore, was very supportive, and I never had any difficulty with the higher command. The only thing which I remember about the sole visit of the Divisional Commander, Maj. Gen. Chapple, was the extraordinary fuss he made about the absence of a grease trap in the H.Q. Company cookhouse. The Company Commander, the Company Subadar, the Subadar Major and I were all admonished as though we had committed some heinous crime, putting the security of the realm at risk. A wink from the Brigadier let us know that we were forgiven. The General took little interest in anything else except the lunch which we gave him.

I was glad to see David Amoore and Peter Jones when they arrived as C.O. and 2 i/c respectively, for I was due home leave and could not go until I had handed over. This was completed by the end of May but I did not get permission to go home for another month. G.H.Q. quibbled about my right to have leave, saying in effect: 'You have been out east for more than six years, you should have gone home three years ago, you have no right to be here and thus you are not entitled to any leave'. It took many letters from the C.O. to sort out this nonsense, but I left Taiping at the end of June, spent a few days in Raffles Hotel in Singapore, and managed to book a seat on B.O.A.C.'s regular flying boat service to the U.K. Although the flight took the best part of a week, it was by far the quickest way of getting home in those days and much more restful than present day jetting. The plane took 20 passengers who were seated four to a table, two on each side as in a railway carriage. There was a bar and a little lounge up a small staircase and plenty of space to stretch one's legs.

Shortly after daybreak, we were ferried out to the aircraft from Clifford

Pier and climbed aboard. The four engines were started, one at a time, and we then 'sailed' in a leisurely fashion to the start of the take-off section of the harbour where we swung round in our wash, the wavelets lapping the cabin windows. After each engine had been tested at maximum revolutions, all four were opened up and we were on our way. At first the aircraft seemed to sink down in the water, which partially obscured the windows, but as the speed increased we rose up and the waves started to hammer against the hull until one wondered how it could stand the strain. More speed brought less buffeting and suddenly all was smooth as we lumbered into the air like a gannet full of fish. Slowly we gained height over Pulau Bukum and banked right-handed with St John's Island on the starboard beam. Gradually the peninsula came into view, fishing kelongs standing on stilts in the calm blue waters along the coastline of the Malacca Straits, and great white masses of cumulus clouds banking up out to the west over Sumatra. With a maximum ceiling of about 10,000 ft., and the clouds bubbling up to 20,000 ft. or more, the captain soon had to alter course to find a way through or over them. Thus we flew on skirting the cloud banks and occasionally entering the wispy edges for a little buffeting, emerging again to catch a glimpse of Penang Island, the tip of Sumatra and the white-flecked blue of the Indian Ocean. After about seven hours, the sea began to show signs of muddy silt from the Irrawaddy and we were soon losing height in our approach to Rangoon. We swooped over the city and planed down to the wide river, skimming the surface, a rushing sound growing louder as the aircraft settled down on the water.

After a night at Steele's Hotel, the second day's flight took us to Calcutta, where we landed on the Hoogly and were driven to the Great Eastern Hotel through squalid streets. Karachi was our next stop after the longest stage of the whole journey. As we flew for hours over parched and mainly rocky country in an aircraft designed to land on water, the captain assured us that he would rather make a forced landing on that sort of country in a seaplane than in one with wheels. Neither then nor at any time until the service ended did the occasion arise. We flew on sedately through a cloudless sky with a bump now and again as we hit convection currents from the baked country beneath.

Bahrain gave us a hot and airless night in the B.O.A.C. hostel on the sandy banks of the Gulf. We were glad to rejoin the plane in the clammy dawn and climb up into the cool air above the shimmering desert which stretched endlessly on all sides as we headed for Cairo. No sign of life did we see until we crossed the Suez Canal – a silvery ribbon etched in the brown sand – followed by the amorphous mass of Cairo's suburbs and suddenly the pyramids rising from the sand, and the Nile, brown and sluggish, down to which we swooped to land between two bridges.

Shepeards Hotel lived up to its reputation. Vast, with high ceilings, it swarmed with eager waiters clothed in white shapeless gowns and red-tasseled tarbushes. They seemed to anticipate one's every whim and in so doing expected constant baksheesh. Staying there was an experience, now gone for ever in fire and revolution.

A Nile bridge flashed just beneath us as we rose slowly above the city on the morrow and headed north-west over the pyramids and the sphinx to the Mediterranean Sea and our last night stop, Augusta on the south-west coast of Sicily. We knew we had left the East behind as we sat on the hotel verandah with white villas dotting the hills on either side and tall spire-like cypresses framing our view of the placid sea.

Poole Harbour was our journey's end after a flight up the Italian coast and across France, each mile of which became greener as we headed north. Then the Channel and our first sight of England; such a thrilling moment for a returning native, to be compounded by the rail journey up to London with all its familiar yet half-forgotten sights. To be transported 8,000 miles in but six days seemed almost unbelievable in those far-off days and it was no easier to comprehend as we drew into Charing Cross.

CHAPTER 17

CAN YOU HELP ME SAHIB?

I spent three months' leave at home, mostly in Northumberland, with a week's fishing holiday in Inverness. In August during my leave India had become independent and it seemed unlikely that the new Indian Government would wish its regiments to remain in British colonial territories. Added to this uncertainty was the future of British officers in Gurkha regiments and, indeed, that of the regiments themselves. When I reached Calcutta, on my return journey, I discovered that the Battalion had been ordered back to India and I was advised to go to Delhi and await its arrival. We had been posted to Khyber Barracks in the cantonment and the Battalion eventually arrived in a troop train which was 22 hours late. As it happened, we had returned to a land of increasing chaos and tragedy. Two letters, written in late October, 1947, which had somehow escaped the censorship imposed by the new Indian Government, give some idea of what we saw and felt:-

'I haven't received any letter from you this week – not surprising, considering the muddle which exists in this country at present. The administration seems to have broken down. We are having an awful time at the moment because we come under their Military Administration and they don't seem to know what they are doing. The escorting of Muslim refugees to Pakistan has fallen to our lot. I personally have not yet done any escorting, but the Bn. has been responsible for removing some 20,000 souls by train, two of the trains holding 8,000 each. On one train 10 people died and 4 babies were born. I saw a train being loaded and a greater concentration of human misery I never wish to see.'

'Another awful week; nothing but orders and counter orders. Twice we were told we were going to Kashmir and, thank goodness, twice it was

156

cancelled. The whole of India is in absolute chaos from an administrative point of view and they are now trying to fight a war in Kashmir. I am glad to see that H.M.G. has decreed that no British officer will be allowed to go there. None of us British officers can leave this Bn. because they haven't produced any Indian officers to take our place. We should have gone to our British Gurkha Bns. yesterday; I must say I shall be glad when we get there.

We have moved to a place called Gurgoan, which is about 20 miles south of Delhi, and tomorrow we start escorting a foot convoy of 40,000 Muslim refugees part of the way to Pakistan. During the last day or two we have been besieged by wretched Muslims who, seeing a white face for a change, think that salvation has returned and ask to be allowed to stay here. One old man came to me (he had served the British since 1914 in two wars) and asked me why, having served us for so long, he was being turned out of his ancestral home. It is impossible to make them understand that we British no longer have any say in matters Indian. Consequently, one feels thoroughly ashamed that we have let them down and that we are absolutely powerless to help in any way. If only the British public knew what is going on in India now they would hang their heads in shame. Tomorrow 40,000 people of all ages are being turned out of their homes near here simply because they happen to be Muslims (the same thing is happening to Hindus in Pakistan) and are being forced to march over 200 miles with as much of their possessions as they can carry. It is our thankless task to escort them on their way. I very much doubt whether half of them will survive the journey.'

Little did I realise when I wrote this letter that the people at home did not care two hoots about what was happening in India. They had been conditioned to think that the British in India had been repressors and that all that was required for the Indians' future happiness was the removal of the British from government. In fact, the departure of the British administration heralded a degree of massacre and misery never before seen even in Moghul times.

At one time my company of Gurkhas and I were given an open area of fields, without any shade or shelter, into which the Police herded thousands of Muslim refugees. Many were old and infirm, many were babies in arms, many were ill, some with smallpox; all were frightened and had been rendered homeless overnight. They had no food, were totally bewildered and without hope. From amongst them we sought out army pensioners and put them in charge of groups and sections; we provided them with basic rations and attempted to treat some of the less hopelessly sick. Those with smallpox were beyond our help, except that we were obliged to bury those who had died of this disease, for the relations would not own up to the corpses for fear of being excluded from the parties which we were putting on to the trains destined for Pakistan.

Each morning a long train would be shunted on to the line bordering the fields, to be surrounded by a struggling mass of desperate people whom we tried to control, at times even having to threaten to open fire. The police were supposed to supervise the loading and most of them made a real effort to do so, but on one occasion I caught a constable demanding a rupee from each passenger before he let them on the train. He had a knapsack absolutely full of rupee notes. I arrested him and took him to the local magistrate, who promptly let him go free. He was a Hindu persecuting a Muslim and thus he had committed no crime in the current state of affairs in the new India. But this was a very minor incident compared with what happened to refugees after they set out on their train journey. Crammed into the carriages like animals, hanging on the outside and sitting on the roofs, they faced some ten hours of travel in temperatures of 90 to 100F. They carried little or no food with them and no water. Unless there was an army escort with the train, commanded by a British officer, the station masters deliberately and with malice turned off the water. Thousands must have died of thirst and thousands more were butchered by gangs which ambushed unescorted trains.

It was a dreadful time, particularly so for us British officers of the Indian Army. We watched the biggest volunteer army in the world, one which had played a vital part in the war, disintegrate as Muslim companies of previously mixed regiments were disbanded or were sent to Pakistan; we saw Hindu companies, ousted from Pakistan, arrive in India bewildered and leaderless; and, most shaming of all, we were witness to loyal pensioners, forsaken by the army they had served, being herded amongst the refugees. In one respect we who served in Gurkha regiments were more fortunate than those in Indian units. At least, our battalions remained intact and the men were not Indian subjects with divided loyalties. I know of no incident in which a Gurkha unit behaved other than impartially, despite their being Hindus. Indeed, it is fair to say that had it not been for the Gurkha regiments in the Indian Army, the chaos and carnage would have been much worse. Yet, despite the loyal support which we gave the new Indian government, we were spied upon and our letters were opened. Our adjutant, Johnnie Johnston, writing to his mother, made some uncomplimentary remarks about the new rulers, and our C.O. was warned by a British officer at G.H.Q. that he was in danger of being arrested by the Indians. He was put on an R.A.F. plane that very evening bound for the U.K. – a sad way to end several years of active service with the regiment. At least he was spared the hurried and heartrending handover which was to follow his departure.

A week after our postings to Gurkha regiments which had been transferred to the British Army, ordering us to proceed 'with immediate effect', we still had no Indian officers to whom we could handover. Eventually, they started to come and I had but a few hours to hand over my company to Lt. Cariappa, who came from the Kumaon Regiment. He was very sympathetic and appreciated the emotional stress from which I was suffering. I felt that I was abandoning to the unknown men who had served me loyally through thick and thin. They were my friends of dangerous moments and happy times, some of them had saved my life, all of them had trusted me without question. What was I now to say to them? They had a fundamental distrust of Indians, in no way diminished by what they were currently witnessing, and now their future was to be placed in the very hands of these people. I do not remember what I did say but I do recall tears and lingering handshakes, accusing glances and a forest of waving arms as I was driven away out of their lives. No more than a few weeks later they were to fight in Kashmir under their new masters. Many of them were killed, including that most faithful of all, Subadar Indrabahadur. It took many years before these memories could be recalled without pain.

In August, 1947, four of the ten Gurkha Regiments of the Indian Army were transferred to the British Army; they were the 2nd. King Edward's Own Goorkha Rifles, the 6th. Gurkha Rifles, the 7th. Gurkha Rifles and the 10th. Gurkha Rifles. Who made the choices for transfer and why they were made, we were never told; neither were we given any choice about which regiment we were to go to. My posting was to the 2nd. G.R., which in any case would have been my choice. Their depot had also been in Dehra Dun and contacts had been close.

After the uncertainty and misery of recent weeks, it was an enormous relief to join my new regiment, 1/2nd G.R., at Santa Cruz, near Bombay. Here was stability again and a future amongst those most loyal and loveable of men in a regiment of long and proud tradition. Some half dozen of us came from the 1st., 8th. and 9th. G.R. and some of us were senior to officers of the regiment already there. This was due in part to many of the senior officers being away on leave and others, disillusioned by recent events, having retired or transferred to British Regiments. Contrary to our fears, we were received with marked friendliness by the officers and, in particular by the C.O., Gordon Richardson, and were in no way made to feel interlopers, which was generosity indeed. I found myself in command of

D Company and my first job was to move it, with the Battalion, to Poona where we arrived on Christmas Day, 1947.

Poona may be a joke name but it is a delightful place, especially in December, when the weather is cool and the sunshine constant. Our short stay there is one of my most pleasant memories of my service in India. We were busy with the reorganisation entailed by our imminent transfer to the British Army but there was time for shooting and each evening saw us out at one or other of the 'jheels' in search of duck. At that time of year enormous numbers of wildfowl migrate to India from northern latitudes, and the flighting we enjoyed with Mallard, Teal and Shoveler, as well as with native species, was remarkable. The mess cook was at pains to invent new recipes for the daily bag of wild duck. I was elected Mess Secretary and I was determined to maintain or even improve the standard of messing. Some months later there was a minor revolt over the cost of my menus. At a meeting of the committee I was reported to have said 'If you want to eat swill, so be it, but you will have to find another mess secretary.' They did, but I am sure we never ate swill.

Although the British and Indian governments had signed an agreement about the future of the Gurkha regiments, as mentioned above, the arrangement was one-sided; every man in regiments going to the British Army was to be given the chance to say whether or not he wished to be transferred, but none of the men of the regiments remaining in the Indian Army were allowed any choice. The reason was obvious; had the Indian Army regiments been allowed to 'vote' there would have been a huge majority in favour of the British Army. The agreement also included other restrictive measures aimed at reducing 'defection' to the British, such as keeping the rates of pay, pensions and leave regulations the same in both armies. In practice the patent inequity of pay rates being the same for those serving in Malaya and Hong Kong as for those remaining in India was resolved by a generous overseas allowance. Subsequent pay settlements were such that there has never been any shortage of Gurkha recruits for the British Army.

The 'Opt.', as it was called – each man giving his decision about future service – had to be conducted in all eight Battalions at the same time on the same day throughout India. Each Gurkha Officer and other rank had to come before a panel of the C.O., the Subadar Major and an Indian Officer of the Indian Army, to answer the question 'Do you wish to continue serving in the Indian Army or to serve H.M.G.?' Company Commanders were also present when their men were 'opting' and I watched with interest as they came in one by one. Almost all of them said 'H.M.G.' with enthusiasm; only those who were domiciled in India, such as clerks and some boys born in the lines at Dehra Dun, and by no means all of them, opted for India. Indeed, the proportion of the whole Battalion wishing to join the British Army was around 90%. In 2/2nd G.R., for reasons which no one really understood, the boot was on the other foot, with an opt. for India of over 80%. Most of the men of that Battalion had been prisoners of the Japanese in Malaya, for whom that country had nothing but bitter memories, and it was also possible that the Indian National Army's (I.N.A.) anti-British propaganda, to which they had been subjected, had influenced some of them. The opt. in 6th. and 10th. G.R. went quite well, but in 7th. G.R. things went badly with a very low percentage in favour of H.M.G. To some extent the result depended upon where the units were stationed at the time of the opt., and also greatly upon the attitude of the Gurkha Officers. The Indian authorities tried their best to persuade the men to vote their way and they had allies in Gurkhas Officers nearing pension age and with homes in India, who, whatever their private opinions, clearly had an interest in keeping on good terms with the Indians. This was particularly so in the 7th. and 10th. G.R., which recruited Limbus and Rais in E. Nepal and which had many Gurkha Officers born in or retired to Darjeeling. Another factor which affected the 7th. G.R. opt. was the advertised plan to convert the Battalions into an artillery regiment. This ridiculous decision to turn first-rate infantrymen into gunners found no favour with either the Gurkhas or the British officers and, within a year or so, the regiment reverted to its infantry role.

Apart from the fact that those regiments which opted badly lost many of their Gurkha Officers and N.C.O.'s, the setback was not serious for the Gurkha Brigade as a whole. There was no shortage of recruits and there was something to be said for starting afresh with men who had not known service in the old Indian Army. Furthermore, those officers who opted for transfer against the trend in their regiments were obviously staunch in their loyalty and formed an excellent cadre upon which to raise what were virtually new Battalions.

The opt. over, we were able to set about reorganisation with confidence and enthusiasm. The old Indian Army ranks were changed; the Subadar Major became the Gurkha Major; the Subadars Gurkha Captains; the Jemadars Gurkha Lieutenants; the Havildars Sergeants; the Naiks Corporals and the Lance/Naiks Lance/Corporals. As far as British Officers were concerned, the establishment remained the same, around 15 per Battalion;

but the 'amateur' quartermaster (any junior officer appointed by the C.O. for a spell of duty) was replaced by a long-serving professional attached from a British regiment.

New Year's Day, 1948 was when we became part of the British Army and I a seconded officer with a short service commission in the Rifle Brigade, replacing my emergency commission in the Indian Army. There was much administration to be done, such as filling in attestation forms for the Gurkha ranks, all of whom had to re-confirm their oaths of allegiance to the British Crown, and the inspection of all the arms in the Battalion by the Chief Civil Master Armourer (C.C.M.A.). Some 75% of the rifles had been made before 1917 and were thus barely serviceable. Nevertheless, they were bought by H.M.G. from the Indian Government in order to arm us until we arrived in Malaya. The advance party, which I was detailed to command, was due to leave for Singapore on 23rd, Jan., 1948.

CHAPTER EIGHTEEN

CHANGING ARMIES

The Advance Party, which consisted of two Gurkha Officers, 46 men and me, left Poona by train early on a Friday morning. Our first change was at Kalyan, where we had a scheduled wait of eight hours, but when the Calcutta mail arrived they gave us only ten minutes to load all the men and our kit; the result was complete chaos. Furthermore, I discovered that our coach had been booked only as far as Jubblepore and was to be detached from the mail at that station. When we arrived there on the Saturday evening, I tried to fit our party into the public coaches of the mail, but they were so full that it was impossible; we had to wait four hours for the Allahabad Express, on to which, with much pushing and shoving, we managed to squeeze ourselves. We arrived in Allahabad at 0500 hrs on the Sunday. When the Dinapur train came in some three hours later, I piled all the men into an empty coach at the rear marked 'For Minority Community Only' and then, to my horror, I discovered that this coach was to be taken off at Benares. There followed a hectic few minutes trying to cram the party into the rest of the crowded train; after enduring much cramped discomfort, we eventually reached Dinapur late that evening for an overnight stay and a chance to eat a decent meal. Without much more ado, we finally reached Howrah Station in Calcutta on the Tuesday morning, where we were pleased and not a little surprised to find two lorries waiting to take us to the empty workshop lines at Bhavnagar. Rail travel with a large party in the new India was stressful indeed.

There was to be no reduction in the pace of our progress; half our number were due to fly to Singapore on the very next day and there was much to be done in completing loading manifests and dealing with Indian officialdom. On the Wednesday, leaving Tony Wright, who had joined me in Calcutta, to bring the rest of the party later, I went to Dum Dum Airport at 2200 hrs.; but we did not take off until 0400 hrs due to fog at Rangoon, where we had a refuelling stop. Mingladon Airport was looking more than usually dilapidated, although the Shwe Dagon Pagoda was as impressive as ever from the air. The direct flight from Rangoon to Tengah R.A.F. Airfield was a very long one for a Dakota, the longest the Squadron Leader captain had ever done in that type of plane. In all, it took us 11 hours flying from Calcutta, and the whole journey from Poona just under a week.

I had expected that the Battalion would be housed in one of the relatively modern barracks in Singapore and that all we would have to do as an Advance Party, would be to 'March In' and generally adapt things to suit a Gurkha Battalion. Not a bit of it! When I went to see the G.O.C. on the morning after our arrival, I discovered that we were to go into a 'temporary' tented camp at Ulu Pandan – a hilly area of open scrub country where once a transit camp had been. I went out there to be greeted by a scene of desolation almost beyond belief. It had been raining for 24 hours without stopping, and everywhere was mud and water. The paths and tent standings had at one time been covered with roofing felt which was now full of holes and torn by the wind. The only permanent buildings were the officers' mess, some cookhouses with storerooms attached, and a row of wash-houses and latrines. There was no barrack accommodation or married quarters either for officers or other ranks. As I stood and contemplated these neglected, rundown acres, I felt angry and really let down by the British Army; and I suspect that the Gurkha officer who was with me shared my outraged opinion, but he said nothing other than to remark on the mammoth task which faced us; we had less than a month to build a camp.

A company of the Ceylon Pioneer Corps was put at my disposal and, on the whole, they worked very well, relieving us of some of the heavy work. Day after day was spent in erecting tents, often in the pouring rain; and often too, the tents would turn out to be defective and leaking, and down they would have to come. What surprised me was how cheerful the Gurkhas remained, for not only was the work hard and tedious, but the future prospect of living in this city of sodden tents could not be contemplated with much enthusiasm. I had found, during the war, that Gurkha soldiers could convert part of a wilderness into an oasis of comparative comfort when conditions made it necessary, but they could reasonably have expected something better than Ulu Pandan on joining the British Army. Nevertheless, the labour had its moments; almost the last thing we took over from the old Transit Camp was the Hindu Temple and, within minutes, one of the many adopted cats moved in and produced kittens – good luck, it seemed, for anything which suggests fertility can be interpreted as a good omen in the Hindu religion.

The only permanent married quarter was a converted gun emplacement – one of the sites of the famous guns which could only face seawards and were thus useless when the Japanese attacked from the land side in 1942. This was allocated to the C.O., Gordon Richardson. Three other officers, Monty Ormsby, Gordon Shakespear and Bill Scotter, were bringing their wives. For them we pitched large 4-pole tents with wooden walls and partitions to form a bedroom and living room. Behind them were semi-permanent bathrooms and loos connected to the main sewage system. Years later Bill Scotter became Commander-in-Chief of Rhine Army and one wonders with what strange nostalgia Jean, Lady Scotter, must have recalled her first married quarter when living in her grand house in Germany.

Single British Officers either had rooms in the Mess or tents with 'facilities', as did the married Gurkha officers. Married other ranks had similar tents but the latrines were communal. The bachelors lived six to a tent. Heavy rain and the occasional 'Sumatra' (strong off-sea winds accompanied by torrential rain) made life a bit uncomfortable, but on the whole everyone got used to the conditions. Rory Ormsby started life in his parents' tent and Nigel Shakespear came there at a very early age. As the months went by, the glaring deficiencies were made good and the camp became a model of contrivance and a worthy example of Gurkha ingenuity and adaptation. Few other soldiers could convert, with undiminished cheerfulness and good humour, a scrubby wilderness into a happy and contented township where for three years some 1500 men, women and children lived in good heart and health. They never once dwelt upon the undoubted slight given to their regiment and their race by the failure of the British Army to give them barrack accommodation on arrival in Singapore. Furthermore, from this far from satisfactory base the Battalion conducted highly successful operations during the early years of the Emergency.

During the first month as O.C. Advance Party, I had many other things to keep me busy. I was besieged by contractors vying with one another to supply fresh rations, tailoring, swill removal and so on. All offered bribes and other inducements. A Sikh seeking the swill contract, which was much sought-after by many, brought with him five chickens and 40 eggs. Those who won contracts always asked 'And what can I do for your goodself?' I was careful to accept nothing in any shape or form.

I spent the whole of one morning with the Chief Engineer, and some hours later with his officers, inspecting the draft plans of the new barracks which were to be built for us. Modifications were made at my suggestion but on the whole the plans were well thought out, and the final result, Slim Barracks, was vastly superior to anything we had in India. I used to attend the G.O.C. Singapore District's weekly conference, which I found both interesting and occasionally frustrating. Trivia often claimed our divided attention, such as an officer taking some of our time telling the General how slow the Military Forwarding Officer (M.F.O.) had been in sending on his kit, and similar matters of no import whatever. But I did find the District staff very helpful when I went to discuss various points of Gurkha administration. Naturally there was much ignorance about these matters, but it was ignorance freely admitted and the staff certainly had the Gurkhas' well-being at heart. At no time did I ever have any difficulty in persuading them to accede to my reasonable requests.

I did have some difficulty in finding a midwife to attend the Gurkha wives. Eventually, after many interviews, I found a pensioner nurse who used to work in the Kandang Kerbau civil maternity hospital. She, unlike other candidates who were unwilling to live in a tent, was happy to accept the same accommodation as her charges, and she was soon accepted by the families despite her modern methods.

One morning I went out to R.A.F. Tengah with the G.O.'s to watch a demonstration given by the latest jet fighter, the Vampire. It was the astonishing rate of climb which was so impressive, as indeed was the speed in level flight. The pilot made one run over the airfield at 480 m.p.h. which took our breath away. The Gurkhas were astonished beyond measure. The plane was in the Far East on exhaustive tests in tropical conditions.

I see from my diary of 18th. Feb., 1948 that Ulu Pandan, despite its early disappointments, had begun to grow on me:-

'This part of Singapore Island, Ulu Pandan, in spite of our canvas dwellings, has its attractions. It is undoubtedly one of the coolest parts of the Colony, as there is always a breeze either from the Malacca Straits or from the China Sea. The view too is lovely. To the west are the blue waters of the Straits with the islands of the Riouw Archipelago dotted here and there. To the north is the tip of the Malay Peninsula, green and hilly, and to the south are the rooftops of Singapore City, with landmarks such as the Cathy Building as well as the great oil storage tanks.'

One morning I was telephoned by Singapore District and asked to write a speech of welcome for the Governor, Sir Franklin Gimson, to make on the

Battalion's arrival. I was not so presumptuous as to write it word for word, but merely presented him with a number of facts about the regiments' history which he subsequently strung together to form an excellent speech. As the time for the Battalion's arrival drew near, I started to receive a succession of contradictory signals about the personnel aboard R.M.S. *Strathnaever*. One message would include 1/2 G.R. on the manifest, the next would not; and so it went on for days, making one wonder how any organisation could be so inefficient.

The *Strathnaever* arrived in the Western Anchorage on the afternoon of 13th. March, 1948, and I went out on the Embarkation Staff launch to meet the Battalion. The 2/10th. G.R., commanded by George Bolton, was also on board bound for Hong Kong. On the following morning the ship docked at Keppel Harbour and the Governor welcomed the Battalion officially. He read his speech, passages of which I recognised, and General Charles Boucher, Maj. Gen. Brigade of Gurkhas, translated it into Gurkhali. The Police Band played incidental music and, later, the Pipes and Drums of the Seaforth Highlanders marched and counter-marched on the dockside. It was altogether a very colourful welcoming ceremony.

After a day or two at Ulu Pandan, there was a feeling of great depression in the Battalion. Something better than tented accommodation had been expected. I told everyone that I too had felt much the same at first but had later begun to appreciate the advantages. As I have mentioned before, time and hard work converted the place into a tolerably comfortable base, with airy tents much cooler than stuffy barracks and a hilly terrain not unlike a village in Nepal. In later years it was talked about with something like affection.

Some diary extracts, written at this time, are, perhaps of interest:-

'Over to Nee Soon this morning with the C.O. to look at the accommodation proposed for the Regimental Centre. Most of the people there were fairly callous, an exception being the Q.M., an old soldier, who was most outspoken about the lack of proper arrangements for the G.O.'s families. One of the officers going there is a V.C., Capt. Lalbahadur Gurung, who certainly deserves proper consideration.'

'To a cocktail party at Brig. Sparks' home. I didn't know a soul there but they were all very friendly. One good lady was complaining bitterly because the Padre kept a pet python, which had just eaten her cat. She lives out on Blakang Mati island, her husband being in the Malay Coastal Battery stationed there.'

'The first lot of families arrived today on the S.S. Rajula from Madras. At the best of times this ship is filthy and the uncongenial atmosphere this trip had been further sullied by the fact that the Captain had been unable to make his usual 'packet' on excess deck passengers and was consequently in poor humour. The Gurkha officers' wives refused to leave their cabins and feed in the dining saloon; as a result the cabins could not be cleaned.'

'Went round the shops with a G.O. this morning, with a view to spending our £190 amenity money which must all be used up by the end of the month. The novelty of many things in the shops quite surprised the G.O. He was keen to buy himself an egg-whisk to stir his dhal; other expensive items which took his fancy included an electric gramophone and a patent vegetable pressure cooking pan.'

In May, 1948 I went on a month's leave. We left R.A.F. Tengah, the only airfield then able to take large airliners, in a B.O.A.C. 'Constellation' at 0800 hrs., and flying at 20,000 ft., we reached Calcutta seven hours later. It was dreadfully hot there and we were glad to leave, after a two-hour stop, for Karachi where we arrived after a five-hour flight. Next morning, after an uncomfortable night in the B.O.A.C. Hostel, which was no advertisement for the airline, we took off for Basra. When we arrived there five hours later, the temperature was 130°F and, owing to a cholera epidemic, we were confined to one small room where, for the first time in my life, I was badly affected by the heat. I soon recovered when we got back on to the plane, but I was glad to get to bed in the Heliopolis Palace Hotel when we arrived in Cairo at 1830 hrs. On the third and final day of the flight, our first stop was at Castel Benito in Tripoli, from where it took seven hours to reach Heathrow. The custom officials there were very doubtful about my Palembang bird skins, some of which I had brought home for fly-tying. Eventually they let me take them in. A night rail sleeper to Alnmouth in Northumberland completed my three-day journey – half the time it took in the flying boat barely a year previously.

I much enjoyed my leave. I played a lot of golf and I joined my parents on a holiday in Scotland, staying at the Stronvar House Hotel at Balquidder, which had rods on several lochs. The fishing was not particularly good but the picnic places were delightful. My leave ration of five gallons of petrol made this holiday possible.

I returned to Singapore at the end of June by the same route. We were delayed a whole day in Cairo by engine trouble, which gave me the chance to go out to the pyramids and the Tombs of the Kings. We had a four-hour stop in Karachi and I was interested to find that the complaints we all made about the hostel there on the homeward journey appeared to have borne fruit; everything was excellent, especially the food. The final stage of the flight over the Bay of Bengal was extremely bumpy, but we were not delayed and I was only a day late returning from leave after a journey of 16,000 miles.

The Author with his orderly, Rfn. Yembahadur Chhetri, in 1948.

A painting by Felix Lewis, now in the Senior Police Officers' Mess, Singapore, of Yembahadur as a Piper in the Gurkha Contingent in 1958.

P.C. Yembahadur and his family in Singapore, 1961.

Yembahadur in retirement in Darjeeling, with his wife and daughter in 1993.

CHAPTER NINETEEN

THE FRAGILE PEACE BREAKS DOWN

Although I had been away only a month, I found that the security situation in both Singapore and Malaya had deteriorated drastically. My diary of 7th. July, 1946 records:-

'The Communist threat to Malaya is very considerable although its real extent is impossible to gauge from official statements, which naturally will not admit to a situation which the government should never have permitted to exist. The topography of Malaya lends itself to warfare by small bands of terrorists having local knowledge and innumerable spies and sympathisers. It is going to be awfully difficult to stamp it out.'

How right I was! Almost a decade went by before the Communists were beaten.

An emergency was declared and our Battalion was one of the units responsible for the internal security of Singapore, Keppel Harbour being my company's responsibility. The crucial V.P.'s (Vital Points) there were the three dry docks with their huge mechanical gates, which were as vulnerable as they were difficult to mend. We carried out a number of exercises in conjunction with the Police, such as a raid on a squatter area near Bukit Panjang, when 375 people were rounded up, including the local schoolmaster, who was found to have a Japanese helmet, detonators and subversive literature in his school. But by the middle of August the situation up-country had become so bad that the Battalion was ordered to South Johore.

On the 15th. of the month I went up to Kluang, some 70 miles north of Singapore, to meet the C.O. of the Seaforth Highlanders, under whose command I was to operate. I was ordered to set up my H.Q. on the Rengam

174

Estate and operate in the area 'intensively'. The Company arrived on the following afternoon and almost immediately I was asked to send a guard to Layang Layang Police Station to reinforce the flagging morale of the men there. No sooner had I done that when the phone rang and a detective told me that there were some bandits about half a mile from my H.Q. I went out with ten men but we failed to find anything, although we arrested a Chinese who was thought to be behaving suspiciously.

During the following day I visited the rubber estates in my area and found that the planters were having a very hard time. They had to be planters all day and policemen all night. One of them had his car shot at that very night on the Layang road, so I took out an ambush party next evening. We sat concealed on a track some five miles south of Rengam but saw nothing; on the way home we arrested a Chinese whom the detective with us suspected of being implicated in a double murder. The trouble was that one never knew whether these Chinese detectives were making genuine arrests or were merely paying off personal scores.

A few evenings later, I set out on an operation in the Bukit Jintan area. We had received information that there was a bandit H.Q. in an old sawmill there. We split into two parties, I with one and the O.C.P.D. (Officer in Charge of Police District) with the other, planning to meet at dawn. Unfortunately, the OCPD's party lost its way and came down the track on which I had set an ambush. Some shots were fired before we realised who they were and as a result of this debacle surprise at the sawmill was lost and we abandoned the operation.

When I returned to my H.Q. I found that the Sembrong Estate had been attacked during the night and the factory had been burnt down. A European assistant manager from a nearby estate had been shot and killed as he came to give assistance. In addition six estate workers had been killed and 15 wounded. The attackers, estimated to be 100-150 strong, were reported to be very well organised and had two Bren guns as well as a Tommy gun, Jap rifles and revolvers. They were dressed in jungle-green uniforms and carried packs.

There was little we could do about it; it was a situation typical of the difficulties which we faced at that time. We had to act on information which we received from the police, such as that about the sawmill, and so often either misinformation or police inefficiency drew us away on wild goose chases, rendering us unable to respond to genuine emergencies. In this instance we returned to base after having only about the equivalent of two nights in bed out of five, and I could not go on pushing the men or myself beyond a certain limit. Later that day I was awakened to learn that we were to be relieved by the Devon Regiment and move south to Pontian Kechil under command of 1/10th G.R.

Two extracts from my diary, written whilst we were at Rengam, show that there were other interests:-

'The oil-palm estate at Ulu Remis is an amazing place. The yield is about 1,000 tons a month and the present price of vegetable oil is just over $200 a ton. Rats are incredibly numerous amongst the palms and the estate pays 5 cents a tail for each one caught. The average payout per month is $500-10,000 rats. I noticed that snakes were very numerous too, presumably preying upon the rats.

'This morning I took out a platoon patrol into the jungle at the back of Rengam Estate. Whilst we were filing along a path through the primary jungle, a ten ft. python fell from a tree on to the ground at my feet. It quickly made off into a nearby stream. On another path I noticed two little white eggs in a sort of nest, and bent down to investigate. I was surprised to find a flying lizard sitting by them, quite fearless and determined not to move; in fact it tried to bite me.'

I took over my new area on 24th. August; one platoon at the Pontian Waterworks, one at Pontian Kechil and one at the Linden Estate where I had my H.Q. The waterworks was very important as it supplied most of Singapore. At that time work was in progress on a tunnel through the mountain, Gunong Pulai, to tap the watershed north of the range. They were about halfway through after nine month's work. On the night of our move, Amber Estate, in another company area nearby, was attacked; the Tamil dresser was killed and several workers were wounded. The attack was carried out by masked men in civilian clothes, who communicated with one another by bugle calls. They numbered 20 to 30, armed with rifles and Stens and at least one Bren.

A day or two after our arrival an operation was planned called 'Soccer' – a series of sweeps to try and flush out bandits reported to be in the area. We had little hope that much of value would result as the bandits' intelligence service was vastly better than ours. They were ruthless in their dealings with anyone who informed against them. In fact, while I was out arranging Operation Soccer, I heard that a Malay informer had been murdered by three Chinese four miles from my H.Q. and this information was 15 hours old when I received it.

We started the operation at 0500 hrs. with a sweep through a wide area of lallang scrub and marsh. Nothing was found but I heard a loud beating of tins in the area just after we started, which was probably a warning signal. One of the English stretcher bearers attached to us came to me and said he had been bitten by 'one of them snakes with yellow legs'. As he seemed in good health and only nipped, as it were, the creature must have been a large centipede, the bites of which are painful but not dangerous.

The second phase of the operation involved placing platoon patrols in selected places; all mine were out next morning by 0900 hrs. and I visited two of them. One had seen a very large tiger pug mark seven inches in diameter, another had shot a twelve-ft. python and also a gibbon. I was angry with them for shooting this inoffensive primate and ordered them not to do it again. One of the early morning sounds in these jungles was the whooping calls of these gibbons – a wonderful chorus passed from one group to another, echoing round the hills.

On the morrow, we went to an area where a group of bandits were reputed to have a hideout in an overgrown rubber plantation. We found it, a low hut, and the bandits ran out into the thick undergrowth nearby where we tracked them down. Three of them, two women and a man, were wounded and captured. Thus we ended this operation with this very modest but hard-won success. That evening we returned to Ulu Pandan for a rest.

During the operation I had attached to me a Chinese gazetted officer from the Singapore Police. I found his help invaluable as he could recognise all types of Chinese at a glance – something which I never found the Federation police officers could do.

Some diary extracts written during our short rest period are of interest:-

'Had an interview with Singapore's Commissioner of Police concerning the proposed raising of a Gurkha flying squad. I might be asked to raise it.'

'A piece of Kipling's Gunga Din should be quoted at the Ordnance people: "The uniform he wore was nothing much before and rather less than 'arf o' that behind." They lay down that the life of a P.T. vest is eight months in this climate. They should come and see them after only two. They also say that the life of a gym shoe is 20 months; I have seen one become unserviceable after one game of basket ball.'

'A Gurkha child undergoing a minor operation in the British Military

Hospital (B.M.H.) died under the anaesthetic today. At this stage of our joining the British Army it is a blow to Gurkha confidence in the R.A.M.C. which will merely reinforce the Gurkha womens' fear of hospitals.'

After three weeks in Singapore, we were ordered up country again to relieve Alistair Langland's company at Kulai. I went with marked lack of enthusiasm. I found these operations extraordinarily frustrating and very exhausting. My Gurkha officers, extremely competent though they were operationally, spoke no English and thus, being on my own, all liaison with the British units and the Police was my job and mine alone; I had to be everywhere at once and on constant call. There was no mess and I had to eat what my inexperienced, but extremely willing, orderly cooked for me; fare soon began to pall. Even on the day I took over we had two false alarms and an order to mount an operation early the very next morning. It went very well as far as troop movements were concerned, but there was no sign of the enemy. The informer, having failed to produce the armed bandits he promised, started to accuse some of the estate coolies of collaboration, which raised a storm. Finally, the Gurkhas ducked him in a stream and he admitted that he had made it all up.

That afternoon the assistant manager of the Kulai Yong Estate was fired on by 12 Chinese while driving along the estate road. They were evidently surprised, for they left behind a full Tommy gun magazine. A couple of days later, at 0200 hrs., we were woken by shooting near the Kulai Besar Estate factory, both rifle and automatic fire. But the shots did not appear to be aimed at anything and the whole incident was a mystery. Maybe two bandit parties met one another and opened fire in error. But no sooner had the investigation into this incident been completed, when on that very evening, violent firing started from the direction of the Senai Estate. I rang up to ask what was happening and the manager said 'Come quick, we are being attacked'. We rushed over there to find complete calm. Apparently, an employee of the estate had come home drunk after curfew and one of the Special Constables had opened up, followed by all the others. Such were the frustrations.

There was no doubt that the extensive illicit rubber tapping, which was rife on all the estates in my area and elsewhere, was providing cash for the bandits. The squatters who lived near the estates were tapping in the furthermost and least frequented parts of the plantations and were using the cash from the sale of the latex to cover the extortion demands of the Communist bandits. It was virtually impossible to stop it, and it was not until years later, when the squatters were collected together into protected villages, that this source of cash, and indeed food, was denied the bandits. In this way, in particular, were the cards stacked against us in the early years of the emergency. We were lucky that this spell of duty was interrupted by a three-day break for the Dashera celebrations, for which we all returned to Ulu Pandan. This occasioned a *cri de coeur* in my diary:

'Returned to Singapore this morning from Kulai Besar. It is always depressing to arrive back and find that no one is in the least interested in what one has been doing. One works really very hard indeed, in fact one is on duty for 24 hours a day, and no one in Battalion H.Q. is really in the least interested nor cares what has happened or realises what one has been doing.'

After this brief rest, which, I suppose, we were lucky to get, considering the state of affairs up country, I returned to S. Johore and again set up my H.Q. on the Linden Estate, this time in what must have been the assistant's bungalow. I occupied the back verandah of the building, which was nice and cool with a view across the well-tended garden. The rest of the H.Q. staff disposed themselves in various rooms of the house and we were all very comfortable. The manager and his much younger wife were most kind to me and quite often asked me to dinner with them. They were, of course, glad of the protection which our presence gave them, but this solicitude for the comfort and well-being of us all was far beyond anything which we could do for them. Such could not be said of many of the estates on which troops were stationed.

The wildlife which I watched from my verandah was a welcome diversion from the wearisome task on hand. Occasionally I was able to have a leisurely breakfast when I could watch the Sunbirds flitting amongst the hibiscus blossoms, sometimes accompanied by Orange-breasted Flowerpeckers. Once I watched a pair of flying lizards feeding on trees not many feet from where I sat. They climbed to the top of the bole of one tree, picking up insects the while, and then vol-planed down to the base of the next. Their flight was remarkably well controlled and the alighting very gentle. In flight their bodies were arched like ducks settling on water and their tails were depressed between their legs. They had flexible sacks beneath their chins which they constantly inflated and deflated, probably a method of keeping cool.

In the evening, when Gurkha Captain Pirthilal Pun would often come and have a drink, we would watch the fruit bats flighting to their feeding trees and listen to the tonking of the Nightjars, as the velvety darkness swallowed up the distant jungle-clad hills and the fireflies starting twinkling in the crowns of the garden trees. Pirthilal would tell me tales about wildlife in Nepal, some more probable than others. Leeches in Malaya, he said, were nothing compared with those in his village. They were called 'Bhainsi jhukas' (buffalo leeches) because they were enormous and often entered and clung inside the nostrils of water buffaloes. The only way to get rid of them was to take the animals to drink, when the leeches, also thirsty, would poke their heads out of the nostrils and could then be snipped off with scissors. The Jungle Fowl which we often heard crowing in the morning, reminded him to tell me about their action in Nepal when a family is disturbed; the chicks immediately seize a leaf in their feet and lie on their backs, completely hiding themselves. I have never seen this happen but certainly young partridges and quails are adept at hiding themselves.

Pirthilal was a tremendous help to me during the year or so that we operated together in S. Johore. He was a natural leader, gaining immediate respect and obedience. He advised and supported me in everything we did and I never had a moment's qualms about any of my operational or administrative orders, discussed beforehand with him, being unsound or unreasonable. Later he became Gurkha Major of the Battalion, and years later still, in 1977, long after he and I had retired, we met at a reunion in Hong Kong. He died in Nepal in 1984.

Back in the Pontian and Glang Patah area again, I decided that I should have a look at it from the air and I arranged a flight in an Auster light aircraft. Flying low at a comparatively slow speed, I obtained a very good idea of the lay of the land and I was able to see how much change there had been in the general appearance of the countryside since my 1928 maps had been made. The biggest change was in the vastly expanded area of rubber plantations, as well as improvements to the roads.

On 19th. October, I heard an astonishing piece of news. A Japanese had come out of the jungle to give himself up at the Johore Bharu police station. He had been in hiding since the surrender in 1945 and said he was now 'fed up with it'. That he could remain hidden for so long, with presumably all hands turned against him, showed how difficult was our task of dealing with the bandits, who had the support, albeit through fear in most cases, of many local people.

We spent five weeks in the Pontian district searching patches of jungle, deserted squatter areas and pineapple plantations. Often we found hideouts, some long disused, others only recently vacated, the occupants presumably warned of our approach. Now and again the murder of an informer or sniping at night on a rubber estate would find us dashing here and there in futile attempts to contact the culprits. Then for a day or two, a combined operation of several units would carry out a sweep of a more extensive area with, perhaps, a brush with some bandits. But for the most part there was little change in the situation. The planters lived behind barbed wire and somehow managed to continue running their estates, protected by Malay special constables in the charge of Police Lieutenants, late of the defunct Palestine Police. The main roads were safe to travel on, the minor roads less so, and estate roads in some areas were dangerous to use unescorted. Life in the villages went on with apparent normality but there was much intimidation – too much for anyone to give us any useful information. We floundered about, just holding the line, but could see no end to the emergency as long as the squatters, much too scattered to control, could continue to feed and succour the bandits.

With all this patrolling in largely uninhabited areas, there was much of a natural history interest to be seen. One morning after a night spent in thick jungle on the edge of a pineapple plantation, I was delighted to see a number of Great Hornbills. They were calling to one another, a weird bovine sound, before they flew off on loudly whining pinions. Also in the trees, sitting high up in the canopy, were some completely black monkeys with very long tails, possibly dusky leaf monkeys.

On 7th. December, we were detailed to take part in 'Operation Hammer and Sickle' under command of the Seaforth Highlanders, in the Segamat area. I drove up there via the Muar Ferry, a distance of about 150 miles, and Tony Wright, with the Company, arrived on the following day; we all settled into a very reasonable camp at Batu Anam. After visiting some of the estates in the area in search of information, we planned two 'ops' for the morrow. The first started at 0300 hrs. and we reached our objective at first light. The bandits had gone but the hideouts were there and we burnt them. Two days later one of our Chinese informers was murdered by a party of seven bandits only two miles from our H.Q. His wife and grandchild were both seriously wounded by bayonet stabs. Small wonder it was difficult to get information when even women and children were subjected to such savagery! Nevertheless, another informer came and told us that he knew of five men living in houses on the edge of thick jungle who might be able to help us catch the murderers. We picked them up in the evening and Jock Neill, the O.S.P.C., persuaded them to talk. One of them 'agreed' to lead us to a camp some three miles from the Batu Anam-Jementah Road.

As we approached the camp shortly before dusk, a bandit sentry saw our leading section and fired two bursts of Sten. We rushed into the camp but the birds had flown. There were 19 huts, a stage, an armourer's shop, a school, dining halls and a kitchen. Cooked food for about 50 men was ready, steaming in pots. There were two parade grounds and targets attached to trees for weapon training. Here and there were posters displaying, in Chinese and Javanese, such exhortations as 'Fight the British until Victory' and 'Russia is the only Country where Men are Really Free', and suchlike faint hopes and gross falsehoods. I thought it a good idea to discomfort the bandits further after our return to camp, so I asked for an air strike on the adjacent jungle whither the bandits had fled. Two Spitfires strafed the area on the following day.

The next few days produced nothing much, but on one patrol we were attacked by a swarm of savage bees. Their stings were excessively painful and I received five of them. It was lucky that there were not bandits about at the time as chaos was complete, with everyone dashing about trying to escape the buzzing hoards. Oddly enough, on the same patrol, we found a huge hornet's nest in an old squatter's hut. By burning the hut we were able to obtain the nest, which had five stories. The Gurkhas extracted the grubs which they subsequently ate. We also came across the tracks of several elephants, one of which was of considerable size. The spoor was near a stream in an area of young rubber and only about six miles from the main Muar-Segamat road. At that time both elephants and tigers were not uncommon in South Johore; there can be few if any there now.

Out shooting that evening, round the reservoir on the South Senarut Estate, I saw an iguana surface near a White-breasted Waterhen and pull it under the water. Both on this estate and at Batu Anam, Red Jungle Fowl were very common. One evening a cock bird came to the camp and was seen to mate with one of the Company chickens.

A few days before Christmas we started to have some real success. On 22nd. December, Tony Wright, with 7 Platoon, led by a guide, crept up on a bandit camp and saw five men in uniform standing talking in a hut. A grenade was lobbed into the hut, killing one bandit instantly whilst the others ran for their lives into the surrounding paddyfield. The excitement was too much for some of the recently-joined riflemen and it took some time to calm them down and stop them firing. By that time the fleeing bandits were some 200 yards away struggling waist-deep in the muddy water. Rain was hissing down and bouncing off the water, and mist swirled over the field. The Bren gunner was sure that he had hit them all but visibility was so bad that this could not be confirmed. A search of the camp revealed an unwounded and very frightened bandit, who surrendered with his bugle and became very talkative. He said he was a member of 21 Troop which had been in the camp for three months, and the man killed by the grenade was the deputy leader. The following morning a further search of the area was made and another dead bandit was found in a nearby squatter's hut; presumably one of the party which had been fired on while crossing the paddyfield.

Our luck was to hold. On Christmas Eve the captured bugler agreed to lead a platoon to a camp where he had once lived, saying that he was able to show us a route which by-passed the sentry point. The going turned out to be extremely laborious through thick undergrowth, with the final approach through water chest-high. Unfortunately, there was only one bandit in the camp, quite unaware that the Gurkhas were only a few yards from him. He was wearing uniform topped by a blue Trilby hat. He was despatched with all the humanity that five Sten guns can command. Perhaps we should have lain doggo for a while in the hopes that some of his companions might return to the camp, but the excitement of actually finding an armed enemy at the end of a tedious march was not easily controlled. The camp, with accommodation for 30, had been partially dismantled, the wooden bed-boards and stocks of food already removed. The inmates had probably heard the firing two days previously and had decided to leave.

Christmas Day, 1948 was more than usually unreal – hot and sticky and far removed from family and friends. After drinks with the G.O.'s, Tony Wright and I had lunch with the Seaforths and then went and arrested a communist agent in Jamentah. The police questioned him and, on Boxing Day, he agreed to take us to an ambush position. When we got there he became frightened, sat down in the long lallang grass and refused to go any further. In a voice of despair he announced that to go on would mean certain death and to go back certain torture. Having made this profound statement, he bit off the end of his tongue. The resulting haemorrhage was so severe that we were obliged to return to base; not that we could have had much success without his guidance. Nevertheless, after hospital treatment, and much to our surprise, he said he would show us a house where three Communist agents lived. We went there and arrested three men. One of them was so shaken when he saw his betrayer that he agreed to take us to a camp the next morning. It turned out to be empty, but it had accommodation for 40 and a large well-stocked vegetable garden; it was obviously well-established and only recently vacated.

The operation ended 30th. December. The results had been good by the standards of those early days. We had certainly stirred up the bandits and dispersed them, but with so little reliable information to go on, the whole exercise had been like a game of blind man's buff.

We returned to Singapore on the second day of 1949, and as we passed Kulai Police Station I noticed two corpses lying on the lawn. They were bandits killed in another operation by our Battalion. One of them was a much-wanted leader.

We had a week in civilisation, during which I sold my ancient Morris 8 and bought a new Citroen 15, and held a Company nautch in honour of winning the volleyball competition, during which two men poisoned themselves by drinking tea poured into a jug taken from the M.I. Room. They were laid low within minutes but recovered in hospital in a matter of hours.

Back in S. Johore again, I set up my H.Q. in the Pineapple Factory at Glang Patah. Although, by virtue of being in the back of beyond, this was strategically a good place from which to operate, the 12-mile laterite road from the main highway always presented us with the possibility of ambush by bandits, and thus vehicles had to travel in pairs, adding to the problems of getting about. The factory was a pleasant cool place at night but my sleep was often disturbed by civet cats which lived in the roof.

One of the first operations we mounted from this place was by launch up the Sungei Pulau to Kampong Redang. On the way we came across some Orang Laut (Men of the Sea), a race of Malayan aborigines. They were living in a little shack by the river mouth; all the children seemed to have reddish hair and the adults had sloping foreheads above rather dull-witted faces. Needless to say, when we fired our 3 inch mortars at a supposed bandit hideout, they were terrified.

We spent many days patrolling and searching jungle, scrub and plantations in the Glang Patah area but found little except illicit stills and stale evidence of bandit occupation. Just when I was due for three week's leave, I was ordered to take the whole Company up north to the notoriously 'bad' jungle area near Poh Lee Sen. After we arrived there, I was taken right back to the Chindit days when we settled down in a bivouac near a woodcutters' kongsi some miles from the nearest road. Lying down on the ground on a mattress made by my orderly from bamboo leaves, with the pinging of mosquitoes often drowning the grating of cicadas, I could see the stars twinkling through the gaps in the tree canopy and half imagined I was back in

Northern Burma. There was no pleasure in recalling those days; indeed, I wondered why, in this time of peace, I was again lying out there under the stars; there were surely better ways of living one's life. And yet, as I listened to the Gurkhas chatting as they smoked their issue cigarettes, I was forcefully reminded of how privileged I was to be serving with them, and at once felt there was a purpose in what I was doing. They never questioned their role, they never complained about being sent here and there at a moment's notice or feared the dangers which they faced. They had solemnly promised to serve the Queen, as I had, without question wherever they were sent and in whatever role might be expedient, and this was what they were doing with courage and patient good humour.

In the morning we found an empty camp and, while following the track which led out of it, we came under fire from three Bren guns at a range of about 20 yards. We were lucky to escape without any casualties. We followed the bandits' retreat but made no further contact. There were some bloody bandages in the empty camp, suggesting that this was the refuge of the gang which D Coy. had 'bumped' on the previous day. We patrolled the area for several more days, based on Roscote Estate, without finding any more traces of the bandits, but the men reported having seen signs of elephants and tigers; one of the elephant spores showed that its nails were as big as 'soup spoons' which would make the animal very large indeed. Another patrol brought back the beautiful secondary wing feathers of Argus Pheasants – a rare species which I thought I had heard calling. These feathers seemed to confirm that I had.

At the end of this operation, I went to Singapore on ten days leave, during which I was officially offered the appointment of the shortly-to-be-formed Gurkha Contingent of the Singapore Police Force.

CHAPTER TWENTY

THE GURKHA CONTINGENT

The Japanese surrender in August, 1945 and the re-occupation of Singapore found the Police Force a shadow of its former self; morale had collapsed, corruption was rife and, indeed, the re-instituted Colonial Government had virtually nothing with which to enforce its authority. The pre-war Sikh Contingent had disintegrated in dishonour under the impact of foreign invasion, and this para-military unit, an essential part of any armed police force, no longer existed, Against this background, the Commissioner of Police, Mr R.E. Foulger, started negotiations with a view to replacing the Sikh Contingent with a similar unit of Gurkhas. In the autumn of 1948, after many tedious delays, permission was finally given to raise the unit and the Nepalese Government sanctioned the recruitment of its nationals. An establishment was worked out and, true to form, the total manpower came to the nice 'square' figure of 149. The Gurkha Contingent, as it was to be called, was to have a British Officer (subsequently increased to 2), 5 Gurkha Officers and the usual complement of N.C.O.'s and men to make up a company of 4 platoons. It was decided that the Gurkha Officers should be former V.C.O.'s of the old Indian Army and that all the men should have previous military experience. It was also decided that two thirds of the men should come from West Nepal and one third from the East of that country.

The ill wind of procrastination at least blew us something to our advantage. While the Colonial Office dithered, the bricklayers and carpenters were being much more constructive; the new barracks for the Contingent at Duxton Plain, in the centre of the city, grew apace and were virtually ready when the men began to arrive. There were family quarters for all the Gurkha Officers and men, with the usual stores and offices and a modicum of space for games.

In February, 1949, Bill Cowan, who had been in the 9th. Gurkha Rifles at the end of the war, and later in the 6th. G.R., and who had joined the Singapore Police as an Assistant Superintendent, went to India to recruit the 149 officers and men. I had just been offered the post of O.C. of the Contingent, but I was still in the army. Pending leave due to me after the resignation of my commission, I was lent to the Police to help with the reception of the men and smooth their settling in. In March I went up to Port Swettenham to meet the S.S. *Sirdhana*, the ship on which the men had sailed from Calcutta, and accompanied them to Singapore. When we arrived I was astonished to discover that the Gurkha policemen, being civilians, would have to endure 48 hours' quarantine on St. John's Island. This was no way to introduce the men and their families to their new home but my pleas to the Immigration Authorities were of no avail. I had to go ashore and seek help elsewhere, and it took most of the day finally to persuade the Secretariat to issue a certificate and enable me to take the men ashore.

For the next month, until Bill Cowan returned from India, I acted as adviser to the Police on matters Gurkha and I was, in effect, in sole charge of the Contingent. None of the Gurkha Officers spoke English or Malay, so it fell to my lot to do all the administrative work and the documentation, as well as acting as interpreter at the attestation parade. It was an interesting time, laying the foundations of a unit I was to command for a decade. After three months' leave pending retirement from the army, I was appointed to the Colonial Police Service and, on my return to Singapore, I was officially gazetted as O.C. Gurkha Contingent.

The *raison d'etre* of the Gurkha Contingent was to provide a strongarm squad in times of civil disturbance and to mount security guards for vital points, as well as to provide personal protection for important people and mount ceremonial guards of honour. Apart from the ordinary conventional drill, we also had to learn a riot drill in which baton sections, gas sections and rifle sections had their own particular roles as the riot situation deteriorated. Another high priory subject was the teaching of Malay. This was done by two Punjabi sergeants, old hands in the Police Force, who used Urdu as the medium of instruction, the language being understood by the Gurkhas, although not their native tongue. They picked up colloquial Malay very quickly, but unfortunately they shut up like clams when spoken to by Malay-speaking British officers of the Force. Thus we gained the reputation of being a fairly unintelligible bunch, adhering to its own mumbo jumbo with an obstinacy scarcely rivalled by the early Hanoverians. This was, of course, a misconception, as the men conversed with astonishing fluency with their Malay colleagues and they had no difficulty in giving orders on crowd control duties. The rudiments of law were also taught by the same Punjabis but they found this more difficult than teaching Malay; to kindle in the breast of a Gurkha other rank in those days even the smallest spark of interest in the Right of Private Defence or the General Exceptions to the Penal Code required instructors of rare ability.

The headgear worn in those days for ordinary duties was a dark blue beret. Gurkha hats, with blue pagris, were worn on quarterguard and at other times when we wanted the public to know who we were, as it was surprising how closely many of the Gurkhas resembled the Malays when dressed alike. The uniform shirts were of blue-grey flannel worn with silver buttons. Khaki shorts with black leather belts, dark blue hosetops and ankle puttees with black boots completed the uniform. Kukhris were worn on quarterguard and other special occasions. The Gurkha Officers, who had the ranks of Gurkha Inspector and Gurkha Sub-Inspector, wore a similar uniform but with shoes and stockings instead of boots. They wore their 'pips' on their collars and not on their epaulettes.

One of my greatest worries in the early days was the welfare of the families of the 40 men who had brought their wives and children with them, the children ranging in age from 11 years to minus 6 months. Flushing a toilet came no more naturally to a Gurkha wife straight from the wilds of Nepal than did the removal of yards of cloth from around her waist or the freeing of her baby from the stifling mass of swaddling clothes which permanently imprisoned it. But the hot and humid climate, combined with encouragement from the G.O.'s and me, eventually persuaded her to do all three. The Kandang Kerbau Maternity Hospital was not, initially, a popular place for confinement, nor, indeed, were mothers keen to leave their ailing offspring in the Childrens' Ward at the General Hospital. As time went on, the excellence of the Maternity Hospital and the kindness and sympathy of the staff created a great impression, and we eventually reached the stage when a quick discharge after a confinement was a matter for complaint and a longer restful sojourn an occasion for satisfaction; and the childrens' wards at the General gradually ceased to hold any terrors. In fact, the Gurkha babies thrived in Singapore; of the 40 babies born in the first three years, only three died and these were premature births. The older children remained very healthy and two of the boys went to schools in the town as soon as their English was good enough. The rest of the children attended classes held by the Brahmin teacher, classes chiefly remarkable for their total lack of discipline and the permanent cacophony of sound which emanated from them throughout their duration.

Gurkha Wives and Children, Singapore, 1950.

Until the unrest in December, 1950, which will be described later, there had been no riots in Singapore since the Contingent was raised. It thus became necessary, after the initial training had been completed, to find how best the Gurkhas could be employed and give maximum help to the Force as a whole in the conditions of emergency which existed in the Colony and in Malaya. Our first assignment was to send two platoons over to Johore to assist the police there in their struggle against the Communists in the jungle. Units of this strength, under Bill Cowan, were maintained there on and off until April, 1950, when acts of terrorism in Singapore made it necessary for the whole Contingent to be present in the Colony. Our incursions into the Johore jungles, despite Bill's determined leadership, were never marked by that positive proof of success which dead bandits provided, but our presence was certainly of assistance both to the Police and to the Gurkha regiments with whom we worked. During these operations, our Sergeant Major was killed in an ambush and a P.C. was severely injured and partially paralysed when his back was broken by a falling tree. The men undoubtedly enjoyed these forays into the jungle as a change from the tedium of guard duties, and many of them who had taken part in the war in Burma relished the opportunity to display their erstwhile skills in jungle warfare. But the dispersal of a small unit administered from Singapore had its disadvantages and a return of all the men to Singapore to assist in maintaining its security was not unwelcome to me.

Communist activity in Singapore took the form of arson of buses, taxis and rubber factories; murder of prominent Asians by shooting and grenade throwing; and the more innocuous but widespread posting up of subversive literature. All these things were extremely difficult to counter, particularly when, as in Singapore at that time, the public made no effort to co-operate in the apprehension of criminals. Nevertheless, we tried by mounting guards on rubber factories, placing armed men in plain clothes on the buses and patrolling poster areas in jeeps. These precautions, which could not be maintained indefinitely, had the desired effect where they were staged, but the initiative was always with the Communists, who just switched from one area to another and varied their activities at will. Whilst all this was going on, Special Branch was gradually gaining the upper hand as far as intelligence was concerned, and many leaders were arrested; this had a salutary effect upon the situation.

In April, 1950, an attempt on the life of the Governor was made at the Happy World Stadium. He had just finished watching the finals of the Amateur Boxing matches and was walking out of the door when a youth threw a grenade at him, which, by good fortune, only flaked open, doing no harm. Following this incident, we had to provide a two-man bodyguard to protect His Excellency both in his office and in his car. These men were a great success and soon learnt to close a Rolls Royce door with the aplomb appropriate to so prestigious an appurtenance.

Another duty was maintaining a small garrison on Pulau Tekong, a little island north-east of Singapore, halfway between the Penggaran Peninsula of Johore and the island of Singapore, and the scene of considerable bandit activity before we arrived there. In consequence, it could have provided a staging post for undesirables coming to the Colony. The presence of our section there was to give the local population confidence enough to report suspicious strangers. The fortnightly duty on the island was very popular, the generous 'camping out' allowance being one of the reasons.

The Contingent soon gained a reputation for controlling crowds. The arrival of a Chinese football team from Hong Kong, a frequent occurrence, was the occasion for a vast concourse of Singapore Chinese to gather in the Jalan Besar Stadium to cheer the Hong Kong team and boo the referee. Before the game started, there was a marked tendency amongst the younger fans to regard queues at the ticket booths as long lines of the unenterprising who should give way to the go-ahead, and during the game these same pushers tried to move seats and benches on to or inside the touch-line to enable them to cheer or boo more effectively and catch out the referee with greater certainty. Tact and firmness were necessary to deal with such crowds. Visits from Pandit Nehru gave the Indian community an excuse for coming together, making a great deal of noise and blocking all the ramifications of the Queen's highway within the vicinity of Panditji, restricting his movements and making him quite inaudible. Here again, persistent and firm action was required to keep the situation under control.

In November, 1950 I went to India to recruit more men for the Contingent. I travelled via Calcutta, Benares and Gorakhpur to Lehra, where the British Gurkha Recruiting Depot had been established since 1948. It had been formed, largely in tents, round a large and rambling bungalow, the former property of an old world English zemindar named Bridgman, who had built it before the Mutiny on his indigo plantation. It was a delightful place, only seven miles from the Nepal border, with the Himalayan snows clearly visible from the verandah. All round about was unspoilt Indian countryside. After the humid heat of Singapore, the crisp sunny days and cool nights of the Indian cold weather were very welcome. To step out of the Mess before breakfast and see the far-off perpetual snows glinting in the sun, to hear the harsh calls of House Crows and the ringing notes of the Dayal Robins, all accompanied by the sounds of a military camp – the bugle calls, the words of command, the rhythm of marching men – brought back vividly days of yore in Dehra Dun.

I spent 17 days in Lehra and enlisted 18 recruits; somewhat unproductive, on the face of it, but I wanted a mix of races, both Magars and Gurungs. Although the Gurungs had all come in during the first week, the Magars, mostly from the more remote and inaccessible parts of W. Nepal, were slow to appear at the Depot. And there was an additional difficulty caused by a minor revolution in the country. The King, the titular Head of State, had fled the country after an apparent disagreement with Maharajah Joodha Shamshere, the hereditary Prime Minister, and there were wild rumours and unrest in the hills. It was said that the King was sympathetic to constitutional reform, unlike the Maharajah, but he may have just become tired of his prison-like existence. He was treated like a kind of god and allowed no freedom of movement or expression. At first the Indian government supported the Nepali Congress, which sided with the King, but later changed their tune, calling the leaders 'greenhorns and self-seekers' (which, of course, they were), although two years later they supported the second revolution which ousted the Maharajah and restored the King as a constitutional monarch. All this resulted in the movement of recruits through Thansing being stopped, seriously interrupting the flow. The Gurkhas seemed to show little interest in these political activities, regarding them as Khatmandu capers unlikely to have any effect on their lives in the hills.

Rough shooting in the countryside around Lehra was excellent. On several evenings Norrie Wylie Carrick, the Deputy Recruiting Officer, and I went out after Snipe and Duck when we always saw, apart from our chosen quarry, Dabchicks, Egrets, Darters, Black Ibis and Green Sandpipers. On one occasion the Gurkhas shot a porcupine. We sometimes saw cheetal and wild pig, particularly in the sal forest, and on one beat a leopard cat was flushed. Both rhesus and langur monkeys were often seen.

After securing my 18 recruits and arranging their despatch with a party of army men, I left Lehra. I had dinner at the Indian Recruiting Depot in Gorakhpur where I met Naik Karnabahadur Khattri who had been in the Signal Platoon of 3/9th. G.R. during the war. We recognised one another with mutual pleasure.

That evening, as arranged, I met Col. Ran Davidson, the British Gurkha Chief Recruiting Officer at Gorakhpur Station, where we caught the Katihar train which left at 2230 hrs. We had an utterly miserable journey, as we could not find seats in the 1st. class and had to travel 2nd. At that time of year, large numbers of peasants travelled up to Assam for harvesting and many hundreds of them were on the train, some with 2nd. class tickets. At one time there were 13 of them in our compartment, meant for six. In these cramped and smelly conditions, with no chance of even a snack, we did our best to remain cheerful until we reached Katihar 18 hours after leaving Gorakhpur. Here we had a wait of six hours for the Siliguri train, which was less crowded, and we accomplished the 11-hour journey in only moderate discomfort. Gone, it seemed, were the days when travel on the Indian railways was an interesting pleasure, although the Darjeeling Himalayan Railway, which we next boarded, was as delightful and remarkable as ever. The little puffing engine hauled us up the 6,000 ft., away from the dusty heat of the plains, its frequent strident whistles heralding its bustling progress through the main streets of many villages, until we reached the cool clear air of the Himalayan foothills at Darjeeling, with the shimmering white mountain, Kanchenjunga, towering above the town. We took a taxi up to the Eastern Recruiting Depot at Jalapahar; the driver was an ex-6th. G.R. rifleman.

I had last visited Darjeeling in 1942 and I was shocked to find how much the place had changed for the worse. Although the man behind the counter at Lloyds Bank was the self-same person who had cashed my cheque eight years previously, everything seemed neglected and decayed. An air of dejection surrounded the Everest Hotel, which in the old days had some 300 guests; now there were only seven. The long-standing distrust of the Indian Government by the inhabitants of Darjeeling, mostly hillmen and many of them Gurkhas, had been further fuelled by the well paid jobs being given to Bengalis instead of locals. This had encouraged latent political unrest to flare up, with trouble in Nepal adding to the uncertainty. While I was there, Indian and Nepalese troops clashed on the border near Pashupattinagar, prompting Nehru to rant like Hitler with dire threats of acting to restore stability to Nepal, exacerbating the tension in Darjeeling. Not that I, a Britisher, should have been concerned, but as our men came from Nepal, the welfare of their country and its attitude to recruiting was of crucial importance.

I spent a fortnight in Jalapahar, from where, at 8,000 ft. (1,200 above Darjeeling) the views were magnificent, particularly in the early morning when Kanchenjunga seemed nearer than ever in the clear air, with sprays of snow blowing off the peak in attenuated white ribbons. It was a wrench to leave this enchanting place, but I had enlisted my Limbu and Rai recruits and could not prolong my stay. Furthermore, on the day before I left, reports from Singapore spoke of serious rioting. This was confirmed when I arrived in Calcutta by a letter from Bill Cowan giving me first-hand news of the riots and telling me how well the Contingent had done. Indeed, it was the only part of the Police Force which had done its duty. The Contingent was to be expanded and negotiations with Nepal for permission to recruit had been set in train.

As I had been granted a month's leave, and permission for further recruitment would take some time to come through, I decided to go home and spend my first Christmas there since 1939. Whilst there I received a signal confirming our new establishment as 300 and ordering me to go back to India and recruit the extra men. I returned to Calcutta in mid-January, 1951, spending a few days visiting the British High Commission in search of news about recruiting. Eventually, I heard that the Nepalese Government had turned down the request, the stated reason being that it would be too great a strain on their manpower. This was clearly nonsense, the actual reason probably being that the Rana regime was on its last legs and wished to appease the Indians by opposing the British and thereby fend off India's meddling in Nepalese affairs. Thus did our expansion fall victim to international politics; more than a year was to elapse before we were again allowed to recruit.

I was instructed to return to Singapore, where I arrived at the end of January to find the Contingent in very good heart but most of the Force feeling guilty and unsure of itself.

CHAPTER TWENTY-ONE

THE HERTOGH RIOTS

The riots which I mentioned in the last chapter, and which resulted in the expansion of the Gurkha Contingent, were caused by a legal dispute about a girl called Maria Hertogh. The progress of the disputes and the disorders which followed are summarised in this chapter.

Maria Hertogh was the daughter of Adrianus Hertogh, a Sergeant in the Royal Netherlands East Indies Army, and his wife Adeline, a Eurasian, who had been brought up in Java. Maria was born in that country in April, 1937. Her parents were Roman Catholics and she was baptised into that Church. When the Japanese invaded Java in 1942, her father was interned as a prisoner of war. In December of that year Mrs. Hertogh gave birth to her sixth child and Maria was sent to stay for a few days with a friend, Che Aminah, the Muslim wife of an Indonesian businessman. Five days after Maria's departure, her mother was arrested by the Japanese and interned for the duration of the war. When she and her husband were eventually released, they went to Holland, having lost all trace of Maria.

For more than six years Maria was brought up as a Muslim by Che Aminah, who maintained that the girl had been handed over to her for permanent adoption and had been given the name of Nadra binte Ma'arof.

In September, 1949 it was discovered that Maria was living with Che Aminah at Kemaman in Trengganu, Malaya and in April, 1950 a representative of the Dutch Consul General in Singapore applied for an order to be made for Maria to be delivered to the Social Welfare Department in Singapore. An interim order was made and Maria was placed in the York Hill Home in the city. A month later the Court passed an order giving the Consul General custody of the girl with liberty to restore her to her parents in Holland. But Che Aminah successfully appealed against the order and Maria was returned to her custody. Three days later, under the name of

Nadra, Maria went through a ceremony of marriage to a Malay Muslim, Mansoor Adabi, a teacher and the son of the President of the Muslim Welfare Association in Singapore.

After a series of legal battles, Mr. Justice Brown, on 24th. November, 1950, held that Maria was legally domiciled in Holland and, under Dutch law, had no right to contract a marriage, being under the age of 16. The marriage to Mansoor Adabi was thus invalid and Sgt. Hertogh was entitled to the custody of his daughter. The Judge directed that Maria be handed over to her mother, who was, at that time, staying in the Colony. Her mother placed Maria in the Roman Catholic Convent of the Good Shepherd. Che Aminah and Mansoor Adabi appealed against this order but the appeal was rejected on 11th. December.

While all this was taking place, Mansoor Adabi's father – a trouble-maker if ever there was one – set up a body called the 'Nadra Action Committee', aided by one Karim Ghani, who had spent most of his life in Rangoon and had consorted with Chandra Bose, the founder of the Indian National Army (I.N.A.). This committee kept the pot boiling during the legal wrangles, and Karim Ghani's speeches and articles in the Malay press were clearly aimed at suborning Malay members of the Singapore Police Force.

On 7th. December, Alan Blades, Director of Special Branch, advised the Colonial Secretary, W.L. Blythe, that Maria should be removed from the convent and be placed back at the York Hill Home. This advice followed much ill-feeling expressed in the Malay press about her presence in the convent, whereas there had not been any complaint when she was in the Home. The Colonial Secretary declined to give the order. As it turned out, this was perhaps the biggest mistake made by the Government during this affair.

The disorders which broke out on 11th. December had their beginning in front of the Supreme Court, where crowds had gathered carrying banners calling for the removal of 'Nadra' from the convent. As the crowd became more hostile, Eric Linsell, the officer in charge, asked for a Gurkha Riot Squad to be sent as a reinforcement. At 1030 hrs., Bill Cowan, with 48 Gurkhas, arrived on the scene and formed up in front of the Supreme Court. About two hours later, the crowd which had grown to about 3,000 strong, broke through the Malay police cordon and the Gurkhas were ordered to clear the road from in front of the Court. This they did without much difficulty, and they also chased away people who were stoning police officers from the Padang. The Gurkhas were then ordered to return to the

Victoria Memorial Hall (V.M.H.). The situation continued to deteriorate and the Gurkhas were again called up, but a Malay, Mansoor Adabi, no less, told the officer in charge that if the Gurkhas were withdrawn he could manage the crowd. So the Gurkhas were once more ordered back to the V.M.H., and as they withdrew the crowd became aggressive, throwing stones at the bewildered Gurkhas as they went. With this sign of weakness the crowd became more violent, turning its attention to Europeans standing on the roof of the Cricket Club before moving on the Sultan Mosque.

At about 1415 hrs. John Parks, an Assistant Commissioner, arrived at the Mosque with 30 Gurkhas in two vans. He found a crowd of about 300 watching a truck burning. He tried to reason with the leaders and some of them said that if the Gurkhas were sent away they could control the crowd. So Mr. Parks sent the Gurkhas back to Beach Road Police Station in spite of the fact that hooligans had already smashed some of the windows of one of their vans. After this second sign of weakness, and many instances of Malay policemen refusing to obey orders, the crowd soon sensed that they had nothing to fear from them; the situation at the Mosque and elsewhere quickly got out of control. In another incident, at about 1645 hrs. in Victoria Street, Bill Cowan and 20 Gurkhas dispersed a crowd of about 60 rioters using tear gas. Later, around 1845 hrs., a mob started to advance along Beach Road towards the Police Station. They were confronted by Bill Cowan and 40 Gurkhas and they were told that if they did not disperse the Police would open fire. Fortunately there was no occasion for this, for when the Gurkhas advanced the rioters ran away; but by this time the situation overall was completely beyond the capacity of the Police to control.

While religious fanaticism may have been behind the rioting in its early stages, by the afternoon it had clearly assumed a racial basis and the object of the mob was to carry out murderous attacks on Europeans and Eurasians. The attacks spread over a widening area of the Colony, resulting in nine deaths and 131 injuries.

It was not until Mr. Wiltshire, the Acting Commissioner, fully realised that the Malay element, the vast majority, of his Police Force was failing to do its duty, that he called upon the Army for assistance. This was at 1845 hrs. on 11th. December, when two Internal Security Battalions were immediately deployed and other troops were ordered to proceed to Singapore from Malaya. These included the Green Howards, 13/18th. Hussars, 2/6th., 2/10th. Gurkha Rifles, and one Company each of 1/2nd. and 2/2nd. G.R. With their arrival in force, the situation immediately improved. Some riotous incidents continued to occur on the 12th. December, but by noon on the 13th. law and order had been restored.

The Riot Inquiry Commission's Report laid the chief blame for the situation getting out of hand on the failure of senior officers to take resolute steps to quell the riots in the early stages and the failure to arrest the ringleaders at the Supreme Court and at the Sultan Mosque was deemed a serious error; but what was more astonishing to the Commission was that no attempt was made to use the Gurkha Police effectively in either area. The report went on to say 'We are convinced that if the Gurkha Police had been used effectively in front of the Supreme Court, the crowd would have been dispersed and prevented from reassembling at the Mosque'. In its final summing up the Commission stated that the primary reason for the debacle was 'the failure of officers at the Supreme Court and the Sultan Mosque, and in later stages of the Acting Commissioner to take vigorous measures to disperse rioters by the use of the Gurkha Contingent.'

Although certain senior officers were criticised for their handling of various situations, their personal courage was never in question. The Commission particularly noted that 'Mr. Cowan showed conspicuous qualities of efficiency, initiative and personal bravery'.

Even before the Commission reported on its findings, the Singapore Government had approved an increase in the establishment of the Gurkha Contingent to 300 men, as well as authorising additional transport and agreeing to the building of new barracks to accommodate the increased numbers.

CHAPTER 22

THE CONTINGENT EXPANDS

The early months of 1951 saw much agonizing about the riots as the Commission of Enquiry took evidence and eventually made its report, as noted in the previous chapter. The senior officers who had been criticised left on pension and the new Commissioner,Mr J.P. Pennyfather-Evans, set about his task of healing the wounds which the Malay members of the Force had inflicted upon themselves by their failure to remain impartial. The Contingent warmed to the new Commissioner because of his obvious admiration for Gurkhas and his ability to speak to them in Hindustani. His help in satisfactorily finalising the Contingent's rates of pay, in the face of Government parsimony, was greatly appreciated.

The political situation in Nepal remained tense. In January the Maharajah issued a proclamation – sent to all Gurkha regiments and to us – in which he admitted that reforms were overdue but added that they must be implemented by the Nepalese themselves. This situation appeared, from past events, to bode ill for our recruiting prospects, and the attitude of Sir George Faulkner, H.M. Minister to Nepal, did not seem to further our cause; he warned against any attempts to 'press the Nepalese'. Neither was the Major General, Brigade of Gurkhas, Gen. Osborne Hedley, much help. When he came to the Gurkha Officers' Club one evening he was quizzed on the subject of recruiting and as good as said that if the Army could not get recruits, why should the Singapore Police? As it happened, by the end of the year we both had our wish granted.

Before we received permission to resume recruiting, the Singapore Government was informed that there were large numbers of Burma-born Gurkhas who, disenchanted with their treatment following independence, wished to leave the country. I was asked to go to Burma and see if any of them were suitable for enlistment. I had my doubts from the start, but on

24th April I flew up to Rangoon with David Cotton of the Malayan Police in an R.A.F. Dakota, stopping at Penang and Mergui to refuel. We stayed in the Strand Hotel, formerly the best in the town and by then decaying like everything else in Burma. On the following morning we met the Nepalese Consul, who was a Rana. He told us that there were two political parties reputedly representing the Burmese Gurkhas, one basically pro-British with which he was in sympathy, and the other, the All Burma Nepalese Association (A.B.N.A.), left wing and anti-British and supported by the Burmese. We interviewed over 70 of these Burma-born Gurkhas; they were a very mixed bag as far as castes were concerned, and nearly all of them were over 30 years old. We gained the impression that continuous ill-treatment by the Burmese government had made them highly suspicious of authority and despite the obvious pro-British feelings of most of them, I was confirmed in my doubts about the wisdom of enlisting them; they had but a tenuous connection with Nepal and both from age and attitude would not be suitable additions to our Contingent. Another circumstance which showed the influences under which they were living occurred during our last day of interviews. As we spoke to the men, two opposing political meetings were being held within earshot, one encouraging and the other discouraging the enlistment of those who had come to see us; and to make matters worse, A.B.N.A. officials had the temerity to interrupt our interviews. This was intolerable and it was clear that should we enlist any Burmese Gurkhas, we would become involved in Burmese and anti-British politics. There was one amusing incident: the spokesman for A.B.N.A. who came to the Consulate to protest about our activities was none other than Dharamsing Sharma, who had been for a time Intelligence Havildar in 3/9th G.R. He was more than a little embarrassed when he saw me and quickly fled. David Cotton, who was setting up a Gurkha Jungle Squad in the Malayan Police and was desperate for recruits, did take 120 of these Burma-born Gurkhas, but the unit turned out to be a failure.

Our eventual expansion to 300 was fairly certain and this would mean new barracks as already authorised by Government. Those at Duxton Plain had been designed for half that number and their location was neither salubrious nor sufficiently central for island-wide operations. An army camp at Pasir Panjang had been taken over by the Government and it was suggested that it might be suitable for the Contingent. I went to look at it in June 1951 but found it to need so much alteration and so many additions that it would probably be cheaper and certainly more satisfactory to start afresh elsewhere.

On 22nd September, Singapore was presented with a Royal Charter and officially became a city. The Contingent was on stand-by from early in the morning until 0430 hrs the next day, as it was thought that there might be disturbances. But the huge crowds which collected to watch the ceremony and the evening processions, in spite of being larger than anyone could remember, were generally very well behaved. The only incident, starting a temporary scare, was an 'explosion' in the crowd near Beach Road Police Station. Some 30 people were slightly injured by broken glass caused, it was thought, by a bursting mineral water bottle.

A fortnight later the complacency about security was shattered by the murder of the High Commissioner of the Federation of Malaya, Sir Henry Gurney, when he was ambushed by Communist terrorists. He and Lady Gurney were travelling over the Gap en route to Frasers Hill, when bandits opened fire on the car, killing Sir Henry outright, his wife escaping injury. This tragic incident finally prompted the British Government to take the emergency seriously with the appointment of General Templer as High Commissioner, followed by the remarkable improvement in the situation which his dynamic personality engendered.

This same autumn, the new De Havilland Comet jet airliner flew into Singapore, after a 25-hour flight from London. The Captain of the plane presented the Governor with the previous day's *Times* and everyone marvelled at the speed of the aircraft and the elegance of its lines. The last leg of the flight from Bangkok was flown at 40,000 feet and at an average speed of 380 mph including landing and take-off. I was at Kallang when it landed; it still had ice on its wings. Little did we foresee at the time the tragedies which were to follow when scheduled services started. Three planes were to disintegrate in flight at high altitudes. Metal fatigue was eventually found to be the cause, but by the time that the fault had been diagnosed and cured, the Americans had overtaken us with the size and range of their jet airliners. Comet services became uneconomical, although they lasted long enough to fly me and the family home when I retired from the Force in July 1959.

As far as our general duties were concerned during the year, there were no serious disturbances, despite the usual worries on May Day and during the Hertogh appeal. Crowd control at football matches, an air display and a huge gathering of Chinese school teachers, as well as security patrols following bus burnings and factory strikes and currency escorts to Kuala Lumpur relieved the boredom of many guard duties. These currency escorts involved huge sums of money being taken by train, usually overnight, always with the risk of derailment; a circumstance which fortunately never happened, although there was occasional sniping.

In November I went to India again, following permission to restart recruiting. This time I went in a Quantas Constellation and the flight was uneventful apart from bumpy weather over the Andaman Islands. It took more than an hour to get through Calcutta customs, after which I engaged a room in the Grand Hotel and on the following morning visited the High Commission before catching the Doon Express that evening, sharing a coupé with the Lehra courier. I left the train at Benares in the morning and spent the day at Clark's Hotel, where a fellow guest was Dr Schacht, who had been Hitler's financial adviser during the war. I never discovered what he was up to in Benares. That night another train took me to Gorakhpur and I reached Lehra in the afternoon to find the place as delightful as ever.

I eventually enlisted 55 recruits, all excellent men, mostly Gurungs – Magars seemed to be in short supply – before going on to Darjeeling. I caught the Katihar Mail and this time I had a 1st class compartment with a travelling companion, a Mr Khanna, of Indian catering fame, who was on a tour of inspection of his many establishments. Although we arrived at Katihar half an hour early, we stood outside the station until the Assam Link train had gone through, which meant a 12-hour wait for another train or 3rd class travel in an earlier one. I chose the latter and soon regretted it; it took nearly 10 hours to reach Siliguri, where I spent the night in the back of a station wagon.

I went up to Darjeeling and Jalapahar in a taxi, which, at one of the hundreds of bends in the road, went into a ditch. Here we remained for 45 minutes while the driver and a few conscripted onlookers contrived, with much order and counter-order, to get the vehicle back on the road. Peter Prentice, the D.R.O., kindly put me up in his bungalow. He had some potential recruits lined up for me and I eventually took 15 Limbus and Rais, all seemingly excellent men.

During my short stay, I spent a night with David and Anne Purves on their Chamung Tea Estate near Sukia Pokhri. The weather was clear, crisp and fine in spite of a cyclone reported over the Bay of Bengal. Kalij Pheasants and Partridges were often to be seen in the garden, and the cold weather was forcing barking deer to come down from the higher ground. Plucking the tea had stopped and would not start again until the first flush appeared in March. All the coolies were engaged in pruning, weeding and road repairing.

The tense political situation which I had noticed a year ago still pertained. At Ghoom one morning I met a Communist procession about 50 strong, of

Gurkha Police Recruits, Jalapahar, 1951.

Five Gurkha Police recruits on Selection Parade at Lehra, November, 1951.

The same five men in Singapore 3 months later.

Gurkha Contingent recruits swear allegiance to the Queen at an Attestation Parade in Singapore, 1954.

whom half were women. They were chanting slogans originated by two Gurkhas carrying megaphones. Trouble was also reported from Sikkim, where the Indians seemed bent on undermining the age-old régime and replacing it with a so-called democratic government.

In mid-December I returned to Calcutta, taking a station wagon as far as Baghdogra and a 1 hr. 45 min. flight from there by Indian Airways. I dined with Brigadier Armstrong, who asked me if I would escort a Gurkha draft due to sail for Singapore shortly before Christmas. This I was glad to do, particularly as 70 of the men were my recruits. Also at the dinner party was Chota Morris, ex 7th G.R., who was agent for Elastoplast in Calcutta and was reported to be making a fortune.

I embarked on the S.S. *Santhia* together with 500 Gurkhas and an Indian Field Ambulance destined for Korea. Also on board were 21 Chinese Communists, members of a so-called Cultural Mission. One evening during the voyage, one of them, a professor of philosophy, came and talked to me. He was remarkably shrewd and had travelled widely. It was distressing to find that someone so intelligent should be so unreasonable about the Korean war and Communism in general; everything bad (and most things seemed to be in his opinion) was America's fault.

We arrived in Singapore on 3rd January 1952, a year in which we started to build up the Contingent to its eventual 300. The first incident of note was in February, when rioting was reported on the Indonesian island, Pulau Samboe, threatening the Shell oil installations established there. A directif from the Prime Minister, no less, ordered the Singapore Police to go there and ensure that the Indonesians maintained law and order. Sixty men of the Contingent in five launches, with Assistant Commissioner Joe Anderson in charge, landed first of all on nearby Pulau Blakang, from where Anderson, with two other officers, went over to Pulau Samboe to find that the local police had the situation under control. During the night, a Marine Police launch, patrolling in Indonesian territorial waters, was threatened with shooting and withdrew. Our launches patrolled all night and one of them was surrounded by three heavily armed Indonesian boats. However, nothing untoward occurred, largely because H.M.S. *Amethyst* and H.M.S. *Morecambe Bay* were standing by. We all returned to barracks by late morning. The whole incident was really a storm in a teacup, brought about by a wild rumour, but it was exciting while it lasted.

General Sir Gerald Templer was appointed High Commissioner for the Federation of Malaya and on several occasions during the year we provided security at the airport when he visited the Colony. On one occasion, when I escorted him to his plane, he shouted to me as he went aboard, 'Give my love to your Gurkhas'. The improvement in morale amongst both military personnel and civilians following his appointment was most remarkable; he was a born leader. Also at this time the Governor of Singapore retired and was replaced by Sir John Nicholl.

On 6 February, on the evening news bulletin, we were all very shocked to hear that the King had died in his sleep. A day or two later Princess Elizabeth, who was visiting Kenya at the time, was proclaimed Queen in Singapore at a very impressive ceremony outside the Victoria Memorial Hall. We were on crowd control duty while the Governor read the Proclamation in English; it was also read in Malay, Mandarin and Tamil, followed by prayers for the new Queen said by Bishop Baines. A Royal Salute of 21 guns was also fired.

In April there were reports of intimidation on Pulau Tekong and we mounted an operation in conjunction with the Johore Police. To achieve surprise, I embarked 60 men in launches one evening and we spent the night on board before landing at dawn and rounding up all Chinese on the island between the approximate ages of 16 to 40, collecting them together in Kampong Pulau. One bandit courier and the wives of two known bandits were arrested. All three were identified by 'tame' bandits (Surrendered Enemy Personnel – S.E.P.) from Johore, who were wearing uniform and carried arms.

In May the postal workers went on strike and the Contingent was made responsible for the security of all bulk mails, escorting them to and from the airport and the docks and standing guard over the distribution centre at the V.M.H., where the public came to collect their letters. To complicate matters and increase our workload, the bus drivers also came out at the same time. Their strike ended after a day or two but the postal strike lasted for a fortnight.

The training of the new recruits had been another important part of our activities. As far as drill was concerned, so keen to learn had they been that I was able to take a squad of 30 of them on the Queen's Birthday Parade. Here they acquitted themselves so well that they were generally considered to be the best on the parade.

Security at the Detention Camp on St John's Island was a worry to Government and I visited it several times. It appeared that there was collusion between the guards and the detainees. Stricter supervision was started and in order to prevent a probable revolt by the Communist detainees, I moved 25 recruits and a Gurkha Officer over there to keep an eye on things. They were able to continue with much of their training while performing the security role. On one day when I went over to St John's East with the Commissioner to inspect the magazine, we found all the jagas (guards) asleep. This typified the general lax attitude to security on the island, which we hoped the Gurkhas' presence would improve.

In June three Indian Navy Sloops visited Singapore. On board one of them, the *Kistna*, was Chief Inspector Harkajung's nephew, together with three other Gurkhas. He told us that there were also Gurkhas on the other ships. U.S. Navy ships too were visiting Singapore at that time and there was a considerable alarm when someone threw a home-made bomb into a café in Jalan Besar, wounding three American sailors. The Governor 'flapped' and had us dashing hither and thither on various wild goose chases. The culprit was never found.

Just before I went on home leave, one of our men struck it lucky; he won $2,500 on the Selangor Turf Club's unlimited sweep and put it in the Post Office Savings Bank to grow there until his leave was due. I left on a B.O.A.C. Argonaut, flying direct to Colombo where we had an overnight stop, staying in the Mount Lavinia Hotel. I had stayed there in 1941 but this time I found it a shadow of its former self. During the morrow's flight to Karachi we flew right over Ootacamund, looking superb in the sunshine. We were delayed in Karachi by an air display put on by the Pakistan Airforce but eventually left at 1800 hrs., to reach Bahrein four and a half hours later. We arrived in Cairo in the early hours of the following morning and were put up at the Heliopolis Palace Hotel after being told that there would be a 24-hour delay due to mechanical trouble. So they arranged a guided tour of the Pyramids. On driving through Cairo it was interesting and distressing to see how much damage January's riots, resulting in King Farouk's abdication, had caused. Shepeards Hotel had completely disappeared. On the following day we were taken out to the airport three times and thrice came back to the hotel. We were told that one of the plane's propellers kept going into reverse thrust for no apparent reason. Neither was the fault put right on the next day which we spent in the hotel, pestered by fortune tellers and touts. However, at 0430 hrs. on our fourth day in Cairo we actually took off and flew to Rome and Zurich, arriving in London in the evening after a journey which had taken six days; as long as the flying boat trip in 1947. Nearly all my flights before the advent of jet engines suffered from delays due to engine trouble. Modern air travel is much more reliable.

I spent five months at home on leave, returning to Singapore in January 1953.

CHAPTER 23

SINGAPORE 1953/54

The year 1953 was chiefly noteworthy for the Coronation, which was celebrated by parades, street decorations and float processions. Apart from all the planning involved – the rehearsals, the practices – in the few months before the event, the Contingent was involved in many much more mundane activities. The Commissioner General, Malcolm Macdonald, decided that he needed a permanent guard at his residence, adding to the pressure on our manpower; escapes from Woodbridge Mental Hospital during a warders' strike had us scouring the Yeo Chu Kong area; a search for an escapee from Outram Gaol ended when he was caught riding a bicycle towards Tiong Bharu by one of our patrols; a threatened strike by Singapore Harbour Board personnel was called off after I had spent two days planning security measures.

As the Coronation drew near, so did the sense of occasion and preparations for it increase. The Gurkha Brigade Coronation Contingent, commanded by Dudley Spain, set sail on the *Empire Orwell*, wonderfully proud and happy to be chosen and the officers and men much smarter than those of other units on board. The decorations, both public and private, throughout the city were both lavish and tasteful; most buildings were festooned with bunting superimposed with crowns, and the illuminations were magnificent. They were turned on a few nights before the actual event, and the crowds were so dense that it took 45 minutes to go from Robinson Road to the National Dancing outside the City Hall, watched by a crowd estimated at 50,000. We held the final parade practice on 1st June; it went off very well, the only worry being what the weather would do on the morrow. That evening a Sunderland flying boat dropped flares and fireworks over the harbour.

The actual day was fine and the parade was a spectacular success, our squad generally acclaimed as being the best; we received a letter of congratulations from the Commissioner. During the morning we heard that Everest had been conquered by a New Zealander called Hillary and the Sherpa, Tensing. They both reached the summit on 29th May – a really wonderful piece of news to break on this historic morning. In the evening the vast Chinese procession of floats started at Collyer Quay, where I was on duty with 50 men. It was four and a half miles long and took many hours to wind its way through the city. The Chettiar Community put on an excellent fireworks display.

Four days later Bill and I and 100 men took part in the Queen's Birthday Parade and on that evening the illuminations were switched on for the last time. They were very spectacular and unlikely to be equalled again. Thus was Coronation Week brought to an end; it had been a huge and inspiring success.

Earlier in the year our strength had been increased by the arrival of 51 recruits, enlisted on our behalf by the Army, and bringing the Contingent's numbers up to around 270.

Even something as momentous and, one would have thought, as uncontroversial, as the conquest of Everest managed to fall victim to political wrangling. Both India and Nepal claimed Tensing as a national, and he was prevailed upon to sign several different statements on the subject which all contradicted one another. As a result his proposed visit to England was cancelled amidst a deal of ill-feeling, which the *Straits Times* was happy to foster by a series of articles claiming strained relationships amongst the team and even racial discrimination. The paper proudly proclaimed that its articles would 'raise further controversy'. However, much of this was forgotten by the time Hillary and Lowe visited Singapore and jointly gave a two-hour lecture on the expedition. It was given without notes and illustrated by beautiful colour slides. The superhuman effort to reach the mountain and climb to its summit was graphically described.

In August I took our tug-of-war team up to Kuala Lumpur. I went up by car, the men following by train, taking seven hours, including a half-hour stop for lunch at Tampin. Some measure of the improvement in the security situation was to be seen by the extensive re-planting on the rubber estates, which in some areas had completely altered the landscape, particularly in South Johore. Our team won the tug-of-war convincingly, creating a great impression amongst the Federation Police Officers.

In October I accompanied the Commissioner on an official visit to Bangkok. We flew up there in an R.A.F. Valetta, landing at Penang to pick

Traffic in Bangkok, 1953.

up the Federation Commissioner. On arrival at Bangkok, we scarcely had time to change before being whisked off to the British Embassy for a cocktail party, followed by a repeat performance an hour later at the house of the Director General of Police with a display of classical dances as a diversion. To keep the hectic pace going, a dinner with another senior Police Officer followed to conclude the evening's entertainment. In the bedroom allotted to me, which I was very glad to get to, I found everything provided, including a dressing gown, pyjamas, toothbrush, toothpaste and a variety of soaps.

On the following morning we were bidden to the official opening by the Prime Minister of the new Police Headquarters, followed by a visit to the Royal Palace and the Emerald Buddha Temple, both very lovely in their own particular way. In the afternoon we attended a most impressive police parade in which more than 3,000 police personnel marched past the King, who arrived in a large yellow Daimler closely followed by an equally large yellow Rolls Royce, empty but for the driver. I asked one of the Thai officers why the second car followed the King's, and he said it was in case the Daimler broke down. Several senior Thai Police Officers were presented to the King and they approached him literally lying on their tummies and snaking their way towards his feet. In the evening we were guests of the C.I.D. Chief at an excellent dinner, followed by a boring succession of boxing bouts at which kicking as well as punching was allowed.

The final day was quite the most enjoyable. We left Bangkok at 0700 hrs. in a special train bound for Ayuthaya, the ancient capital sacked by the Burmese in the 1730s, thence by bus to the King's Summer Palace at Bang-pa, where we had lunch. After this we boarded a launch and steamed for five hours down the river to Bangkok. Iced beer, tea and cakes and enchanting riverine views accompanied our sedate progress. But the day's entertainment was not yet over; there was a supper and a dance at Police H.Q. yet to come, and the small hours of the following day were well spent before we got to bed.

A Garuda Indonesian Airways Convair took us back to Singapore, where we arrived, just after midday, and I was just in time to attend the 'Mar' (the head-cutting of a buffalo calf) at the Contingent's Dashera celebrations, which were continued that evening by a series of parties lasting until 0400 hrs. next morning. But there was little respite. Within 24 hours there was a 'flap' and at 0600 hrs. I took out 100 men to search for a pistol in the Bedok area, joined by 500 Malay police. After two hours we found the pistol; an important find because the ballistic experts showed that it had been used for a murder and an attempted murder. A few days later the U.S. Vice-President, Richard Nixon, arrived in the Colony and we had to mount a permanent patrol around Government House.

Another duty fell to our lot at this time, namely a permanent guard at the Chief Justice's House. He was not keen to have such a guard but he had been persuaded by the Commissioner that he was at risk. I met a P.W.D. officer at the house and we decided upon the location of the guard house; modifications to an outhouse were agreed and the conversion made adequate accommodation for yet one more boring duty.

In November I went to India again for the last batch of recruits. When I arrived in Calcutta I found that the Maj. Gen., Brigade of Gurkhas, Lance Perowne, was also on his way to Lehra, accompanied by Col. John Stephens, and he invited me to join his party. We flew by Indian Airways to Benares via Patna and spent the day in Clark's Hotel. The night train from Benares took us to Gorakhpur, whence we travelled to Lehra by road. That evening there was a party in the G.O.'s Club at which 28 Gurkha officers, serving and pensioners, were present, their service totalling 658 years – an average of twenty-three and a half years each – some much less and some a great deal more.

On the afternoon of the morrow we set out for the recruiting camp in Nepal at Pakhli Hawa, a mile or so south of Bhairawa and two miles north of Sanauli on the main road to Nepal proper. Although the distance was only 22 miles, the road was so bad that it took us three hours to get there. We were accommodated in tents. It was delightful to sleep under canvas again, in cold, crisp weather, the distant howls of jackals competing with the nearby dual chucklings of a pair of Spotted Owlets as soporific aids; and as dawn broke, the sounds of rural India grew in intensity – the cawing of House Crows, the mewing Kites, the clear notes of Dyal Robins and, a delight to hear, the strident calls of Grey Partridges – as well as all the hubbub of a military camp – the bugle calls, the parade-ground commands, the clatter in the cookhouses. Here I found 22 recruits waiting for me, all excellent men; it was a pity that I could not take more. I spent some hours completing their documentation and testing the clerk candidates, but I did have time to accompany the General on an excursion to Bhairawa and Batoli, from where we walked to Dobhan and then climbed over the hill through Nawakot and back down to the Batoli suspension bridge. The Parakeets, both Alexandrine and Rose-ring, were dashing everywhere in little noisy flocks and Sunbirds were feeding in large numbers on the parasitic loranthus flowers.

I left Pakhli Hawa a few days later with the recruits, taking the train from Nautanwa, but when we arrived at Parandapur we found that the promised lorry had not arrived, so we walked the six miles to Lehra along a road bordered by rice fields, which were supporting an unusually good crop due to heavy winter rains. On one of the jheels which we passed there were large numbers of Mallard and Cotton Teals, and hundreds of Jacanas, Coots and Moorhens, and in the reeds round the edges were numbers of Scarlet Minivets and hoards of Ring-neck Parakeets feeding on the seeds of tall grasses.

After the recruits had all passed their medicals, I left Lehra for Jalapahar, travelling the same route as on previous occasions with much less bother. I arrived in Siliguri in the early evening and took a taxi, arriving in Jalapahar at 2200 hrs. after a very pleasant drive in bright moonlight. Ten recruits, including a clerk, were ready for me in the morning and after I had inspected them, and found them to be excellent men and keen to join us, I went down to Darjeeling where I met Tensing and his wife in the bookshop. I found him very unassuming and very easy to talk to, with no hint of his bearing any ill-feelings about the way the press and the politicians had treated him. While in the town I bought a Kashmiri carpet for Rs.22 – a bargain.

Before leaving Jalapahar I visited Kalimpong with Douglas Carter, the D.R.O. We went in a Landrover, taking one and a half hours to reach the Teesta Bridge on a dusty road which drops 4,000 feet in 10 miles, to climb again an equal height and distance to Kalimpong, which at that time was very Tibetan both in population and influence. We walked up the road towards Tibet and met convoys of mules carrying woolpacks which almost smothered them from view. I felt that Communist influence must also be strong in Kalimpong, as there were many Chinese walking about and a Communist banker from China was a fellow guest of ours in the quaint Himalayan Hotel, run by an Anglo-Gurkha named Annie Perry.

Next morning we walked on the hill above the hotel. The weather was perfect and we sat in the sun looking N.E. towards Tibet. As far as the eye could see, were small homesteads clinging to the hillsides, the terraced fields all neat and tidy after the pre-Dashera harvest. The recent heavy rains had caused severe erosion, scarring the countryside to an alarming degree. We returned to Jalapahar that evening.

My return to Calcutta was by taxi to Baghdogra, with lunch at Kurseong en route, and thence by plane to Dum Dum, a fellow passenger being Prince Peter of Greece. I stayed in the Transit Camp and spent a day in the city, which had deteriorated even further since my last visit. The streets were

filthy and the Maidan was covered with homeless paupers. I had lunch at
'Princes' in the Grand Hotel. Col. Guinea Graham was also staying at the
Transit Camp, having just finished a recce in search of a site in Nepal for a
new Brigade of Gurkhas Depot. The chosen place was Dharan.

I arrived back in Singapore, after a six and three-quarter hour flight, on
the day before the City Council elections. The Contingent had to escort all
the ballot boxes and we were on duty at the Victoria Hall in the evening
when the results were announced, to control the boisterous crowd, mainly
Indians, who came to cheer or boo according to their political persuasions.

The Queen and the Duke of Edinburgh were on their Commonwealth
tour and had reached the Antipodes. I was made responsible for meeting the
Queen's mail at Kallang and escorting it to and from the G.P.O. The first
instalment arrived shortly before Christmas, consisting of no less than 15
bags, mostly, I was told, Cabinet documents. It certainly made me realise
how much work she has to do. Her New Zealand visit was marred by a
tragedy on Christmas Day when 160 people were killed in a train crash
while on their way to see the Queen.

An interesting diary entry shows how trouble was brewing in S.E. Asia.

28 December
'A serious threat to Laos and the whole of Indo-China has developed.
The Vietminh have appeared in strength on the Mekong and have taken the
French by surprise. Siam is also alarmed as the Mekong forms the frontier
with Indo-China for some 300 miles. American physical help to the French
seems unlikely because of the general anti-overseas service attitude which
has forced an armistice in Korea.'

1954

The main domestic event of the year was the setting up of our Pipes and
Drums. The Army enlisted for us a retired Pipe Major from the 4th
Gurkhas, Puransing Thapa, who was an excellent teacher. We asked for
volunteers for the band and had no difficulty in filling all the posts, mostly
with 1952 recruits. The C.O. of 10th. G.R., stationed at Majeedi Barracks
in Johore Bharu, very kindly offered to train the drummers, who spent
several months over there. I was astonished at how quickly they learnt their
trade; by the end of the year, with the pipers, they were able to put on very
respectable performances. When two new sets of bagpipes were presented
to us by 7th. G.R., the Pipe Major insisted that the only way of softening the

leather bags was to pour a tin of golden syrup into each of them; it seemed to have the desired effect.

Trouble arose at the Bin Seng Rubber Factory, where the workers refused to accept what they considered inadequate 'Ang Pows' (New Year bonus); striker threats to *Straits Times* workers developed and a Communist threat to the life of the Government Public Relations Officer, Mr Thomson; the shooting and wounding of D.S.P. Thurai Rajah occurred in a house at the junction of Kampong Java and Thomson Roads, as well as the killing of a Chinese detective who was with him. All these events and other minor problems kept us well occupied early in the year, with guards, searches and patrols, as well as mounting a Guard of Honour for the Opening of the Assizes. In addition, there was a ghastly accident at Kallang when a B.O.A.C. Constellation aircraft, coming from Sydney, crashed on landing and caught fire. All 31 passengers and two of the crew were burnt to death. It was impossible to open any of the doors or hatches because of the buckling of the fusilage. I had gone down to meet the plane and the Queen's mail, which escaped the flames as it was in the front of the cockpit with the captain, who also survived.

A new pay scale for all Government servants was approved by the Legislative Council, following recommendations by the Ritson Report. This brought to a head long-standing opposition to the Gurkha Contingent's right to rations, as written in their terms of service. The Government maintained that their increase in pay made rations unnecessary and unfair to the rest of the Force, who did not receive them. At a meeting which I had with the Commissioner, the Deputy Commissioner and a government representative, I argued that the agreement could not be overturned and, in any case, everyone had received an increase and the extra which the Gurkhas received in rations in no way made them better off than they had been before, as compared with the rest of the Force. The reason for this was that the Gurkhas were expatriates without the support of nearby homes and families. Opposition was withdrawn.

Late in the previous year the Legislative Council had passed a bill requiring all males between certain ages to register for part-time national service. This gave the Communists an excuse to cause trouble. May 12th., 1954 was the last day for registration and children from the Chinese High School spent the day trying to send a deputation to the Governor asking for exemption. He refused to meet them and on the following day students from several Chinese schools formed up outside Government House and had to be dispersed by force. Some 46 were arrested and a good many others were slightly injured in the fracas. The *Singapore Standard*, a new paper started in opposition to the *Straits Times*, predictably accused the police of brutal fascist methods against defenceless students and demanded an enquiry. The date for registration was advanced a few days but the students failed to register, holding indisciplined meetings at many of the schools. At 0530 hrs. on the day of the deadline, 22nd May, I was at the Chung Cheng School with a squad of Gurkhas. About 3,000 students from six different Chinese High Schools congregated in the grounds and refused to move out. We laid siege to the place, cut off all food supplies and waited to see what would happen. In the evening some parents came and tried to persuade their young to come home, to no avail. But early next morning a number of parents appeared and started to break down the barricades which the children had erected. Having got inside, they found their children and took them home. This action by the few responsible parents started the rot and by 1130 hrs. all the students had left and the show was over without our having to do anything but surround the area. Nevertheless, ill-discipline continued in Chinese schools, prompted to some extent by the conviction of 28 students for rioting and failure to register; they were bound over for six months. Seven more, who obstructed police in Penang Lane, were sentenced to three months' rigorous imprisonment. These students had difficulty in finding competent lawyers to defend them but it so happened that a famous left wing Q.C. from Britain, called Pritt, had been in Malaya defending university students in a sedition trial. He agreed to act for the Singapore students and on the day of their appeal we were at the Supreme Court expecting trouble, but only about 400 fellow students turned up and caused no bother, to some extent because heavy rain damped their spirits. The judge reduced the sentences from three months R.I. to 18 months bound over to keep the peace. But the students refused to sign the bonds, so they went back inside to serve the rest of their original sentence.

These events and the probability of future trouble resulted in the Contingent being issued with two fire tenders and some of the men going on a course run by the Fire Brigade. It was thought that jets of water played on unruly crowds would be an effective way of dispersing them without inflicting any injury; and so it turned out to be, as events in 1955 were to show.

As 1954 drew to a close, some of the buildings in our new barracks at Mount Vernon began to take shape. The date for occupation was given as July 1955.

Towards the end of the year I left Singapore on the *Sangola* for a round trip to Hong Kong and Japan.

CHAPTER 24

ROUND TRIP TO JAPAN

On 17th December 1954 Guy Matthews and I embarked on the S.S. *Sangola* en route for Hong Kong and Japan. At Pulau Bukum the ship sucked in tons of fuel-oil before moving to the Western Anchorage where a collection of indeterminate bundles was swung aboard from lighters and large numbers of deck passengers swarmed up the gangways. All had bicycles, most carried baskets of sweet potatoes and some clutched pails containing goldfish. As dawn rose the following morning, we sailed round to the Eastern Anchorage and really began to think that we were on our way. But no, the compass must be tested and a man came aboard who, had we been in a temperate climate, would have surely worn a bowler hat. We spent the whole morning describing small circles in the Anchorage, and every time we looked up from our books, the Sea View Hotel was coming up on the port bow. Teatime saw us passing Horsburgh Light, dipping gently in the N.E. monsoon swell. It was here that the only alarm of the whole voyage took place. A French frigate, on a parallel course, suddenly altered direction like a Parisian taxi and cut across our bows. A blast on our siren and a sharp turn to starboard were our only reactions but the Captain was far from amused by this exhibition of Gallic seamanship.

During the next four days we sailed N.E. straight into a strong and increasing headwind, whilst we ate a great deal and imagined that each morning was colder than the last. We saw no ships but there was some elation one morning amongst the ship's officers because we had overhauled another of the Company's vessels during the night and by dawn she was well below the southern horizon.

Hong Kong looked delightful in the morning sun and, on coming out on deck, we found it unnecessary to pretend that it was colder. There was no doubt about it; the wind was blowing from the general direction of Outer

Mongolia and the sun could not yet reach us as we anchored in Kowloon Bay. Small boats descended upon us like ants on a sugar bowl, and we were very soon enveloped in all the tiresome chores which the bureaucratic control of travel imposes.

At that time Communism was a sinister creed creeping over much of S.E. Asia, and when we visited the frontier between the New Territories and China it was almost as if we expected to see a sharp geological and botanical difference between the two sides of the border. But we gazed over the wire fence at country exactly similar to that upon which we were standing, expecting perhaps to hear the crack of a rifle shot announcing the end of a misguided diversionist or to see a gang of selfless youths tilling a collective rice field. Yet everything was disappointingly normal, the vegetation and its supporting geological strata passing under the fence unchanged as far as the eye could see.

The drive through the New Territories was a pleasant experience, especially to anyone who had spent an unbroken year or two in the harsh green of Malaya. The coastal parts reminded me of Southern France – intensely blue seas lapping pale brown rocky shores, with pine trees covering the surrounding slopes. The hills were bare of anything but grass and creeping plants; the sun and a seasonal drought had baked them all to a golden brown. While the eye could feast upon big and beautiful scenery, the nose was prompted to send urgent messages to the brain by the Chinese farmers' ancient and highly efficacious method of returning nitrogen to the soil.

More cargo was quickly loaded and, joined by Dudley Spain and a number of other 'round-trippers' from England and America, we set sail for Japan on the morrow. The Formosa Straits in a gale is not the sort of subject which Christmas card painters are wont to portray as an ideal locale for seasonal activities; but this is where we spent the day. The N.E. monsoon, channelled between the mainland and Formosa, beat down upon us and, although brave attempts at breakfast were made by all except an 82-year-old lady, who always had it in bed anyhow, most of us were feeling very jaded as midday approached. The Captain came to the rescue by suggesting that we should all repair to the bar and taste the wine and make sure that it would be suitable for dinner. By the time we had decided that it was, we had forgotten the weather and were even able to laugh at the American couple's 'Republican-Democratic' jokes with a tolerable semblance of amusement. The rest of the day was all that it should have been; we ate a great deal too much, drank more than enough and were altogether surprised that it was so late when it was.

As we approached Japan, we became aware that we were playing second fiddle to the cargo. Rumours were flying around, all beneficial to the cargo and detrimental to us passengers. We were only going to Kobe to stay but two days; cargo was crying out for a passage to Singapore and Calcutta and it would not be inconvenienced by a stay in Japan; we might even turn round and go back again straightaway. In the event it turned out that although we only docked in Kobe, the Japanese New Year holiday stopped all loading and unloading for several days and the ship stayed there for a full week.

We arrived in Kobe on a cold, misty morning and at once went ashore. Our decision to stay in a Japanese-run hotel was not a wise one; it was cold, noisy and primitive and as disappointing as Kobe itself. Imagine the most unattractive seaport which the British Isles can provide, place in it close on a million Japanese and almost as many cars, scatter bars here and there in every street to the total of six hundred and ninety-two, forget most of what you know about mending roads and do not worry too much about American soldiers' inability to walk without the physical support of indigenous females. There you have Kobe as it was in December 1954.

One of us was a person who could stare at a temple, breathe the air of an ancient city or contemplate the processes of some archaic custom with all the serenity of the Buddha himself. So off we went to Kyoto, the ancient capital with a thousand temples. There we chose a centrally heated European-style hotel, booked in and straight away went on a bus tour designed to cram a thousand years of history into three hours of hectic bustle. We dashed hither and thither in a garishly-painted bus, resembling a Wimbledon tennis crowd as we glanced from side to side at passing temples. Now and again we were herded into shops and encouraged to buy things 'very popular in the States'. Sometimes we just stopped at street corners while the guide gave a fluent but largely unintelligible dissertation on Japanese history and we were told to get ready for the plum of the tour – the old Imperial Palace. At last we approached it, standing nobly in a pine-studded park. It was shut; its ancient gates would open to no visitors for the next four days. We must content ourselves with walking in the grounds where centuries before the Shoguns had trod while visiting their imperial masters. Then a rude shock: the guide, talking in less assertive tones, told us that the 'old' Palace was only a full scale model built 50 years ago. And the site? Well, it was not the actual site, that was over there; and he flung his arms in the general direction of the setting sun. Then it started to rain, a circumstance by which the guide was highly diverted. This particular precipitation was peculiar to

Kyoto, he said, called 'Foxes' Wedding Rain', but quite why this so ordinary shower should be unique to Kyoto and relevant to Reynards' nuptials even the loquacious guide failed to give the faintest clue.

Kyoto was a pretty place. Surrounded by hills lightly sprinkled with floury snow, its gardens, parks and temples were all laid out in the bamboo-pine-cherry tree style so typical of Japan. Huge department stores stood erect beside more humble establishments, while old one-man rickshaws competed with American taxis in a confusion of traffic to which a constant blowing of horns gave no hint of resolution.

The train journey from Kobe to Tokyo was over 300 miles and we accomplished it with a degree of speed and comfort which would have made the Shoguns envious and should have made British Rail ashamed. The seating arrangements in the coaches resembled those in an airliner and the hostesses were as decorative and even more numerous. Rice fields and bamboo-pine covered hills flashed past, giving way to an occasional glimpse of the sea. Every piece of flat land was cultivated, every human being was working or walking. Of idleness and waste there was no sign. At lunch in the swaying dining car we found ourselves beside an American psychology professor who waxed eloquent on the wifely virtues of Japanese women. American women, he said, were spoilt, pampered and lazy, while Japanese women were affectionate, selfless and attentive. Although we only attended to his ramblings with half an ear, we felt that there was something in his theory when, at breakfast in Tokyo's Imperial Hotel the following morning, we noticed an American colonel being obliged to cut the top off his wife's boiled egg.

Tokyo was vast and teeming. It was New Year morning when we walked the crowded pavements. Japanese families in their thousands were flocking to the Imperial Palace, the women and children dressed with colourful good taste, the men with drab indifference. In what straitened circumstances the makers of combs and hair clippers must live, we thought; the Japanese male hair-do, would not have disgraced a Skye terrier at Crufts.

We joined the multitude converging on the Palace. It was impossible not to be touched by the simple loyalty which this demonstration portrayed. But recently prostituted by an evil clique, this blind faith in the Imperial Person did incalculable harm. Nine years after defeat it was a stabilising influence in an area threatened by Communism. The Palace occupied a vast area in the centre of the city, surrounded by a huge moat on which swans were swimming in stately pairs. There were no military guards. Policemen stood here and there with fixed expressions of fierce boredom while Tokyo's citizens gazed with awe towards their sovereign's abode.

A taxi took us through the streets at a speed quite beyond all safety margins to the Meiji Shrine, built to the memory of the moderniser of Japan. Inside were many paintings depicting the various stages of Meiji's reign: the overthrow of the Shoguns, the abolition of the clan system, the despatch of men to Europe in search of technical skill, the Russo-Japanese War, and so on; a pictorial record of doubtful artistic value showing the remarkable rise to power of a vigorous and industrious people. Beyond the precincts of the shrine, in a nearby stadium, a vast concourse of American servicemen and Japanese civilians was watching a game which the New World calls football. The roar from 20,000 throats which greeted the success or failure of a padded player must have seemed to Meiji's spirit like a 'banzai' of long ago.

At night Tokyo winked and twinkled like any modern city and all the streets were filled with swarming crowds. Ginza on New Year's Eve presented a remarkable spectacle. All the shops and stalls were open and neon lights lit up the street. Camera shops full of mirrored images of Teutonic optical skill, milliners with furs and silks and tweeds in glorious profusion, fruit stalls piled high with mandarin oranges half enveloped in shining silver paper, dirty urchins hawking gladioli with cries like parrots well versed in American slang. A forest of neon signs beckoned pleasure seekers to an astonishing profusion of night-clubs where dancing with well-dressed girls was punctuated with dancing by well un-dressed girls; and everywhere milling crowds clutching parcels.

Another day and we were on the train again, hurrying back to the dingy grime of Osaka and Kobe, passing Mt. Fuji on our way. Time and weather have yet to destroy the beauty and symmetry of this giant volcanic cone which, tipped with snow, reached 10,000 ft. towards the blue heavens. Small wonder it is divine. We broke our journey to visit Nara, an even more ancient capital than Kyoto, where we stayed in the wooden-built Nara Hotel situated on a hill above the lake and surrounded by an extensive deer park. In this old-world town we made our only really serious attempt at Japanese food. Our wartime contention that the Imperial Armies seemed able to live on very small quantities of almost anything gained valuable support. Although the quantities were small, the 'almost anything' part of the description fitted well. The soup, which contained small sections of octopuses' tentacles and various portions of piscine viscera, tasted like the smell of water in which a kippery plate had been washed-up; but at least it was warm. The rest of the meal was cold, congealed and rubbery, and of most unappetising hues –

pale green lumps of this and bluish lumps of that. But the saki was good.

We embarked again on the *Sangola* in Kobe on the cold wet morning of 5th January 1955, passing through the Inland Sea between various small islands and along the coast of Shikoku before night fell. In the morning, as the southern tip of Japan fell below the horizon, we were pushed along by a N.W. gale which continued as we entered the Formosa Straits and made it no more hospitable than it had been when we came north.

We spent two days in Hong Kong, visiting Repulse Bay, the Peak and, of course, the Peninsular Hotel in Kowloon, before sailing for Singapore, joined on board by Betty Dunkerley, who in the following year was to become my wife. At that time she was working as an Almoner at the Tan Tock Seng Hospital in Singapore, and had been on holiday in Hong Kong. The weather improved as we sailed south until it became quite warm again, and the deck cargo of cabbages and onions, destined for Chinese New Year in Singapore, gently reminded us of their presence as the tail wind kept the air on deck more or less static. This favourable wind and the calmer tropical seas resulted in the ship's speed reaching sixteen and a half knots with the final daily run of 399 miles – a record for a B.I. boat of this type, and the Captain threw a party in the evening to mark the occasion. It had been raining when we left Singapore and it was still raining when we anchored there again on 15th January, 1955.

CHAPTER 25

RIOTS AND SELF-GOVERNMENT

The year of grace 1955 saw our Pipes and Drums playing in public with increasing confidence and acclaim, our new barracks at Mount Vernon taking very satisfactory shape, and the Colony making somewhat faltering steps towards self-government, in no way helped by wide-spread strikes ending in disorder and riots.

On Election Day, 2nd April, we endured 23 hours of continuous duty starting at 0400 hrs, escorting ballot boxes and standing-by in case of trouble. After the count, everyone was surprised by the Labour Party's victory and the Peoples Action Party (P.A.P.) gaining three seats. After several days of negotiations David Marshall was appointed Chief Minister of a government with considerable autonomy, but within a month strikes and unrest caused it serious embarrassment. It fell to the Police Force and to the Contingent as part of it, to try and maintain law and order in an atmosphere of mounting indiscipline and muddled thinking. A rash of strikes spread across the island like measles in a prep. school dormitory. Strikes were soon followed by intimidation and, inevitably, by violence. The situation was greatly aggravated by an altogether unhealthy interest which the 'children' from Chinese schools took in the 'welfare' of the workers. They drove around the city in open lorries making the air hideous with dreary slogans. Quite what political independence had to do with the working conditions in a sauce factory or the duration of maternity leave due to a worker in an aerated water plant seemed obscure. The tension grew by the day and we brushed up our trailer-pump drills; the time soon came when we had to use these machines.

On May Day political rallies were held; some 12,000 people, half of them students, turned up at the P.A.P. meeting which moved en masse to the Hock Lee Bus Co., whose drivers were on strike and where we had a platoon on duty. We were jeered at for an hour or two, but there was no violence. In factories and at the Harbour Board workers downed tools, ostensibly to demand more pay but actually to make a political point in favour of the quasi-Communist P.A.P. At the bus company, workers had split into two factions and, in keeping with current fashion, had formed two unions. It takes only one union to make a quarrel but if there are two, a bigger and better quarrel is certain, especially if one calls a strike and the other does not. The striking section of the employees decided that they would not allow the non-strikers to take the buses out of the depot; they squatted down in front of the gate, knit together with linked arms in a defiant mass. For days and nights they sat there, fed by students who arrived in lorries bearing edibles and chanting slogans, while we sat and waited for the bus owners and the government to summon up courage enough to take some action. Fruitless haggling with the unions eventually broke the owners' and government's patience and on the morning of 10th May we were ordered to open the gates and let the buses, driven by non-strikers, come out. When the obstructors at the gate refused to move in spite of several warnings by a magistrate, we turned the hoses on them. For a few minutes the human barrier remained firm, held against the gate by pressure from the hoses, but the immense buffeting from the jets began to tell and the strikers gradually broke towards the flanks, helped on their way by carefully aimed jets. Thus was the gateway cleared and the buses drove out.

This was by no means the end of the matter. The drivers who had taken their vehicles out of the depot soon found that the warring factions meant to prevent them from working at all costs. Stones were thrown at the buses and the drivers were threatened with violence unless they returned to the depot. In a very few hours all the buses were back in the garages and the strikers had reformed at the gate. Posters sprang up here and there consigning employers to the devil, and visits from students became more frequent and increasingly noisy. That the strikers were permitted to remain in the vicinity of the depot was unfortunate and interpreted as a sign of weakness by strikers, who assumed that they could continue to defy authority and break the law; their insolence and indiscipline reached intolerable levels.

On the morning of 12th May, the government decided at last that the strikers should be removed from the vicinity of the depot, and we again used our hoses. The human barrier broke up and the buses came out, to be greeted by showers of stones. Many of the stone-throwers were arrested and the crowds were removed from the area. We then withdrew, returning to barracks. In the early afternoon crowds began to collect in Alexandra Road and lorry loads of students converged on Alexandra Circus. The Reserve Unit had to make baton charges and fire tear gas to disperse them. In the evening we returned to the bus depot to protect it from angry strikers. Two of our platoons, accompanied by John Worley and me, found themselves confronted by a crowd whose size and hostility was rapidly increasing. We deployed across the road and tried to reason with the mob but were met with nothing but defiant insolence. Soon some stones were hurled at us from the back of the crowd. Several Gurkhas were struck and Worley received half a brick on the top of his head; he staggered about with knees half bent and was clearly concussed. It became obvious that the mob's intention was to attack the depot after overcoming the Police. A City Councillor, with more courage than realism, made a final effort to make the crowd see reason, but to no avail. Then we charged them and victory was as instantaneous as it was complete. With a yell of horror some 2,000 hooligans took to their heels pursued by 50 very angry Gurkhas. Those who could not run fast enough received the sort of treatment they deserved and within five minutes the area round the bus depot was virtually empty. Though some youths tried to attack our flanks, were kept out of stone-throwing range by tear gas shells fired by Ben Gard and another platoon while we pursued the main mob, dispersing them before returning to the depot.

The fury of the mob reached a crescendo at about 2200 hrs., and in several places foul murder was done by fire and 'chungkol'. The Reserve Unit, out in force while we were resting, managed to confine these savage excesses to just a few areas and, considering what might have happened, Singapore was let off quite lightly. The Contingent toured round the affected areas for the rest of the night, clearing away road blocks made of anything from torn-up bus stop and street-name signs to Chinese sauce jars. Often we were stoned by unseen gangs of hooligans but a Gurkha can throw a stone as well as any and better than most and the opposition quickly melted away. We came across cars upturned on their roofs and battered like much-used toys. The jetsam of four hours of savagery was horrifying; like the margin between sanity and madness, the diversion between orderly administration and anarchy is quickly crossed. Gone is the dignity of a pillarbox upturned; gone is the feeling of security when cars, so lately moving unimpeded, lie charred in the shambles of their cremation; gone is goodwill and tolerance when mindless men hurl stones and abuse. The morn was far from smiling; everywhere the evidence of the past night's excesses lay scattered about. Stones, bricks and bottles, abandoned bicycles, burnt out tear gas grenades, bent bus-stop signs, all told the tale which, by the grace of God and loyal exertions, had not been the great tragedy it might have been, but only a drama of criminal folly.

Shortly before the riots an international conference of Asian leaders was held in Java, many of those attending passing through Singapore. For several days Kallang Airport enjoyed Alice-Through-the-Looking-Glass scenes as planes landed and took off; some carrying delegates from Nepal and Outer Mongolia accompanied by American and British journalists; others piloted by Frenchmen carrying Vietnamese; yet others with Indian crews carrying such men as the ex-King of Cambodia. And when the Chinese Foreign Minister, Chou En Lai, landed unannounced in an Indian Skymaster, a whole crowd of thugs jumped out of the doors and stationed themselves round the plane. He lunched in the VIP room, shook hands with Malcolm Macdonald and flew away, to be followed by a plane-load of Viet Minh Communists who behaved in a similar suspicious manner. On another day the Afghan Foreign Minister arrived without having booked his onward passage and was surprised when he was unable to complete his journey. After a few days they all came back again, but so great was the inefficiency of the Indonesian Consulate that it was impossible to discover who was on which plane, making the planning of security difficult. Throughout this migration to and from Bandoeng, via Singapore, we were on duty at Kallang protecting delegates to a conference the soul aim of which seemed to be denigration of the West. They were lucky to be looked after so well.

In June strikes started to break out, encouraged by the P.A.P., which had no friendly feelings towards Marshall's Labour Government. Following the arrest of some of its members, the P.A.P. called a general strike. The Hume Industries factory at Bukit Timah became the focus for strikers from Singapore Harbour Board, bus workers, intimidated taxi and petrol tanker drivers, rickshaw men and some City Council employees. Altogether some 17,000 people were involved, not really enough to be effective, especially when Gurkha escorts on vehicles reduced the intimidation, and the P.A.P., realising that the strike would break, 'recommended' a return to work.

The weeks which followed the riots and strikes were tense and busy. When workers are frightened and union bosses without scruple, the Police have a very trying time, for whereas they are the protectors of both they are often considered to be friends of neither. For very many weary hours did we sit outside factories and bus depots, and it says much for the Gurkhas' tolerance and good humour that no one had occasion to complain of partiality one way or the other. And so the year wore on, unspectacular and in some ways frustrating, but interesting and not without its lighter moments. We had our share of ceremonial: the Opening of the Assizes, the Queen's Birthday Parade and domestic police parades. Our Pipes and Drums continued to improve amazingly and our new barracks at Mount Vernon were so near completion that we could contemplate a move there within months.

On 30th June I left Singapore on six months' leave aboard the Italian ship S.S. *Asia*, calling in at Bombay, where I had a round of golf at the Willingdon Club, and at Karachi, where I dined at the Metropole Hotel and drank beer at Rs.6 a bottle. At Aden, where it was extremely hot, I bought 8 mm cine films at 22/6d. a reel and a Weston Exposure Meter for £7. Perim Island looked barren as ever and the old barracks were a scene of desolation. A violent wind in the Red Sea denoted a sand storm ashore. We went through the now Egyptian-owned and managed Suez Canal without a hitch with the S.S. *Neptune*, the troopship *Staffordshire* and the S.S. *City of Brooklyn* in the convoy astern. We arrived in the Bay of Naples on 19th July, sailing close to Capri and Sorrento, and had time enough to go ashore to visit Pompeii and see the ruins resulting from an eruption of Vesuvius in 79 A.D. which covered the city in volcanic dust. The excavations started in 1748 and were still in progress. At Genoa, where we arrived on 21st July, I caught the 1900 hrs. Paris train which reached that city at 0900 hrs. the following morning, Calais at 1500 hrs. and London at 1930 hrs.

I was at home on leave until 16th December, when I sailed from Tilbury on the P & O liner *Chusan*. We called at Gibraltar and passed close enough to Malta to enjoy good views of The Grand Harbour and St Paul's Bay. Our passage through the Suez Canal was delayed for the best part of a day by fog both in the Canal and in the Bitter Lakes. Christmas Day was spent steaming at 23 knots through the Red Sea, arriving at Aden on the 27th December and at Bombay on 31st. At Colombo, on 3rd January 1956, I shared a hire car with Col. and Mrs Kerr, driving the 72 miles to Kandy and the marvellous Botanic Gardens at Peridynia which I first saw in 1941. Now I was no less impressed by their beauty. The heady aromas in the Spice Garden of cloves, nutmeg, cinnamon and allspice were especially evocative of the East. At Penang we took the hill railway up to the Peak and saw once again the splendid panorama of the harbour, the city and the bluish mountain spine of the Malay Peninsula. We arrived in Singapore on 8th January, where I was joyfully met by Betty, to whom I proposed a few days later and was accepted, and by all the Gurkha Officers and many of the men. It was the beginning of a momentous year.

When I went to report my return to the Commissioner, he told me that he had detailed me to be the Police Extra A.D.C. to the new Governor, Sir

Robert Black. I was surprised but pleased; the work turned out to be extremely interesting, as many world leaders and other famous persons were entertained by the Governor when they visited Singapore and I often had to meet them at the airport and attend functions at which they were present.

Our first parade of 1956 was one at which the Commissioner presented the Contingent with a Commendation for our work during the previous year's riots, and a few days later Ben Gard commanded a Guard of Honour for the Opening of the Assizes. The Pipes and Drums started to practice with the main Police Band for future combined performances at Beating of Retreat ceremonies. They were also in increasing demand for playing at Golf Clubs, Polo Club and Turf Club Gymkhanas, at which they excelled themselves.

On 9th March I took over the keys to the new barracks at Mt. Vernon and we started to move in. For eight years we had lived in the middle of the Chinatown; highly convenient for shopping and tolerably near the cinemas, no doubt, but not very salubrious. A number of the quarters faced on to a nearby street, one which led to the docks, and many a fascinated Gurkha wife had watched a sweating Chinese driver trying to extricate a shattered half-shaft from the back axle of a grossly overloaded lorry. Many a rickshaw driver too, frightened by the aggressive alertness of the Contingent's dog Pangre, had approached the gate sentry, pointing excitedly to a trivial scratch more likely caused by his own vigorous evasive tactics than by the loose fangs of the old dog. How often did a clattering and clashing Chinese funeral procession pass within a few yards of us, the final noisy journey a never-failing fascination? How often did we hear the monotonous 'clopping' of the mee seller's messenger or the deafening clangour of the Lion Dancers' rehearsals behind the G.O.'s quarters? And what of Chinese New Year? For two days and nights in each twelve months an amplified imitation of a Burma wartime Japanese jitter party assailed our ears and almost entered our bones. Even the slumbering Gurkhas, normally impervious to the biggest of bangs, were woken by the fearful din. And during Singapore's silliest season – early days of the new constitution – we grew weary of the prolix and amplified political outpourings which came to us in daily doses from a trades union H.Q. across the street. We were in the centre of much activity which was far from peaceful. Our move to rural surroundings, with much more space and greatly improved accommodation, was very welcome.

Mount Vernon was a raised piece of ground between Serangoon and Paya Lebar Roads, extending over some 23 acres. Each four-storey block,

The Gurkha Contingent Pipes and Drums, Mount Vernon, Singapore, 1957.

of which there were ten, contained 24 married quarters, and those for whom married bliss was denied lived two to a quarter. A separate block for Gurkha Officers and two British Officers' houses completed the dwellings in Phase 1 of the project. Phase II, which was taking place whilst we were moving, included the Administrative building – a shapely edifice containing offices, stores, armouries, and a guardroom – a large canteen, garages, a drill shed, a children's school and a Hindu temple. For this latter building our Pandit's whims were law unto the P.W.D., who bore his chronic indecision with remarkable good humour. They barely raised an eyebrow when he changed the position of the building; they gladly found more money when he demanded that a four-foot wall should surround the verandah; they merely shrugged their shoulders when he stated a preference for striplighting and asked for two wall-fans; and the carpenters seemed delighted when he found two cupboards with sliding doors essential for storing his religious impedimenta; the plumber quickly found the enormous length of pipe required for an isolated stand-tap, and even the garish colour scheme met with only polite suggestions for more sober hues. But one thing they would not do was move a fire hydrant and dig up the vast labyrinth of pipes to which this red excrescence was attached. The final Phase III comprised a chain-link perimeter fence of tremendous length and a 30 yards rifle range. We were glad when the fence finally enclosed our domain, for when we held our week-end cinema shows a huge band of 'non-entitled personnel' came in from nearby kampongs carrying newspapers upon which to sit and watch the show. Sadly, when they departed, the newspapers remained with us and the morning-after scene was hideous to behold.

Meanwhile the political scene frequently bordered upon farce. The Marshall government, quite understandably, wanted to advance further towards self-government and in March a seven-day period was declared 'Merdeka' (Freedom) Week. A referendum was held, aimed at testing public opinion, but it was fatally flawed because it was not secret nor was it confined to voters on the electoral roll; anyone could sign the form and thus there was no limit to the number of times an individual could vote. We were on stand-by all day when the Merdeka Rally was held at Kallang. It broke up in confusion when the stand on which the Ministers were sitting collapsed, typifying the farcical nature of the whole enterprise. After the rally members of the P.A.P. threw stones at the police and broke windows in the airport buildings. In April Marshall led a delegation to London to negotiate with the Colonial Secretary, Lennox Boyd. The talks went on for nearly a month and day after day we were told that a decision would be announced on the morrow, but on the 16th May they finally broke down because the British Government insisted that external defence and internal security were inseparable and must remain in the Governor's hands. Even after everyone else realised that no further progress was possible, Marshall kept on announcing that he would restart the talks, and did so to such an extent (without any chance of success) that finally everyone ceased to take him seriously. After his return to Singapore on 25th May, he made a speech in the Legislative Assembly blaming everyone except himself for the failure of the talks, and finding that he had little or no support in or outside his party, he resigned on 7th June and was succeeded as Chief Minister by Lim Yew Hock; sanity and stability seemed more likely.

However, in the autumn riots were triggered by recalcitrant Chinese High School and Chung Cheng School children who had barricaded themselves in the main buildings. When, after several days, they refused to come out and the parents seemed reluctant to bring their offspring to heel, the government decided to close down the schools. On 25th October, we arrived outside the Chinese High School at dawn, and after we had warned the inmates to leave peacefully and it became apparent that they had no intention of doing so, we fired tear gas into the buildings. In a matter of minutes the buildings were empty; although there was much wailing and gnashing of teeth, chiefly by the parents who had been sufficiently irresponsible to encourage the children by their physical presence. No one received more than the most superficial of scratches. Attempts by students to form processions on leaving the school were quickly broken up and we were able to return to barracks for the midday meal. In the early afternoon bands of students and hooligans started to collect in various parts of the city and anything which savoured of Government was fair game for their attacks – mail vans, City Council lorries, traffic lights, traffic islands. We were soon out again dispersing hooligans and protecting fire-engines and ambulances by putting two armed men on each vehicle. On several occasions they were invested by mobs of a thousand or more and the men had to open fire, but at no time was more than one round fired. The rioters soon began to give these protected vehicles a wide berth. As to what happened during the rest of the day, a few extracts from my report, written at the time, may help to set the scene:-

'The Superintendent ordered me to take a platoon into Chinatown and disperse any mobs we came across. As we approached a lane, a crowd of hooligans was building a barricade of concrete bricks, traffic signs and oil drums. We charged them and they fled in all directions, the largest party retreating up the lane. To these we gave chase and three of them disappeared up a passageway connecting the lane with the street. We continued in pursuit and as we emerged at the far end of the passage, we saw them enter a house; we followed them closely up two flights of stairs. On entering the room, we found three youths sitting on the floor with their lungs so far working overtime that they were barely able to tell us that they had been in the house for hours. We pulled them out with some difficulty because the women folk, wailing at the tops of their voices, held them in close embrace and wrapped themselves round various articles of furniture. The noise was tremendous and the scene somewhat poignant. On our way back to the Central Police Station with our captives, we came across another mob at the corner of the street. They jeered and threw stones until we charged and caught one of them but for the next hour we were the bull and the mobs the matador. Our cut-off sections, encircling movements and other ruses were to no avail; every front door provided a sanctuary, every back door an escape. Thirsty and exhausted we returned to Central and, whilst slaking our thirst, we were urgently requested to race to the Government offices where trouble was afoot. We arrived there to find the Fire Brigade dowsing two blazing cars while many others were lying on their sides in neat disorder; of rioters there was no sign. Patrols in adjacent areas proved mainly abortive although we did lay our hands on one fugitive. Someone told us that car-burners had retreated into a certain pawnbroker's shop but when we went there those inside were as unhelpful as they were frightened, and if they had been burning cars they had washed their hands and changed their clothes with remarkable expedition. We returned to our starting place and put the cars back on their four wheels. Subsequently all of them (except those which had been cremated) were driven away by their owners. We then acted as escorts to the European members of staff at the Government Offices. Gangs of hooligans roaming the streets fled in all directions as we approached and formed up again as we passed; this was the dispiriting picture throughout most of the rest of the day. Later we escorted 30 prisoners from the Police Courts to Outram Gaol. En route I noticed a gang of hooligans down a side-street and, after we had delivered the prisoners, we came back at high speed and drove into the middle of the rioters. A few bottles crashed against our vehicles and two men were slightly hurt by flying glass, but the helter-skelter dispersion of the hooligans was quicker than our debussing and, apart from scaring them, we achieved nothing. For another hour we patrolled round trying to come to grips with the rioters and dismantling road blocks, and on one occasion we surprised a gang of youths who retreated into a coffee shop; we came to grips with them inside and afterwards I made a mental note that two broken truncheons would need replacing. Some other streets were full of hostile, yelling crowds which we charged and dispersed, and finally, distinctly weary, we made our way back to Central P.S. to find, en route, flames emerging from the 8th Police Court. We rapidly debussed and beat out the flames with our riot shields and for our pains we were nearly shot as arsonists by an inspector. Thus the day drew to a close and we returned to barracks at 0200 hrs.'

Thereafter, for many days, constant vigilance and patrols in conjunction with the Army were our lot. Within a week, thanks to the resolution of the Lim Yew Hock government, the danger receded, but one very sad result of the disorders was the cancellation of the Duke of Edinburgh's visit to Singapore. He was to have honoured our guard at Government House by turning it out and inspecting it. A year later, in more tranquil times, we were thus honoured.

CHAPTER 26

HIMALAYAN HONEYMOON

Betty and I were married by Archdeacon Robin Woods at St Andrew's Cathedral, Singapore, on 5th April 1956. The venue was particularly pertinent because Betty's grandfather, the Rev. W.H.C. Dunkerley, had been Archdeacon of Singapore 51 years earlier. Both our mothers were present and nearly all the Police Officers and their wives, as well as many of our personal friends and those who worked with us in our offices, totalling about 300 – a truly multi-racial gathering. Our three pages were all my godsons, Nigel Shakespear, Rory Ormsby and James Kerr. Betty was given away by the Commissioner of Police, Nigel Morris, and we emerged from the Cathedral through a Guard of Honour of raised swords borne by brother officers and regaled by music from Pipers of the Gurkha Contingent Pipe Band. The reception was held in the Police Mess at Mount Pleasant. Our health was proposed by H.W. Jackson, the Director of Radio Malaya.

The only sadness in an otherwise wonderfully happy and memorable occasion was Betty's mother missing the reception. She had booked a passage on a ship to Perth, Western Australia, due to sail a few days after the wedding, but the date was suddenly advanced to the very day itself. Although they held the sailing until immediately after the wedding, she had to rush out to the ship on a Police launch straight from the cathedral.

After the reception we went to the Seaview Hotel and, on the morrow, caught a plane to Calcutta en route to our honeymoon in Darjeeling, an account of which I wrote a few weeks later.

'With Indian Standard Time covering the whole sub-continent in a materialistic disregard of the relationship between longitude and the hour at which the sun appears above the horizon, dawn comes earlier to Calcutta than the clock admits, and as we emerged from the portals of the Grand

Hotel at 0540 hrs., the sun was doing its best to soften an otherwise hard and sordid scene. A black shabby taxi of New World origin had already received our meagre baggage into its capacious boot and a host of hotel servants were vying with one another for the honour of holding open the door, our gratitude to be measured in their grasping palms. The driver, whose beard and turban had long since given up the struggle to remain white, consigned the lot to the devil, having made sure that they took no annas with them which might later have reached his hungry purse. We drew away from the curb with as much zip as a badly maintained engine in a badly driven car can muster on bad petrol.

Air travel in India is cheap and reliable. The interior of the air terminal at Dum Dum reflected these pleasing facts and no Sahara oasis could have provided a greater contrast to its immediate surroundings, for Calcutta has little to commend it and during our short drive we saw how little. Although the airport bus in which we quickly took our seats had clearly escaped the attention of maintenance crews for longer than we cared to imagine, we were soon to find that our aircraft had not suffered a similar fate. The ubiquitous hack of civil aviation – the Dakota – was standing on the Dum Dum tarmac proudly displaying its name in Hindi script on its snout. The captain was in his seat; rudder, ailerons and other important moveable appendages were responding to his tests with most reassuring obedience. Although charges for excess baggage are very reasonable in India, the reluctance to pay them is underlined by passengers' strange interpretation of 'hand baggage'. To be festooned with half the contents of a photographer's shop, to support a basket of mangoes on your head, to carry a primus stove in one hand and a cage of parrots in the other as you board the plane, is to exercise your right as an air traveller to get something for nothing.

We soon crossed the Hoogly, hidden to some extent by an infestation of jute barges, and flew on north to Bagdogra where the dusty plains meet the Himalayas. The chilly upper air through which we had flown for near on two hours spilled out through the door as we came to a halt on the bumpy grass verge, and the stifling hot breath of the plains soon enveloped us. As we stepped from the plane, a swarm of Darjeeling Gurkhas, who had learnt to drive army lorries during the war and now drove taxis up into the hazy hills beyond, surrounded us, each extolling the virtues of his vehicle. Fortunately, we had booked beforehand and had no hard choice to make. With a prolonged and unnecessary blast of the horn we were off on a journey of 50 miles and a climb of 8,000 feet. The road is tortuous and terrifying; blind hairpin bends succeed one another in breathless profusion.

Mercifully, there is a code of manners amongst the hill-road drivers and all vehicles climbing up the hill have, by gentlemen's agreement, the right of way over those descending. Although two cars may meet one another on a narrow right-angle bend, and come to a horn-blowing shuddering halt, the driver of the descending vehicle, after appropriate comments on the weather and enquiries about friends and relations from his opposite number, will reverse up the hill until passing becomes possible. An additional motoring hazard is provided by the little narrow-gauge railway which, with a total lack of gates, crosses the road countless times. However, the busy puffing of a climbing engine, now and again drowned by a mournful moaning whistle, gives ample warning of its approach and the car driver is apparently as little worried by the giant puffing caterpillar in his path as we are by an errant sheep.

Kurseong is the first and only place of any size on the road to Darjeeling. This little town sits on a spur 5,000 feet above sea level, and on the slopes below it is a green panorama of a million tea bushes; bushes which to the whole district of Darjeeling mean life. Thousands of Nepalis work in hundreds of gardens, pruning, plucking, weeding and road-making so that the bi-annual flush of leaves may, in due course, find its way to Mincing Lane. Left to themselves, the mountainsides are clad in a dense growth of conifers and evergreen oaks, whose roots bind the earth and stones together; but when man interferes and clears the hillsides of natural vegetation, widespread and terrifying erosion removes the soil and sometimes villages too, in an avalanche of unstoppable mud. Here and there the mountains are scarred where the soil has been torn away from the sparkling micaceous rocks yet, despite this desecration, the scene as a whole is one of tranquil beauty.

It was noon when, at 8,000 ft., we reached Jalapahar, the British Gurkha Recruiting Depot where we stayed as guests of the D.R.O., Jimmy Marks and his wife. Despite the strong sunshine, it was cold enough for us to welcome the crackling wood fire we found in our bedroom. From our window we could see the vast mass of Kanchenjunga some 40 miles away, towering above the land of Sikkim like an angry cumulus cloud. Immediately below, clinging to the hillside, was Darjeeling. Now and again the clamour from the open-air market reached us in a diluted, pleasant form, and the wind, soon to bring up the afternoon clouds from the plains, whispered in the cryptomeria trees. In a matter of hours we had reached a new world as unlike the muggy grime of Calcutta as anyone could wish.

A day or two later we set out on a trek into the mountains. A Landrover took us to Manibhanjyang, some 30 miles from Jalapahar. There we started our trek along the border ridge between Nepal and India, eventually to reach a little village called Sandakphu where, at 13,000 feet, the view of the eastern Himalayas is unequalled; this was our objective, to be gained in two days' marches. We had engaged three porters, two women and a man, Sherpas all. The man who, like many Sherpas, was called Nima, had been on the Kanchenjunga expedition, so a leisurely walk up to 13,000 ft. was nothing to him. He was to be our cook and he presented us with a list of provisions which he considered essential, pointing out that rum was not the least important of them. With the skill of an experienced mountain traveller, he deftly apportioned the loads between the two women, carefully securing a live chicken on the top of each and ensuring that his own load of the more stimulating stores was such that he was in no danger of being pressed into the ground.

It was nearly midday when the Landrover left us at Manibhanjyang, where we started our climb up the wooded slopes. We had seven miles to walk and 4,000 ft. to climb to the first Forest Bungalow at Tonglu. The initial two miles were very exhausting; the sunshine was intense and the path exceedingly steep, but eventually we reached a small village where rows of Tibetan prayer flags were fluttering in the stiff and cooling breeze. From there the climb was more gradual through grassy country with rhododendron thickets here and there. We passed small parties of Gurkhas on their way to Darjeeling for supplies of kerosene and other consumer goods. They viewed us with undisguised surprise and always asked where we were going and why; to go to a place just to look at it seemed to them a mad thing to do. Birds were everywhere; Woodpeckers, Nuthatches and Minivets, to mention but a few, and in the valleys the nostalgic call of the Cuckoo, the same call of the same species we have at home. Now and again a Shama sang from a tangle of undergrowth – a sweet nightingale-like song, very appropriate to the surroundings. The din of cicadas still came to us from the valley, but with every step it grew less, to be replaced by the distant crowing of cocks from the hilltop villages and the urgent rattle of cows' neck-bells as small boys collected up their timid charges; although it was scarcely 1500 hrs., the clouds were fast descending upon the hills to envelop them in a cold damp dusk. A constable who had accompanied us for company on his way to the Tonglu police post suddenly started to shake with a malarious ague, but the two aspirins which we gave him had such a psychological effect that he was able to manage the last thousand feet of the climb as well as the rest of us.

The Tonglu Forest Bungalow and Kanchenjunga, 1956.

The Darjeeling Himalayan Railway train, 1956.

Tea Pluckers, 1956.

The Planters Club, Darjeeling, 1956.

The bungalow at Tonglu, a relic of the Imperial past, was still in tolerably good order and the care-taker, anxious to justify his existence, quickly sent off his son to bring in firewood. The two Sherpa women, with a great deal of puffing and blowing, soon had the room full of smoke and a tiny glow in the grate which, with much coaxing, grew into a very welcome fire. In no time at all Nima had made some tea and as we drank this, well laced with rum, cries of gallinaceous distress told us that one of the chickens had met an untimely end for our ultimate benefit. When the fire had started to roar up the chimney, adding its light to the feeble glow from the hurricane lamp, the chilly process of washing and changing our clothes was accomplished without undue discomfort; but another task remained, the inflating of our rubber mattresses. We had been told that the beds supplied in the bungalows were found comfortable only by a vast and fecund population of mice. Actually, this was not so; nevertheless we were glad of our 'lilos', for the beds had no springs. Blowing up these inflatables is no mean feat at the seaside but at 10,000 ft. it is a major and exhausting operation, after which supper was eagerly anticipated. The erstwhile squawking chicken had suffered the post mortem fate of all its breed in the hands of hillmen. No dignified dismemberment for it, but a ruthless chopping with a kukhri from the tip of its beak to the extremities of its gnarled claws. In this mangled state, stewed and savoury, it was borne in by Nima with the same loving care as might have been lavished by a Roman chef upon a dish of larks' tongues in aspic. A healthy hunger proved a worthy substitute for the dentition of carnivores and we soon disposed of this dish and the other bits and pieces which accompanied it, and shortly after, as the saying goes, composed ourselves to sleep.

The dawn was superb. Kanchenjunga, golden tinted by the rising sun, stood in a sea of fluffy clouds submerging the land of Sikkim. A stiff and chilly breeze blew along the ridge, rattling the rhododendron leaves as it passed. To the east the wooded valleys, with magnolia trees standing out white and proud amongst the varied greens, ran down to the Rangit and Teesta rivers. To the south a grey and opaque haze beneath which the dusty plains prepared for another stifling day, and to the west the land of Nepal, where the geological disorder of seismic upheavals has within its midst the delightful symmetry and neatness of hill-rice contour terracing. Such was the scene upon which the sun smiled as we prepared for the next stage of our trek.

We had 14 miles to walk and it was prudent to start early for the sun could be very hot and the day prematurely shortened by early afternoon clouds. Although our destination, Sandakphu, was at 13,000 ft. and our starting height 10,000 ft., we had nothing so simple as a straight 3,000 ft. climb, but an initial and most disheartening descent of 2,000 ft. followed by a steady struggle up 5,000 ft. But the weather was fine when we left Tonglu and God was so obviously in His Heaven. On the shady banks beside the path, where at home primroses might grow, masses of pink primulas escorted us on our way. In the more secluded spots, where the cold spring winds had played but lightly, rhododendron trees showed their gorgeous pink and red flowers against a background of snowy peaks. Again the Cuckoos called and Red-headed Tirmice, in churring noisy parties, searched the pink azalea flowers for insects. Round and down and to and fro the steep path went until it reached the valley bottom, where, after some 50 yards of sober level progress, it again zigzagged up towards the clouds. It was nearly noon before we had made good our early descent, and the sun had ceased to smile. On a grassy saddle at 11,000 ft. we waited patiently for Nima to catch us up with the much-needed lunch. The wind had risen and the gnarled holly-oaks, bearded with shaggy mosses, shook impatiently and sighed. It was cold when Nima arrived and spread before us the unexpended portion of the previous evening's meal, which was much nicer than it sounds. The chill air soon spurred us into fresh activity, and what a weary climb it was. The clouds had come right down and visibility was but a few yards. In the event this was an advantage because we climbed in the mist for hours, always expecting to see the Sandakphu bungalow round the next corner; had we been able to see how far we had to climb, we would have wondered even more why we had ever set out on the trek for pleasure.

Next morning all doubts were expelled; the grandeur of the northern horizon was beyond belief. The whole Himalayan range from Kanchenjunga to Mount Everest was spread before us. Perched as we were at 13,000 ft., no intervening mountains could shelter the summit of Everest from our gaze. There it was, white and smooth and peaceful, its lower slopes modestly obscured by Lhotse and Makalu; many lesser peaks, themselves six times the height of Snowdon, filled up the 80 miles and more which separate the Everest group from the Kanchenjunga massif. All was silent except for the distant sounds of wood chopping drifting up from the deep steep valley. As the sun rose so did the breeze, light with us but a mighty gale above the mountains. Snow, torn from its rocky resting places by the fury of the wind, blew off the peak of Kanchenjunga in a white plume a mile or more in length. This mountain, alone amongst the Himalayan giants, is almost unprotected from the south by any lesser peaks, so its cluster of seven summits ('little storehouses of snow' as the Sikkimese name implies) must be one of the windiest places in the world. On this clear blue morning the only sign of the boisterous turmoil was the snow plume streaming to the north-east.

We climbed a little further that morning, 200 ft. perhaps, and sat in the sun. Higher still some swifts cleft the thin air in screaming rushing dives, and vultures, with slow and measured wing-beats, searched the mountains for their obscene prey. Down in the valleys thin spires of blue smoke hung listlessly about and along the twisty mountain paths laden hillmen trudged wearily along. Three small Limbu boys came in ardent search of firewood, their shrill chattering punctuated by the sharp crack of rhododendron twigs. Presently they noticed us and, seeing our binoculars, asked, in the direct manner of all hillmen, whether they could have a look through them. They were highly diverted and each gave the other advice on how to use an instrument which none of them had ever seen before. Strangely enough, they were more intrigued by the illusion of distance given by looking through the wrong end than by the intended magnification. As we returned to the bungalow by another path, we came across a small patch of snow lurking in the shade of bushes; a reminder of the bleak days not long passed, for in winter time all is white and silent, except the wind.

Sandakphu to Manibhanjyang is 22 miles and we walked it in a day; quite why and how we did it, we are still not sure. To start with, the walk was lovely. We passed a herd of zos (yak-cow hybrids) submitting patiently to a rapacious milking by their Tibetan herdsmen, watched and guarded by a pack of small shaggy dogs; as the summer progressed they would go high into the mountains in search of fresh grazing. We went through a straggling village of bamboo huts where herdsmen come in the warmer months to graze their goats. We noticed again, with pleasure, the primulas and azaleas and heard afresh the whistling nuthatches and the yaffling woodpeckers; but with every mile we found less pleasure in these things. The final descent into Manibhanjyang was torture. The village looked so near, yet always there was another steep rocky path beyond which seemed the final ridge. But eventually we arrived and sank down beside a noticeboard which reminded us, somewhat unnecessarily, that the track along which we had so lately struggled was fit only for pack-animals and travellers on foot.

So ended our trek into country amply armed by nature against the doubtful benefits of civilisation. No traffic problems, no industrial disputes, no politics, no rat race; just splendid unspoilt country and the eternal snows.'

CHAPTER 27

LEAVE IN AUSTRALIA

The year 1957 turned out to be one of comparative tranquillity. Our new barracks were completed; a reasonable percentage of the carefully planted trees, escaping the simian depredations of small Gurkha Tarzans, started to cast welcome and increasing shade; a drill shed of vast area and pleasing proportions gave shelter for a legion of activities ranging from drill to Kalaratri dramas and endless Indian films; the temple became surrounded by a charming garden – a tribute to the Pandit's green fingers, tranquil soul and, perhaps, his religious zeal; a children's school became the focus of much noise and some learning; and a short rifle range with a tall end-wall washed in harsh terra cotta stuck out like the proverbial sore thumb.

What of our activities? The routine, the ceremonial, the unusual, the amusing – they were all there in greater or lesser measure. The guardroom at the Treasury, surrounded by vaults containing many a towkay's ransom, was still protected by an eight-man guard as it had been for nearly a decade. The wireless station on the top of Bukit Timah still provided a change of scene for a resident guard, originally taken over from the Special Constabulary when their nerve broke under the strain of seeing ghosts which, when we arrived, turned out to be flying squirrels. Our sentry at Government House has watched, with mask-like gaze, as princes, politicians and even demagogues have passed through its imposing portals.

We provided more ceremonial guards of honour than was usual. The bewigged dignity of the Opening of the Assizes, from which familiarity has long since banished the desire to laugh, was magnified to a great degree when the Lord High Chancellor of England, Lord Kilmuir, came to Singapore and inspected our Guard of Honour outside the Supreme Court. Our Commissioner, Nigel Morris, left us in October and we were pleased to mount a guard in his honour at the airport. When the Japanese Prime

Guard of Honour for the Lord Chancellor, Lord Kilmuir, escorted by the author at the Supreme Court Singapore, 1957.

The Gurkha Contingent on the Queen's Birthday Parade, The Padang, Singapore, 1957.

Minister penetrated the 'Co-Prosperity Sphere', we were there to meet him and do him honour, and also speed him on his way next morning when he left for the Spice Islands. Our appearance on those occasions was prompted more by good manners than any spontaneous feelings of affection. The Major General, Brigade of Gurkhas, Gen. Anderson, paid us a most welcome visit and was, we felt, delighted to find so many men keen to air their English. We hoped the answer to 'How long have you been in the Police?' was not too often 'Yes' or even 'No'. Colonel Ghana Shamsher, from the Nepalese Army, came to see us earlier in the year and his cheerful, friendly manner delighted us all. Our retiring Governor, Sir Robert Black, who had always shown so much interest in our welfare, paid us a visit just before he left to take over in Hong Kong. He inspected the Quarterguard and a guard of honour before walking round the barracks and the family lines; light refreshments (very light owing to the early hour) in the Gurkha Officers' Mess concluded the visit. Colonel R.A.N. Davidson, always a particularly welcome guest, for he recruited nearly all our men, came and spent some hours with us. General Toran Shamsher, the Nepalese C-in-C, during his tour of Malaya, found time to pay us a visit, a gesture much appreciated.

As to our duties, perhaps the most farcical was an operation to remove a large number of banishees from Outram Gaol and take them to the docks for embarkation on a slow boat to China. When we arrived at the prison it soon became apparent that none of the banishees had the slightest intention of leaving; they linked arms, draped themselves around the prison bars and struck up songs punctuated with shouts which suggested a much more intimate knowledge of our parentage than it was possible for them to have acquired. Eventually, each one of them had to be lifted bodily and carried to the waiting vans, where they continued their uncomplimentary commentary and added a measure of tolerably aimed expectoration for good measure. But down at the ship they filed on board like sheep, their parting gesture being to hurl bottles at us as the ship drew away. It was an intriguing morning for those interested in human nature.

The increase in Secret Society activity in Singapore resulted in a Police drive to try and reduce the activity of the thugs involved. Our contribution was to send out men in pairs, with kukhris hanging ostentatiously from their belts, to patrol the more disreputable streets of the city. As a prophylactic measure it was a huge success; of course we had insufficient men to be everywhere at once, but the thugs were well cowed in those areas where our men happened to be. A Chinese detective, who chanced to be in a coffee-shop where teen-age gangsters were wont to congregate, watched two of our

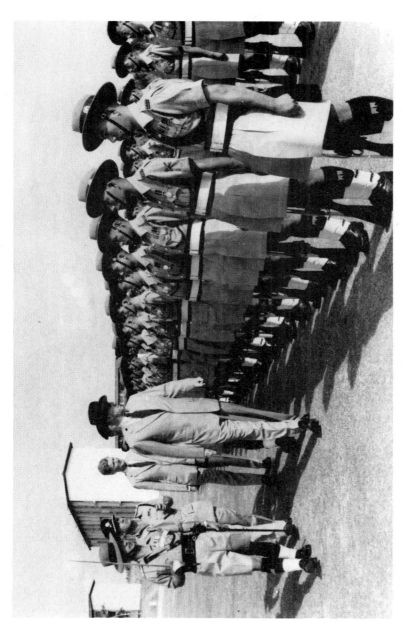

H.E. The Governor of Singapore, Sir Robert Black, inspects a Gurkha Contingent Guard of Honour, Mt. Vernon, Singapore, 1957.

The Governor at the Childrens' School Mt. Vernon, 1957.

Brother Officers and Gurkha Pipers support the Author and his Wife after their wedding at St. Andrew's Cathedral, Singapore, on 5th April, 1956.

men come in and approach a particularly unpleasant example of this noxious breed, eye him up and down for a minute with a contemptuous gaze, and then tell him, in execrable Malay, to go and have a haircut. He departed from the shop in great haste and confusion.

During the year political advancement proceeded apace, with yet another Merdeka Mission beating a trail to London where, so readily were their demands met, that they began to wonder why they had not asked for more. Indeed, the P.A.P. was quick to accuse the Mission in general and the Lim Yew Hock government in particular of failing to obtain more concessions, and in subsequent elections that party made spectacular gains, taking control of the City Council and vastly reducing government majorities in by-elections. The hustings kept us busy; no wad of ballot papers could be moved without a guard, no ballot box could go unescorted to and from the polling stations. So election days and nights stretched our resources and gave us ample opportunity to be amazed by what the people chose.

Our Pipes and Drums were away on leave in Nepal for most of the year, but before they went they had performed in public many times with increasing skill and acclaim. Towards the end of the year Capt. G.H. Moore and Capt. J.F. Clark joined us on two-year secondments.

On the morning of the Queen's Birthday Parade in June, I went to Government House in my capacity as an Extra A.D.C., to escort Lady Black to the Parade. When I met the Governor, he congratulated me on what I assumed to be the recent birth of our first child. Subsequent talk, much of it at cross-purposes, revealed that this was not the subject of the felicitation but the award to me of the Colonial Police Medal for Meritorious Service in the Birthday Honours, of which I had no inkling.

I had three weeks' casual leave due to me. I should explain that I had been lucky enough to marry into a family with Antipodean connections and luckier still because they owned a cattle station one third again the size of Surrey in the Kimberley District of North Western Australia. To this we had been invited, and we now decided to go there.

Making the travel arrangements was not easy in those days. Darwin we had heard of and so had the Travel Agents, but Darwin was some 500 miles from remote Mount House, our destination – 500 roadless and railless miles. Twice a week a plane flew the 200 miles from Darwin to a small sea-port called Wyndham and once in two weeks another plane carried freight 200 miles inland to Glenroy, the main homestead on the cattle station, which was separated from Mount House by 40 miles of 'bush'. Could the international airlines guarantee to deposit us in Darwin to catch all the elusive connections? We juggled with time-tables, we wrote letters which missed the fortnightly connections, we sent cables; it seemed that Wallace's Line was to be as great a barrier to us as it had been to the marsupials at the beginning of time. However, it transpired that Glenroy was no ordinary cattle station; during the Australian winter it operated a meat factory into which were fed the prime bullocks of the year. The daily quota of carcases, some 50 or more, were quick-chilled on the station, loaded into a Dakota and flown to Wyndham where huge freezing plants awaited them. The plane, having disgorged its bloody cargo, winged its way back empty, apart from a legion of flies and a rather raw smell. Why shouldn't we, we thought, provide a little ballast and keep the flies company? Why, indeed? And this is what we did.

For our three-month old baby we paid 10% of the adult fare and a charming little booklet informed us that the baby was not entitled to any baggage allowance but, as everyone knows, the smaller the baby the larger the amount of his luggage, which may be equal to, or even greater than, that of his male parent. Having dashed our hopes, the booklet raised them again by announcing that a carry-cot could be taken containing 'baby's everyday things' provided that it and its contents did not exceed 20 lb. less (and here was a concession) the weight of the baby. Who had ever heard of 'baby's everyday things' weighing 20 lb. or less? So, the three of us and a carrycot cut a comic sight as we staggered out to the Super G Constellation at Paya Lebar on a June evening. The overflowing carrycot was squeezed through the aircraft door, to be met by horrified gestures from the stewards who, in direct opposition to the booklet, announced that we could not bring it in. However, the door was already shut and a kind passenger in the 1st class portion of the plane allowed us to put the offending object by his seat. We were soon airborne, climbing steeply and setting course for Java. Huge cumulo-nimbus clouds were continuously lit by distant lightning vying with the navigation lights winking on the wing-tips.

Djakarta Airport was not the sort of place to move the poet or inspire the painter, even at the best of times; at midnight it was dreary to the extreme. Sleepy, hot and irritated, we had ample time to be amazed at the elaborate precautions taken by rubber-stamping officials to ensure that we did not stay there; they surely flattered themselves. The hour spent there weighed heavily on our hands as we sat in the shabby waiting-room surrounded by posters encouraging us to visit all four corners of the Republic, borne on the wings of a legendary bird.

Airborne again, we were soon roaring over the volcanic mountains, whose cone-shaped symmetry was occasionally illuminated by boisterous flashes of lightning.

As dawn broke we were still flying over the sea, but at about 0800 hrs. we crossed the red and dry-looking coast, with mangrove swamps here and there. The wheels of the plane touched the runway at Darwin with a protesting squeak and a puff of blue smoke; the first and easiest part of our journey was over.

We stayed in a hotel which shall be nameless because it was the worst and most expensive such establishment which we had up to then encountered, and the less said about it the better. Fortunately we spent very little time in it, as some of our relations dwelt in Darwin and they took us under their kindly wing, showing us everything which the town had to offer; the attractive golf course with bandicoot scrapes adding an extra hazard to the not-too-smooth fairways, the brilliance of the bougainvillaeas in the botanic gardens, the ugly modern symmetry of the new housing estates, where the houses were built on stilts to escape the termites, the intensely blue sea and the disappointingly muddy beaches, the expensive but well-stocked shops. (Not many years after our visit a catastrophic hurricane struck Darwin, razing most of it to the ground.)

The flight to Wyndham took two hours and we found the meat freighter waiting for us. We climbed in and sat in splendid isolation as far away as possible from the gory evidence of the recent cargo. The touchdown at Glenroy was exciting; the strip was a dirt one of no very great length and, because of the abattoirs and their attendant offal, vast flocks of Black Kites were wheeling about in the air. I was in the pilot's cabin as we came in, hurtling past surprised and fortunately very agile kites, to bump along the baked red soil and wonder why none of the birds had been sliced up by the whirring propellers.

We were soon in the middle of this remarkable little colony away out in the Australian bush. Every man-made thing which we could see, including the buildings and machines, had been flown in. There, for four months of the year, about 100 men – butchers, engineers, electricians and stockmen – worked the clock round harvesting a meaty crop from 5,000 bullocks. The beasts were mustered in from miles around in large, lowing, dust-raising 'mobs', to be herded between converging fences until finally they found themselves in single file advancing towards their executioners. In a matter of seconds bullocks became beef, the quartered carcases soon on their way to Wyndham and the refrigerated ships which took them to the four corners of the earth.

After lunch, beef steaks no less, we set out for Mount House in a Fargo truck, driven by Doug Blythe, a cousin and co-partner of this two-station enterprise called 'Air Beef'. The truck was fitted with extra-large wheels to lift it above the tussocks and anthills which marked the surface of the track. It was an uncomfortable journey across boulder-strewn plains, up and down the steep banks of dry river-beds and through groups of gum trees whose lower branches bounced off the driver's cab with clattering squeaks. Sometimes the road was 'smooth' and we roared along at 20 m.p.h., glad of relief from tensing our bodies in our lurching and bouncing progress. The country and wildlife were fascinating; now and again a wallaby, with fantastic bounds, would dash away from a nearby grassy clump, usually in headlong retreat but sometimes to stop and turn round with a timid expression and twitching nose, and watch us bouncing and pitching on our way. It was thrilling to see pink and grey Galahs perched on the skeletons of huge and long-since-dead gum trees or hear, at our occasional stops, the cheerful warbling of a flock of Budgerigars speeding past to their feeding grounds. Large eagles circled in the cloudless sky in search of carrion. Sometimes we passed a little mob of cattle – cows and calves and lucky, unmustered bullocks – which, with tails cocked up, would run beside us in seemingly pointless exertion. Here and there a dead dingo would mark the Government dingo-shooter's prowess in reducing the numbers of the only animal which the cattlemen feared; a dingo will attack a cow whilst she is calving and destroy her offspring at birth.

After three hours we came to a fence and a gate; we had arrived at the home paddock of Mount House, around which this fence was some 50 miles in length, and were soon at the Homestead, a large building, every brick and stick of which had been brought in by air. It was a delightful place situated on a bluff above a river, surrounded by a neat little garden – a green and colourful oasis in a dry and reddish world. Beds of pink cannas, great clumps of bougainvillaeas and the greenest of grass watered constantly by sprinklers. Down by the river, gum trees leant out over the water and dipped their leaves in its still surface. A few White Egrets stood erect and motionless, waiting for some hapless fish to come their way. High in the trees hundreds of Corella cockatoos shrieked and squawked with nerve-rending vigour. Small flocks of those most colourful birds, the Australian Finches, were often to be seen near the house in twittering little bands, as confiding as they were restless – Gouldians, Blood Finches, Long-tailed Grass Finches, Zebra Finches and many others.

I built a little 'hide' at a water hole about half a mile from the house and spent several evenings filming the birds which came to drink prior to roosting. The white cockatoos were the most numerous visitors, coming in noisy flocks of 20 or more and pitching a few yards from the water's edge, to walk along with comical stumping gait, raising and lowering their crests and uttering harsh cries. After a few dips of their huge bills, they had drunk their fill and were off to the tall trees by the house where, when darkness descended, a silence fell on their day-long chatter. Some pretty little Spinifex Pigeons used to come regularly and, after a very quick drink, would depart on loudly whirring wings. Budgerigars alighted in nearby bushes but never came to drink; it was strange how timid they were when they are so amiable and confiding in captivity. My largest visitor was a White-necked Heron. I had occasionally seen him on my walks and he had been very elusive, but one evening he suddenly arrived with a thud a few yards from me and stalked into the water, where he had a few sips and, with a terrific heave of his wings, leapt straight from the water and was gone. I hoped that a wallaby might come for a drink, but none ever did. There were many of them about, for they were often disturbed, jumping from clumps of grass and bounding away with a steady 'thump thump', clearing bushes and rocks in their precipitous retreat. They hid all day, only emerging in the evenings to feed on grass shoots near the streams and water holes.

Although my main interest was in the fascinating birds and wildlife, the main concern of Mount House was breeding cattle. There were 20,000 of them, mainly sired by Hereford bulls, and their peaceful, distant lowing was a constant background noise. There was no killing there; only when the bullocks had reached their third year, did they start on their final fateful journey to Glenroy. Once a year the peace of the herds was disturbed when all the cows and calves were mustered for branding. The stockmen rode out and brought in the mobs of cattle to pre-arranged focal points where stockades had been built. Then, some 20 to 30 at a time, the cows and their offspring were ushered in. Each calf was lassoed and branded on its buttocks and the bulls were also castrated, neither operation seeming to worry them in the least.

Most of the stockmen and all the domestic staff were aborigines of both sexes and a variety of ages. The stockmen were superb horsemen and dedicated to their job, cheerful and uninhibited, riding the range in wide-brimmed hats, shirts, jodhpurs and spurred boots, looking very much the part. A lady of great antiquity and astonishingly simian of visage tended the kitchen garden and scared away the wallabies at night, presumably by simply appearing on the scene. Some much younger females worked in the kitchen and the house; a happy, cheerful, unsophisticated little band, glad to have something useful to do between their annual 'walk-abouts'.

When the time came for us to leave Mount House, we were able to arrange for a freight plane to land specially for us at the station airstrip. At the appointed hour, two stockmen galloped about chasing cattle off the strip as the plane, a Dakota, came in to land in a cloud of red dust. An hour's flight took us to Derby, pronounced as it is spelt and claiming no distinction. The next stop, Broome, had enjoyed great prosperity as the centre of the Australian pearling industry some years before, and this occupation was still carried on by many of the inhabitants, some of whom were Malays and Japanese, working as divers. Further along the coast we landed at Port Hedland and then turned south over many miles of barren country including Mount Bruce and the Hamersley Range. As the red evening light began to fade, we landed at a place, much foresaken by the Deity, called Meekatharra, this being followed by a two-and-a-half-hour flight to Perth.

Perth is a beautiful city, standing astride the Swan River and overlooked by a wooded hill, itself the centre of King's Park. From atop this hill, where stands supreme the imposing War Memorial, revered and tended in a way so wholly admirable and so typically Australian, one could see the whole city and the wide expanse of the Swan River making its way to Fremantle and the coast some nine miles to the west. In the distance to the east stood the Darling Range, behind which lay hidden the vast and increasingly arid plateau and the Nullabor Plain. We made several visits to the Darlings, and very lovely was the country. It is odd how one goes to a foreign land and then finds oneself delighted when it happens to look like England. Much of the country west of the range was very English except that the buildings lacked the permanence which makes the home countryside seem so secure. But the green fields with shorthorn cattle standing fly-tormented in the shade not of oaks but of handsome gums, the plum orchards with flocks of white Leghorns scratching beneath the trees, and a tired and elderly carthorse standing motionless by a gate, all reminded us of home. The vulgar laughter of a Kukuburra or the piercing shriek of a Rosella Parakeet soon dispelled the illusion and brought us back from the other side of the world, but the pleasure remained, the more so because we had seen both places.

Three weeks' leave soon came to an end and our departure from Perth Airport, as was so often the case in those days, was seriously delayed by 'technical faults' to the plane. After a brief stop at Djakarta in the same dismal waiting room, we eventually arrived at Paya Lebar to hand over the baby to his amah, who was so delighted to find that her doubts about his parents' ability to feed and tend him properly had been groundless, that she quite forgot to be put out by the fact that they seemed as well able to look after him as she – he had put on two and a half pounds.

CHAPTER 28

FAREWELL SINGAPORE

On 11th January 1958 we went home on five months' leave, sailing on the passenger-cum-cargo liner, S.S. *Hamburg*. The voyage was very comfortable and uneventful except for damage done to one of the ship's propeller blades, caused by hitting some wreckage in the Suez Canal. It had been left there following the ill-fated campaign in the autumn of 1956. We had to reduce speed in the Mediterranean and for the rest of the voyage; we did not arrive at Southampton until 11th February, to meet a cold spell lasting for a month when, in Northumberland, the temperature one night fell to -11.0°C (12.0°F).

We returned to Singapore in a Britannia turbo-prop plane of B.O.A.C. on 26th June, to start my final year with the Contingent. In July, a big Police Review was held on the Padang in which we were well represented both in the marching columns and by the Pipes and Drums, who had become highly skilled performers. During the parade, the Governor, Sir William Goode, presented me with the C.P.M. awarded to me in the Queen's Birthday Honours the previous year. A few days later our second son was born at the K.K. Hospital.

The most important happening during these last months was the agreement reached between H.M.G., the Nepalese Government and the new Singapore Government about the future and the terms of service of the Gurkha Contingent and its members – an agreement laid on the table of the House of Commons, following an official question, which protected and ensured the men's future in an independent Singapore. One of the important items was a promise that the Contingent should be led only by British and Gurkha Officers to sustain the political impartiality essential in a para-military unit of a police force. We held a parade at which the agreement was read out to the men by the Commissioner of Police.

The postponed visit of H.R.H. the Duke of Edinburgh took place in

February 1959 and was a resounding success. Many of the security duties fell to our lot. Despite all the political wranglings and the anti-British attitude of some P.A.P. politicians, the public in general gave the Duke a great welcome, all against a background of impending elections and the implementation of the new constitution.

The General Election, during which we were very busy, was held in May and the P.A.P. won 43 of the 51 seats, a victory exaggerated by a deep split in the right wing votes, but one which foretold the total dominance of the party for decades to come. After his victory, Lee Kuan Yew went to the Governor and told him that he would not take office unless 'those connected with the party and now detained' were released. The Governor bowed to the inevitable and released eight members of the P.A.P. and the new constitution came into force on 5th June when the cabinet was sworn in. No time was lost in getting the 'Peoples Government' into its stride; a number of so-called demoralising publications were banned and radio programmes started to have what was called an 'Asian and Malayan' slant. The Prime Minister set a good example by arriving in his office at 0800 hrs. each day, the Government cut the pay of its employees and ministers took a $600 reduction in their salaries.

At the time, there was, of course, no realisation of how quickly the new island state would develop, especially after its severance from Malaysia, then unforeseen. The British political connection quickly withered away, but the political stability provided by a strong government with an outstanding leader stood the country in good stead. The P.A.P. realised that the Communist threat was a real one both to the political freedom which they permitted and to the economic progress which they sought. They soon took steps to curb the activities of those who thought otherwise.

Shortly before we left, we spent a few days in the Cameron Highlands, a hill station in the central mountain range of the Malayan Peninsula. The drive up from Tapah was fascinating in the way the vegetation changed with the increase in elevation; at about 5,000 ft. the tropical rain forest of the lowlands had changed into more open woodland with a tree-fern understorey and cleared areas where tea-gardens had been established. Now and again we passed small Sakai settlements, where these aboriginal people had come in from the forest to set up more permanent abodes. In the evening we walked up beyond the village of Brinchang for some fascinating bird-watching. Species new to me which we saw included Silver-eared Mesias, Black-throated Sunbirds, Grey-chinned Minivets and Mountain Fulvettas. On the following morning we set out by car to reach the top of Gunong

Brinchang (6,620 ft.) but the car over-heated and we had to walk the final one and a half miles, which was fortunate because we saw many more montane birds such as the Large Niltava, Large Cuckoo-Shrike, Cutias and Golden-throated Barbet. The vegetation at this altitude was mainly of rather scrubby ericaceous species. On the way back to Singapore we spent a night at the other main hill-station, Fraser's Hill, where conditions were very much the same as in the Camerons and the birdlife just as varied and fascinating; Grey-throated Babblers, speckled Piculet, Black and Crimson Oriole and Blue Nuthatch being some of the birds we saw.

In March 1959 I answered an advertisement in the airmail *Times* which sought a Secretary for the Royal Forestry Society of England and Wales, and I was bidden to appear in London for an interview. I took a chance on it and flew home, and on the strength of a forestry degree and a certain amount of administrative experience, I got the job, due to start in September.

As the year progressed, with no very remarkable happenings to disturb our normal run of duties, so came the time for our departure. I looked upon my part in raising and developing the Contingent with some pride and considerable humility. I could have done nothing and the Contingent would have been nothing without those most loyal, honest and hard-working men – the Gurkhas. Although they joined the Police primarily to earn a livelihood, this was not the only reason why they left their mountain homes to serve the British Crown (and subsequently the Republic of Singapore). Most of them were following relatives who had seen similar service. To some extent the Contingent was a family affair, the resulting *esprit de coeur* helping to ensure a cohesive unit proud to serve the authority which employed it. The British and Gurkha Officers were there to manage its affairs and ensure that the demands made upon it were reasonable and directed in the best way possible. No men, however deeply dedicated, can perform their tasks to an optimum unless their well-being and that of their families is closely guarded. This we endeavoured to do by keeping in close touch with the men, both when performing their duties and in their leisure times, which meant, of course, being on duty, as it were, well outside the normal working hours. Indeed, the peculiar nature of our duties, varying between the tedium of 24-hour guards and the uncertainty of constant readiness, was very much at the expense of private lives. Anything which we could do which helped to alleviate this constant pressure on the men and fortify a high morale, was our gratifying duty.

The last two weeks before we left involved us in many farewell parties, including a dinner given at Government House by the Governor and Lady

Goode to which some 20 of our personal friends were also invited – a particularly kind and generous gesture. At a party in the Police Mess I was presented with an Omega Constellation watch which, as I write 36 years later, is on my wrist still keeping perfect time. After the very moving and sad occasion of my farewell parade on 30th June, the Contingent presented me with a silver figure of a Gurkha mounted on a teak base; this is now on my desk and a constant reminder of ten wonderfully happy years with the Contingent.

These final days brought mixed emotions. A decade of intimate involvement with, and personal responsibility for, the lives, duties and the well-being of 350 men and their families whose trust one enjoyed to the full, cannot be handed to others without regret, neither can the prospect of a new life which is to replace it be anticipated without optimism. So the parties given in our honour by the Gurkha Officers and men were on the whole enjoyable occasions, nearness to tears always being overtaken by happy memories of successful endeavours.

Thus did the final departure take place at Paya Lebar Airport when, on 2 July 1959, all four of us boarded a B.O.A.C. Comet. Had I known of it then, I think I would have said to myself, as I watched the waving figures while the plane taxied for take-off, the Prayer for the Gurkhas:

'O God, who in the Gurkha, has given to mankind a race exceptional in courage and devotion, resplendent in its cheerfulness. We, who owe them so much, ask Your special blessing on them, their families and their land. Grant us Your Grace to be loyal to their best interests, as they have been to ours in the past.'

POSTSCRIPT

During the 37 years since we left Singapore, the Contingent has expanded three-fold and serves the Island Republic with the same dedication as it did the Colony in the past.

We have made three visits to the Contingent during this period and have been delighted to find it flourishing, proud of its past and its present and still conscious of the family connections which help to bind it together. On our last visit we met senior men whose fathers had been amongst the original recruits, and we were always given a very warm welcome by every one.

The current rebuilding of the 40-year-old barracks shows a confidence in the future of the Contingent – a story for others to record in due time.

APPENDIX

BIRDS MENTIONED IN TEXT

ALBATROSS, GREAT WANDERING	*Diomedea exulans*
ALBATROSS, YELLOW-NOSED	*Diomedea chlororhynchos*
BABBLER, GREY-THROATED	*Stachyris nigriceps*
BABBLER, JUNGLE	*Turdoides caudatus*
BARBET, GREEN	*Megalaima zeylanica*
BEE EATER, LITTLE GREEN	*Merops orientalis*
BLACKBIRD, GREY-WINGED	*Turdus boulboul*
BUDGERIGAR	*Melopsittacus undulatus*
BULBUL, RED-VENTED	*Pycnonotus cafer*
BULBUL, RED-WHISKERED	*Pycnonotus jocusus*
BULBUL, YELLOW-EARED	*Pycnonotus penicillatus*
COCKATOO, BLACK	*Calyptorhyncus funereus*
COCKATOO, SULPHUR-CRESTED	*Cacatus galerita*
COPPERSMITH	*Megalaima haemacephala*
COOT, COMMON	*Fulica atra*
CORMORANT, INDIAN	*Phalacrocorax fascicollis*
COUCAL	*Centropus sinensis*
CRANE, SARUS	*Grus antigone*
CROW, HOUSE	*Corvus splendens*
CROW, JUNGLE	*Corvus macrorhyncos*
CUCKOO, HAWK	*Cuculus various*
CUCKOO, COMMON	*Cuculus canorus*
CUCKOO SHRIKE, LARGE	*Coracina novaehollandiae*
CUTIA	*Cutia nipalensis*
DARTER, INDIAN	*Ahinga melanogaster*
DOVE, LITTLE BROWN	*Streptopelia senegalensis*
DRONGO, BLACK	*Dicruris macrocercus*

DRONGO, WHITE-BELLIED	*Dicruris caerlescens*
EAGLE, AFRICAN FISH	*Haliaeetus vocifer*
EGRET, CATTLE	*Bubulcus ibis*
FINCH, BLOOD	*Neochmia phoeton*
FINCH, GOULDIAN	*Chloebia gouldiae*
FINCH, GRASS	*Poephila bichenovii*
FINCH, LONG-TAILED	*Poephila acuticauda*
FINCH, ZEBRA	*Poephila guttata*
FLOWER-PECKER, ORANGE-BELLIED	*Diceaum trigonostigma*
FLYCATCHER, CEYLON DUSKY-BLUE	*Eumyias sordida*
FLYCATCHER, PARADISE	*Terpsiphone paradisi*
FULVETTA, MOUNTAIN	*Alcippe peracencis*
GALAH	*Eolophus roseicapillus*
GANNET, CAPE	*Morus capensis*
GREENFINCH, HIMALAYAN	*Carduelis spinoides*
GOLDFINCH, HIMALAYAN	*Carduelis carduelis caniceps*
GREBE, LITTLE	*Tachybaptus ruficollis capensis*
GREENSHANK	*Tringa nebularis*
GULL, ADEN	*Larus hemprichii*
GULL, GREY-HEADED	*Larus cirrocephalus*
HARRIER, PIED	*Circus melanoleucus*
HERON, WHITE-NECKED	*Ardea pacifica*
HORNBILL, GREAT	*Buceros bicornis*
HORNBILL, INDIAN GREY	*Tockus birostris*
IBIS, BLACK	*Threskiornis melanocephalus*
IORA, COMMON	*Aegithina tiphia*
JACANA, BRONZE-WINGED	*Metopidius indicus*
JACANA, PHEASANT-TAILED	*Hydrophasianus chirurgus*
JACKDAW	*Corvus monedula soemmerringi*
JERDON'S CHLOROPSIS	*Chloropsis aurifrons*
JUNGLE FOWL	*Gallus gallus*
KINGFISHER, COMMON	*Alcedo atthis*
KINGFISHER, PIED	*Ceryle rudis*
KINGFISHER, WHITE-BREASTED	*Halcyon smyrnensis*
KINGFISHER, WHITE-COLLARED	*Halcyon chloris*

KITE, BLACK	*Milvus migrans*
KITE, BRAHMINY	*Haliastur indus*
KOEL	*Eudynamys scolopacea*
KOOKABURRA, BLUE-WINGED	*Dacelo leachii*
LAMMERGEIER	*Gypaetus barbatus*
LAPWING, RED-WATTLED	*Vanellus indicus*
LORIQUET (HANGING PARROT)	*Loriculus beryllinus*
MESIA, SILVER-EARED	*Leiothrix argentauris*
MINIVET, GREY-THROATED	*Pericrocotus solaris*
MOORHEN	*Gallinula chloropus pyrrhorrhoa*
MYNAH, COMMON	*Acridotheres tristis*
MYNAH, PIED	*Sturnus contra*
NIGHTJAR	*Caprimulgus asiaticus*
NILTAVA, LARGE	*Niltava grandis*
NUTCRACKER	*Nucifraga caryocatactes*
NUTKA	*Sarkidiornus melanotos*
NUTHATCH, BLUE	*Sitta azurea*
NUTHATCH, COMMON	*Sitta europea nagaensis*
ORIOLE, BLACK & CRIMSON	*Oriolus cruentus*
ORIOLE, BLACK-NAPED	*Oriolus chinensis*
OWLET, SPOTTED	*Athene brama*
PADDY BIRD	*Ardeola grayii*
PARAKEET, BLOSSOM-HEADED	*Psittacula roseata*
PARAKEET, ROSE-RINGED	*Psittacula krameri*
PARTRIDGE, INDIAN GREY	*Francolinus pondicerianus*
PEAFOWL	*Pave cristatus*
PELICAN, PINK-BACKED	*Pelicanus rufescens*
PHEASANT, GREAT ARGUS	*Argusianus argus*
PHEASANT, KALIJ	*Lophura leucomelana*
PICULET, SPECKLED	*Picumnus innominatus*
PIGEON, GREEN, THICK-BILLED	*Trernon curvirostra*
PIGEON, GREEN, CINNAMON-HEADED	*Trernon fulvicollis*
PIGEON, GREEN, YELLOW-LEGGED	*Trernon phoenicoptera*
PIGEON, GREEN, PINK-NECKED	*Trernon vernans*
QUAIL, INDIAN BLUE	*Excalfactoria chinensis*
RAVEN	*Corvus corax*
REDSTART, PLUMBEOUS	*Phoenicurus fuliginosus*

ROBIN, MAGPIE	*Copsychus saularis*
ROLLER, INDIAN	*Coracias benghalensis*
ROSELLA	*Platycercus icterotis*
SANDPIPER, COMMON	*Actitis hypoleucos*
SANDPIPER, GREEN	*Tringa ochropus*
SHEARWATER, GREATER	*Puffinus gravis*
SHIKRA	*Accipiter badius*
SHOVELER	*Anas clypeata*
SHRIKE, RED-BACKED	*Lanius collurio*
SPARROW, HOUSE	*Passer domesticus indicus*
STARLING, COMMON	*Sturnus vulgaris humii*
SUNBIRD, BLACK-THROATED	*Aethopyga saturata*
SUNBIRD, PURPLE	*Nectarinia asiatica*
SUNBIRD, PURPLE-RUMPED	*Nectarinia zeylonica*
SUNBIRD, YELLOW-BACKED	*Aethopyga siparaja*
SWALLOW, RED-RUMPED	*Hirundo daurica*
SWALLOW-WIRE-TAILED	*Hirundo smithii*
TAILORBIRD, LONG-TAILED	*Orthotomus sutorius*
TEAL	*Anas crecca*
TEAL, COTTON	*Nettapus caramandelianus*
TERN, BLACK-BELLIED	*Sterna melanogaster*
TERN, GULL-BILLED	*Gelochelidon nilotica*
TERN, INDIAN RIVER	*Sterna aurantia*
THRUSH, TICKELL'S	*Turdus unicolor*
TIT, CRESTED BLACK	*Parus melanolophus*
TIT, INDIAN GREY	*Parus major caschmirensis*
TIT, RED-HEADED	*Aegithalos concinnus*
TREECREEPER, HIMALAYAN	*Certhia himalayana*
TREEPIE, INDIAN	*Dendrocitta vagabonda*
VULTURE, ASIATIC KING	*Sarcogyps calvus*
VULTURE, INDIAN WHITE-BACKED	*Gyps bengalensis*
VULTURE, EGYPTIAN	*Neophron percnopterus*

These names are all taken from *A COMPLETE CHECKLIST OF BIRDS OF THE WORLD* by Richard Howard and Alick Moore. Published by Papermac in 1984.

GLOSSARY OF INDIAN TERMS

Agewalla	One who goes ahead
Bandobast	Arrangement
Basha	Hut made of bamboo
Bhisti	Water carrier
Bidi	Cigarette made of rolled tobacco leaves
Bistra	Bedding roll
Bund	Division between rice fields
Charpoy	Wooden bed with string base
Chaung	River or stream
Chota hazri	Early morning tea
Chota peg	Small whisky
Chungkol	Two-handed hoe
Chowdhari	Indian shop-keeper or contractor
Dah	Burmese knife
Khana	Celebratory meal
Madal	Gurkha drum
Maidan	Large, flat open space
Malee	Gardener
Mochi	Cobbler
Nautch	Dance
Nullah	Dry river bed
Nimbo pani	Fresh lime juice drink
Padang	Large, flat open space
Pakal	Water container carried on mule
Sangar	Dry-stone wall
Saman	Equipment
Shabash	'Well done'

Sunwar	Goldsmith
Tonga	Pony trap
Towkay	Chinese businessman
Zemindar	Indian landowner